The Telegraph
BOOK OF
THE RUGBY
WORLD CUP

The Telegraph
BOOK OF
THE RUGBY
WORLD CUP

EDITED BY
Martin Smith

Aurum
Press

First published in Great Britain
2015 by Aurum Press Ltd
74—77 White Lion Street
Islington
London N1 9PF
www.aurumpress.co.uk

A catalogue record for this book is available from the British Library.

ISBN 978 1 78131 493 7
ebook ISBN 978 1 78131 535 4

1 3 5 7 9 10 8 6 4 2
2015 2017 2019 2018 2016

Typeset in ITC New Baskerville by SX Composing DTP, Rayleigh, Essex
Printed and bound by CPI Group (UK) Ltd, Croydon, CR0 4YY

For my son, William, a decent fly-half/full-back in his youth – in appreciation of some memorable tries and place-kicks, if not the too-frequent visits to A&E.

CONTENTS

INTRODUCTION

It may seem a tad unconventional to begin a word-heavy book by talking about photographs. However, once the last dropped goal has gone over, the trophy has been presented and the large soprano has stopped singing, what are we left with but our memories? As the eighth tournament approaches, *The Telegraph Book of the Rugby World Cup* will attempt to stimulate the old grey cells, as well as tell the story of what the overexcited organisers call the third-biggest sporting event on Earth. Hopefully the words of the *Telegraph*'s army of rugby writers rolled out here will conjure up, pass by pass, a half-forgotten try, add colour and insight to a famous moment, while you sit back and enjoy your own nostalgia.

Let us start, though, by flicking through a virtual photograph album of iconic images. The stand-out picture of any World Cup is surely that of Nelson Mandela handing over the Webb Ellis trophy to the victorious Springbok captain Francois Pienaar in 1995. Normally a presentation picture is so bog-standard and dull that it would be hidden away in the backwaters of a newspaper's coverage. Not this one; this one had a context way beyond the confines of a rugby stadium in Johannesburg, way beyond sport itself. Conjure up the picture in your mind's eye. It shouldn't be difficult – it has been used everywhere from newspapers, books and magazines to posters for the movie *Invictus*. It shows a beaming white player, fresh from the action, shaking hands with an elderly black guy, decked out in a replica green-and-gold shirt of the other, topped off with a green baseball cap, his smile just as wide. The new, post-apartheid South Africa had been born in monochrome five years earlier with the release from prison of the now President Mandela; the vibrant colours of the emerging Rainbow Nation were painted in as the united country burst with pride at its first international sporting success.

The *Sunday Telegraph* sports supplement carried the picture tip-to-toe on its broadsheet front page, under the headline: 'The waiting is over'. Inside, on page two, the sport itself was celebrated in a shot by staff photographer Russell Cheyne (of whom more soon) of the moment the cup was won. The ball has just left Joel Stransky's boot as he drops the winning goal deep into extra time. As it flies past Andrew Mehrtens's attempted block it almost looks as if the New Zealand fly-half is surrendering. A thousand words told in the click of a camera's shutter.

The front page of the main paper that June Sunday included a single-column portrait of a still-smiling Mandela raising his cap, atop a story signalling the sport section's coverage. The news people had weightier matters with which to concern themselves when it came to that day's splash. And, twenty-four hours later, so did the *Daily*'s sports desk. Bar a small news-based story from the World Cup final, the cover of the sports pull-out was dominated by Phil Brown's shot of Darren Gough's middle stump being ripped out of the ground by West Indies fast bowler Curtly Ambrose in the Lord's Test. Just as life moves on, so too does sport.

That third edition of the World Cup, back in 1995, was comparatively prolific in the number of memorable images it produced. The *Daily Telegraph* Monday sports section was particularly fortunate in the fortnight before cricket reclaimed its place to publish two of the very best, both taken again by Russell Cheyne, the reigning rugby photographer of the year. The first, on 12 June, underneath the headline 'England's dream finish', was of Rob Andrew drop-kicking the decisive points in the quarter-final against Australia. A smile is already forming on Andrew's face as he follows the ball's path. At the same time you can see the despair on the faces of Michael Lynagh and David Wilson as they rush in too late to prevent the impending damage. The image was so powerful that the paper replicated it a few days later, along with a letter from Anthony Robinson of Newark, Nottinghamshire, in which he said: 'The combined results of the work of Russell Cheyne and your production team gave your readers on Monday the finest piece of triumphal sporting photography I have ever seen. The front page of the sport section is a glittering example of pictorial journalism and will make the occasion it celebrates ever more unforgettable.' The marketing department weren't slow in recognising the value of the 'moment that will go down in rugby history'. They responded by offering readers – 'by popular demand' – the opportunity to purchase a poster replica of the front page. You may still have a copy on your bedroom wall.

However, as in politics, so in sport: what a difference a week can make. The following Monday's front page was dominated by a full-length picture of Jonah Lomu charging away to score the second of his four tries in the All Blacks' semi-final mauling of England. Lomu is heading straight towards Cheyne's lens; you can see the power of his six-foot, five-inch, eighteen-and-a-half stone frame, and you want to duck underneath the breakfast table to avoid the inevitable collision. And there, sprawled full-length in the background, grasping at thin air after failing to lay a hand on the man mountain, is the previous week's hero: Rob Andrew. The headline says it all: 'Bulldozed by Lomu'. Indeed.

If Lomu was England's nemesis in 1995, and again four years later, then a slighter, lighter, leaner figure was launched in time to wreak vengeance on the world in 2003: Jonny Wilkinson. All right, opposing backs might not be thumbing through the small print in their health insurance in trepidation, but allow him within range of a kick, dropped or placed, and you were kissing goodbye to three points. Maybe not bulldozed, but Jonny's accumulated points in a match could be every bit as devastating as a quartet of Lomu tries. The mere mention of his name brings up an instant image of that trademark hunched stance, hands together as if praying, or perhaps preying, while he prepares to kick yet more points for England.

Wilkinson was top scorer at the 2003 Rugby World Cup with 113 points. But it was the kick that took him from 110 to 113 that left an indelible imprint in the mind of every red-bloodied, white-shirted England rugby supporter: the last-minute drop at goal that clinched the trophy in Sydney. Who cannot picture the moment? Chris Barry, a regular *Telegraph* freelance photographer, captured it perfectly for the front page of the Sunday paper. So perfect, in fact, that the *Daily* repeated it on an inside page the following day. There is Jonny, in textbook follow-through, as his kick continues its trajectory towards the gap between the posts. The headline? 'The Best', in capital letters; no 'simply' about it. The photograph that led the front of the main paper that Sunday morning was a few frames later as Wilkinson's arms are raised aloft to acknowledge the safe passage of the kick. Twenty-four hours later, the first flush of success over, the front-page shot was of Wilkinson surrounded by a forest of tape recorders ready to capture his every celebratory utterance. A media star was born.

Wind the mental camera on eight years, two tournaments and a hop across the Tasman Sea from Australia to New Zealand. The images become a bit fuzzy and grainy, and aptly so: they are not taken by top-end photographers with expensive kit. These are the type of snaps taken with a mobile-phone camera. Members of the England squad are on a pre-tournament night-out in a Queenstown bar, which is holding a Mad Midget Weekender. This becomes, in journalese, a 'dwarf-throwing contest', and England players appear to be indulging in the competition as well as the local ale. The resulting pictures found their way back to the other side of the world and into every newspaper in Britain. One of those subsequently punished for his involvement was Mike Tindall, newly married to the Queen's granddaughter. Then, to make it even worse, England's premature exit from the tournament was marked by a photograph of a contrite Manu Tuilagi, who had been fined by the management for jumping off a ferry in Auckland harbour and swimming to the landing point. 'Embarrassing to the end' ran the *Telegraph*'s headline.

The various off-field incidents that blighted England's campaign in 2011 might not have mattered much if the team had made a better fist of their quest to regain the World Cup trophy. As it was, the incidents became a metaphor for their total disorganisation and swift disintegration – something about failing to prepare and preparing to fail, as the coaching mantra goes. So from Rob Andrew, Joel Stransky, Jonny Wilkinson, Jonah Lomu and Nelson Mandela to the Mad Midget Weekender: from giants of the game to pygmies. England owe the country a better showing in 2015.

Incredibly, all those images and memories might not have been available to reload into the mind's internal projector had the International Rugby Board (IRB) followed their initial scepticism and rejected the idea of a World Cup. It will seem inconceivable to modern readers that the Rugby World Cup is little more than quarter of a century old. After all, it seems such an obvious concept. Association football established its World Cup in 1930, cricket's first tournament was held in 1975 and, hell, even rugby league was in on the act in the 1950s. It's not as if international rugby was not being played: the Southern Hemisphere triumvirate of New Zealand, South Africa and Australia were darting across the equator to play from the start of the twentieth century, by which time the forerunner of the Six Nations Championship – the Home Nations Championship – had been up and running for nearly twenty years. With improvements in travel, surely it would only have been a matter of time before a global contest was started? However, it required the threat of outside agencies setting up their own competition, and thereby potentially splitting the governing body's autonomy, to bludgeon the IRB into commissioning, then accepting, feasibility studies from New Zealand and Australia. Even so, little more than eighteen months before the inaugural tournament kicked off, England, for one, and Ireland, another, had not accepted their invitations to participate, and it was not by any means certain that they would.

The crux of the problem was the sport's deep-rooted adherence to the amateur ethos upon which it was founded. And the traditionalists in the Northern Hemisphere were not about to give up a hundred years of history easily. At the same time, the handcuffs of amateurism were being loosened Down Under and, though not openly, players were being paid to play. The debate centred on the question of 'broken-time payments', the need to reimburse players for loss of income while away representing their country. It was argued that no employer was going to allow leave for upwards of a month for an employee to head off and play rugby. At the same time, there was an unstoppable revolution at club level with the 'friendly' fixtures of the past being corralled into a coherent league system. Gradually the traditionalists on rugby boards around the world found themselves overtaken by the changing pace of life as professionalism swept all before it. And the Rugby World Cup became the vehicle upon which the change was driven through.

The transition was swift. It went from nought to sixty within a decade. John Eales, the former Australian captain who played in the Wallabies' two World Cup successes to date, summed up the wind of change in an article he wrote for the *Daily Telegraph* in 2003: '[The] 1991 [tournament] was amateur, 1995 was shamateur (or at least on the cusp of professionalism) and 1999 was supposedly full-blown professional, though the largely amateur nature of some of the participating unions probably meant it was more of a pro-am'. He revealed how this manifested itself in practical terms. 'In 1991, against many of our instincts, we sold programmes on the streets of Dublin and tickets to the final just to make a bit of pocket money on the side,' he said. 'Can you imagine Martin Johnson and Jonny Wilkinson selling £5 English team programmes (£10 if they were signed!) on the streets of Perth? It doesn't become them; neither did it become Nick Farr-Jones or Michael Lynagh, but they still did it – they were part of the team and those were the times.'

So amateur was the Rugby World Cup at inception that the men in blazers talked about 'showing a surplus' on the balance sheet; now the men in suits, who have taken over from Will Carling's 'old farts', talk about revenue streams running into millions and millions of pounds. Some of the profits are distributed in accordance with the organisers' original altruistic aim of furthering the game in its outposts. In 1987, just the obvious sixteen leading rugby-playing nations were invited – less the pre-Mandela South Africa, still under apartheid and the blanket sporting ban that entailed; for the 2015 tournament, eighty countries competed in a qualifying process that started less than six months after Richie McCaw held aloft the trophy for New Zealand in 2011. The eight nations who ploughed their way successfully through the qualifying hoops will join the dozen automatic berths awarded to teams finishing in the top three in their pools in the previous tournament. The so-called 'minnows' are still subject to the odd chewing over by the 'big fish', but the one-sided contests are becoming less prevalent. Indeed, performances over the course of the World Cup years have led to Italy being admitted to make the Five Nations the Six Nations Championship, and Argentina, third in 2007, to the now four-team Rugby Championship in the Southern Hemisphere. Meanwhile, Japan will host the 2019 tournament as rugby's tentacles extend into Asia.

The *Daily* and *Sunday Telegraph* have each had only two rugby correspondents in the quarter of a century or so of the World Cup's existence. The Johns, Mason (*Daily*) and

Reason (*Sunday*), were in situ for the conception, birth and toddler years. Reason retired first, handing over in time for the third tournament to Paul Ackford, the lock who played for England in the 1991 final. Mason's retirement ushered in Mick Cleary ahead of the 1999 tournament. They were joined in print at various times by colleagues including rugby writers Brendan Gallagher, Charles Randall and Mark Reason (John Reason's son); rugby columnist and former England fly-half Stuart Barnes; feature writers Michael Calvin, Paul Hayward, Martin Johnson (not that one), Ian Ridley, Brough Scott, Kate Battersby, Owen Slot and Jim White; plus the token Australian, Peter FitzSimons, one of his country's finest sports journalists and a former Wallabies lock. Fitz's gloating piece after Australia's victory over England in the 1991 final, and the literary equivalent of eating humble pie after the reversal in 2003, injected much-needed humour into an often brutal and bruising arena.

Interspersed among the contemporary reports are a selection of readers' letters to provide light relief and a different perspective. At the end of each chapter are the results from the knockout stages as a reminder of how the tournament panned out. In addition, the *Telegraph* has also been fortunate to acquire the services of former and current players who drop in occasionally and offer expert analysis and insight. Not all of them have survived the editor's cut and made it into this book. But here is a *dramatis personae* of the dozen who did, in alphabetical order:

Mark Bailey – the former England winger from the 1980s, capped in the first World Cup, provides a critique of the great Australian David Campese

Matt Dawson – England's World Cup-winning scrum-half offers an insider's view of the 2003 campaign

Ieuan Evans – the former Wales captain and wing runs his critical eye over the performances of his successors in the scarlet jersey

Nick Farr-Jones – scrum-half who captained Australia to the first of their World Cup wins prepares to hail the players who achieved success number two

Will Greenwood – centre for England's 2003 World Cup champions, and a regular contributor to the *Telegraph*'s rugby pages, recalls the pinnacle of his playing career

Tim Horan – World Cup-winning centre for Australia in 1991 and 1999 congratulates and empathises with England's 2003 players

David Kirk – captain of the first World Cup winners despairs in 2007 of his successors in all black *ever* recapturing the trophy

Thierry Lacroix – the top points scorer in 1995 is driven to distraction by contrasting French performances a week apart at the business end of the 1999 tournament

Nick Mallett – coach of South Africa at the 1999 World Cup, and Italy in 2011, analyses the legacy of the Springboks' 2007 success

Hugo Porta – stalwart of Argentina XVs in the 1970s and 1980s celebrates the Pumas' outstanding third-place finish in 2007

Matt Stevens – the England prop describes the impact of the World Cup during his formative years in South Africa ahead of playing in the 2007 tournament

Steve Thompson – England's hooker in 2003, and self-confessed 'Muppet', on what that World Cup win meant to him

Anyway, you've seen the newspaper, now read the book.

MARTIN SMITH
March 2015

PREFACE

THE IMAGE OF GLORY

Shut your eyes and let the images crowd in, and seared forever into the retina is that last-minute Wilkinson moment, the jink right for the drop-kick and the white ball spinning into history. It crowned the ultimate in *Boy's Own* heroics.

Brough Scott on the moment England won the World Cup, 2003

CHAPTER ONE: 1987

HOSTED BY NEW ZEALAND & AUSTRALIA

24 MAY
ENGLAND'S SHORTFALL
John Reason

Most Australians feel New Zealanders have given them a great deal less than nothing down the ages. But chubby little Keith Lawrence, the New Zealand referee for England's opening World Cup match, more than made up for the shortfalls of history. With the scores tied 6–6 midway through the second half, and Dean Richards and the rest of the England back row skinning the Australian giraffes alive for the ball on the floor, Lawrence gave Australian winger David Campese a try after he had literally thrown the ball away in Peter Williams's tackle over the line. Mr Lawrence did not see this, and, sadly, he did not see much else either. He had a disastrous day, particularly in relation to offside, and some of the advantage he played came straight out of *Alice in Wonderland*. All the referee did do was fall like a ton of bricks on England in the line-out, and that presented Australia with a 19–6 advantage in penalty kicks, exactly the same as the score.

Australia were grateful for all the help they could get

because their allegedly awesome pack looked just as vulnerable as giraffes always do when someone takes the leaves and the trees away and makes them bend down to drink among the crocodiles. Not that England deserved to win. But they did make a nonsense of the lordly observations of Alan Jones, Australia's immensely entertaining coach, to the effect that his team were now operating at such a level that they ought to be able to play Beethoven from the sheet music. By the time England had finished with them, Australia looked as if they ought to go back to their two-finger exercises, and no doubt they would have done if England had not been performing them with great relish all through the match.

When it came to grubbing for the loose ball, poor Poidevin had to play England on his own, and he was usually a bad third in the contest. Richards, Rees and Winterbottom really had a day to remember, and Richards showed the world that he is not just a tiger at Leicester. England lost Marcus Rose with concussion in the first five minutes when his head cracked against the ground, but Jon Webb came on to win his first cap and probed forward constantly to release Rory Underwood and Mike Harrison on the wings. Webb was not nearly so successful with his goal-kicking, though he did convert England's try from the touchline, and he could console himself with the thought that Michael Lynagh, Australia's goal-kicker, was even worse, even though the referee gave him every opportunity for practice. Webb kicked one out of three; Lynagh kicked three out of ten.

It was a mistake for Brian Moore, the England hooker, to try to throw so many balls to Richards at the back. Richards had encouraged all his teammates by showing that he could take on anyone around the field, but in the line-out he was as outnumbered as Poidevin was in the loose. Also, Moore's throwing was not accurate enough. England should have made more use of short penalties. Instead, they kicked the few they had straight off the field, and straight back to the Australian jumpers. Lynagh kicked two penalty goals for Australia in the first half, but England came back twelve minutes after half-time with a try by Harrison after a drive by Richards. Webb converted.

As Underwood had already knocked on when he had nothing between him and Australia's posts, Australia were glad to be where they were, and they were even more relieved when Campese was given his try and Poidevin followed up a thrust by Grigg to score another. Lynagh converted that try and kicked another penalty goal but, in a determined finish, the England wings came close to scoring on three more occasions, and Underwood was late-tackled by Gould in trying to follow a kick ahead which ended on Australia's line. The referee? You're quite right. He did not see that, either.

28 MAY
ANOTHER ROMP FOR THE ALL BLACKS
John Mason

In another semi-opposed training session, the All Blacks ran in eleven more tries, were awarded a penalty try for good measure and organised the show in Christchurch precisely as they pleased. For the second World Cup match in succession, New Zealand destroyed the rugby pretensions of the division-two nations. First, Italy were the victims, beaten 70–6; here it was the turn of Fiji, thumped 74–13.

Having caught the Argentines utterly unprepared for a match in which speedy use of the loose ball was the key in their opening 28–9 win, the Fijians decided well in advance that victory was out of the question against the All Blacks. A much-changed team were an incompetent muddle as New Zealand strode to another monumental victory by ten goals, two tries and two penalty goals to a try and three penalty goals. Detailed analysis would be irrelevant.

That will not stop – nor should it – the Gallagher family of Ladywell, Lewisham, in south-east London, feeling extremely proud. There might be the odd cheer at St Joseph's Academy, Blackheath, too. John Gallagher, the New Zealand full-back, late of St Joseph's and London Irish Colts, scored four of the All Blacks' twelve tries, a feat which stole some of the thunder from Christchurch's favourite son, Craig Green, the left wing. Green also scored four tries, the first of which took him to one hundred first-class tries in his career, the fourteenth New Zealander to achieve that figure. He stands equal tenth in the overall list with Stu Wilson with 103 tries.

The World Cup, to an extent, has cheapened some records and it would be ludicrous to pretend that the All Blacks were truly tested here. But Green and Gallagher did play well in contrasting styles and deserve credit for that. The tries against Fiji were Gallagher's first in his fifth match for his adopted country. Like his father, he is also a policeman and when not playing rugby pounds the beat in Wellington where he emigrated three years ago. He is twenty-three. The rout of Fiji has created no illusions for the former Londoner, a modest young man who played one senior match for London Irish. Nor do his All Black colleagues pretend that to date in the inaugural World Cup they have been greatly stretched.

In addition to a penalty try, Kirk, the captain, Alan Whetton and Kirwan also crossed Fiji's line. Fox kicked twelve goals from fifteen attempts and twice hit the posts – a masterly exhibition of long-range goal-kicking. Koroduadua, Fiji's full-back, put over three goals from four kicks. At the end Jioji Cama, the lock, completed a multi-handling raid to secure Fiji's only try.

9 JUNE

ENGLAND AT ROCK BOTTOM AND OUT
John Mason

Even the Queensland skies wept at the sorry state of British rugby. England struck rock bottom in Brisbane, and Wales, though handing another drubbing to the old enemy, had no cause for complacency. But, laboured as victory was, by far the more efficient team earned the privilege of opposing New Zealand in the semi-final. In winning at the Ballymore Ground by 16–3, two goals and a try to a penalty goal, Wales needed to defend stoutly for a time, keep their heads and wait for England's mistakes, of which a large number were unforced. England were dreadful, however. They were shorn of ideas, tactical appreciation and what Clive Rowlands, the Wales manager, the sage of Upper Cwmtyrch, graphically described afterwards as '*calan*' – the Welsh word for heart.

It is popularly supposed through the years that the professional critics (in an amateur game) persistently build false hopes for England. Then, when the team fail, which has been frequently in recent times, out come the knives because aims that were probably never in reach have not been achieved. When Brian Lochore, the All Blacks coach, declares publicly and in detail, as he did in Christchurch, why he thought England would beat Wales, such opinions possess substance, not journalistic whimsy. Lochore was convinced that England would qualify to face New Zealand. He was not alone in that view and, if truth be known, some prominent Welshman, not too distant from the squad, found it difficult to disagree. Yet, come the day in wind, rain and on a soggy, yielding surface, and without adding insult to injury, it is hard to decide what aspects England managed efficiently or which individuals offered a semblance of known form.

From the moment that the vociferous Welsh contingent gave a spirited rendering of 'Land of My Fathers', England backpedalled, taking the wrong options with almost wilful intent. The painful point was that England did not lack for possession. But all that ball was useless without control, as were the decisions to run before a satisfactory platform had been established up front.

The three tries came from English mistakes – the ball popped out of the side of a seven-man England scrum more or less at the feet of a delighted Gareth Roberts. Wales had been attacking and Rendall, England's loose-head, got a finger (accidentally) in his left eye. Thorburn converted easily to make the score 6–0 at the break, Webb having missed two penalty goal attempts for England. A surging raid by Collins, which was stopped initially, regathered momentum and Robert Jones won a long race for a rolling ball that England should have killed. Harding lost that helter-skelter chase and the inhibitions and the nerves began to play havoc, even with the senior hands. Wales, again, had England on the run. Webb, who kicked a penalty goal, almost broke the deadlock, but was firmly held on the last lap. England, their hard work for this competition in ruins, had one last fling. A loop, a miss and a long floating pass created space all right – space for John Devereux, one arm aloft, to score at the posts after a deft interception. Thorburn converted. New Zealand will not be quaking.

14 JUNE
FRENCHMEN ROAR INTO WORLD FINAL
John Reason

Australia's national anthem begins with the first few notes of 'Come Landlord Fill the Flowing Bowl'. Well, the Wallabies and France certainly did that, and they went on filling it until it had run over and France had come back from 9–0, 15–12 and 24–21 to win one of the greatest games of rugby by 30–24. I never thought I would live to see a game to rival the one played between the Barbarians and the All Blacks in Cardiff in 1973, but this one did. It had a few more mistakes and not so many great players. Also, Australia in 1987 are not in the same class as New Zealand in 1973, but so much was happening in so many places for so much of the time that this game will be remembered as long as the World Cup is played. What a pity that a miserable crowd of only 17,000 turned up to watch. The resilience of the French was remarkable. They were much the more inventive and exciting team all through, but for ages they did not get the reward that was their due. Other French teams, at other times, would have given up with broken hearts.

Australia went 6–0 up in the first eight minutes, when Lynagh dropped a rifling goal from a line-out and kicked a penalty goal after Condom had collapsed a maul. France then took over, and constructed a lovely try for Erbani with a short passing move from a line-out only to realise that the referee had not given them advantage and had given them a penalty kick for obstruction instead. Camberabero missed it. But the French heads stayed up. By then, the French forwards were mauling like lions and any ball which was not taken clean off the top of the line-out by Australia finished up in French hands much more often than not. Also, the early departure of the brilliant Papworth with a knee injury meant that France were left with nearly all the class behind the scrum.

Far from closing the gap, though, France saw it increased. Lynagh kicked a penalty goal from fifty-seven yards, and ten minutes from half-time he had a dolly of a kick from in front of the posts. Fortunately for France, Lynagh missed it, France took a quick drop-out, and within a couple of minutes they had scored the try which turned the game and set it alight. It was entirely appropriate, thereafter, that it was scored by Alain Lorieux, who used to be a fireman. Coker, the Australian No. 8, won the ball at a line-out, but had it ripped off him and Lorieux plunged over. Not only that, but Camberabero kicked the conversion from the touchline. That meant that Australia led only 9–6 at half-time and that they had lost their one back who could side-step fresh air. They had also lost Campbell, one of their line-out giraffes, with another knee injury, and it had been made quite clear to their forwards that France had the edge in the scrummaging.

So France were in business and Australia's game of stacking the line-out, and cashing in for position from the ping-pong kicking of Lynagh and Campese before playing a few miss moves in the opposing twenty-five, was nothing like as valid as it had been. By the end of this extraordinary game, Australia had won the line-outs only 25–19. That was enough for France. They scored a marvellous try at the beginning of the second half. Some beautifully controlled forward drives and another remarkable plunge by Lorieux set up a rucked ball that Berbizier and Mesnel used to make an opening for a sweetly balanced run by Sella which gave him a try between the posts. Camberabero converted. That made it 9–12. But then, Lynagh got inside Mesnel from a maul, and Grigg flipped a long pass back inside for Campese to score a try which Lynagh converted for 15–12. And in the next minute he had another easy penalty kick to make it 18–12. He missed that.

France thought that the gods might be on their side after all. Berbizier and Charvet ran a ball out to the left, and Blanco pulled in three defenders, like a sinuous black spider, before launching the sharp-footed Lagisquet on a scoring run. Again Camberabero converted and when he kicked a penalty goal for offside, France led 21–15 and it looked as if Australia were dead and buried. Not a bit of it. As this seething match went into the last quarter, Codey suddenly erupted from an attacking line-out, and with that tremendous man Rodriguez rubbing his eyes in disbelief at an unpunished knock-on, Codey struggled over to score a try which Lynagh converted. 21–21. Mesnel missed a drop at goal, Australia somehow held a brilliant French move and then, at the other end, Blanco made what looked like the mistake of a lifetime by playing silly whats-its in front of his line. The ball he shipped out was a disaster, France were collared and conceded a penalty in front of the posts which Lynagh kicked. 24–21.

Surely, we thought, that was the end. Not a bit of that, either. Camberabero kicked a penalty, which Champ could not bear to watch, after a late tackle, and then at the death, a surging move involving Champ, Lagisquet, Berbizier, Mesnel, Charvet, Berbizier again and Lagisquet again saw Rodriquez in support and Blanco forgetting his injured hamstring and going for his life and a try in the corner. Camberabero converted from the touchline for the second time. Camberabero has had a hair-transplant. It worked for Samson, too.

15 JUNE
WALES DEMOLISHED BY REMORSELESS NEW ZEALAND
John Mason

Wales, the last of the Home Unions in the competition, were ignominiously removed from the World Cup by a merciless New Zealand team who took no prisoners. 'They scored eight tries, didn't they?' said Clive Rowlands, the Wales manager, afterwards. 'We're a proud nation and proud of our rugby players but we had no answer to that.' Neither an answer nor a prayer, I fear, though there was gallantry in the course of an overwhelming 49–6 defeat of seven goals, a try and penalty goal to a goal. In five cup matches New Zealand have not scored fewer than thirty points.

The occasion was not enhanced by the miserable episode in the closing minutes when Richards, the Wales lock, was sent off for punching. As he was semi-conscious at the time, a rough justice of sorts was done. But foolish as Richards was, one New Zealander was equally at fault. I do not doubt for a moment that Wayne Shelford, the All Black No. 8, should have been dismissed as well. It was Shelford, an outstanding forward in all other respects, who laid Richards low with a mighty right cross after the Welshman had attacked Gary Whetton. Two wrongs do not make a right and Shelford, who was not sent off, should be suspended by the New Zealand Union. The chances of that happening, unless there is a dramatic change of heart, are as likely as Wales being able to compete with New Zealand's driving forwards either yesterday, today, next week or next year.

Wales have been fiendishly unlucky. For various reasons they were missing five first-choice forwards for the semi-final. Against the Whettons and Shelfords of this world that is an impossible handicap. Whenever in trouble New Zealand reverted to the pack. McDowell, the loose head, skipped around like a three-quarter and there was thunderous running from everywhere including some, it is a pleasure to record, from John Devereux, who scored the Welsh try which Thorburn converted. New Zealand's tries went to Shelford (two), Drake, Kirwan (two), Alan Whetton, Stanley and Brooke-Cowden. Fox kicked eight goals from eleven kicks and five of those drives went to the forwards.

19 JUNE
WALES LEAVE IT LATE
John Mason

Wales, mischievously labelled the 49-ers after their crushing defeat by New Zealand, came from behind at the last gasp to secure third place by beating Australia 22–21. A huge crowd, comfortably settled in a natural amphitheatre at Rotorua with a breathtaking backdrop of rolling green hills and distant, dark forests, thoroughly enjoyed themselves, not least because Australia were beaten. In some respects due to the largely New Zealand crowd, it was immaterial that Wales – triumphant by two goals, a try and two penalty goals to two goals, a dropped goal and two penalty goals – were successful.

Australia performed wonders while managing to create an impossible burden for themselves: some sort of 'macho' vanity was their undoing and, to a great degree, the Wallabies, I regret, forfeit sympathy. Codey, having been warned after barely a minute following a tussle with Roberts, waded in with his feet three minutes after. As Australia were on the point of winning the ball, his foolishness was unforgiveable. Fred Howard, the referee, called Codey across, turned him round to inspect the jersey number and, with an imperious wave, pointed to the dressing rooms. Codey's offence was more stupid than evil, the unthinking act of a self-styled 'hard man'.

So, from the fifth minute, Wales were playing against fourteen men, a challenge that they fumbled and fretted about for the rest of a highly exciting but otherwise bumbling match. Wales led three times and were behind twice, the second occasion for half an hour before Hadley, his path cleared by Thorburn, thundered into the corner. Still the agony was not over. From the left touchline, the crowd baying and the fifth minute of injury time about to begin, Thorburn had to convert a try to win the match. Suddenly the bank behind the posts erupted and Wales were in front again.

Australia's tries were by the speeding Burke and Grigg, up in support on the other wing. Lynagh kicked the goals, including the dropped goal. The Wales tries went to the gallant Roberts, who was driven over by his colleagues, Paul Moriarty in support of Webster, and, at the end, by Hadley. Thorburn kicked the goals, including the most famous conversion of his career.

22 JUNE

CAPTAIN KIRK LEADS
ALL BLACKS TO GLORY
John Mason

New Zealand's right to be first holders of the Webb Ellis trophy after an emphatic 29–9 victory over France at Eden Park, Auckland, cannot be in question. In six matches they scored 298 points, including forty-three tries, and conceded fifty-two points. Most would also regard the All Blacks as world champions irrespective of the absence of South Africa, though that is not a view that I share. The sporting sadness is that at this point we shall never know whether the All Blacks could have beaten the Springboks.

What is not the slightest doubt is that France, having sought confrontation up front as they did in victory over New Zealand in Nantes in November 1986, could not match the All Blacks' pack. An intermittent sweeping drizzle and a gusting wind that eased later added to the problems of an occasion which offered more in prospect than in reality. Rarely can victory have been so prized in rugby.

There is a raw-boned intensity, a physical presence that is spine-chilling about the way that New Zealanders play rugby. France, for all their new-found discipline which did waver momentarily, could not live with that. As well as stand-in captain David Kirk directed tactical affairs and his own attacking inclinations, one player in this august company and at the pinnacle of an invigorating tournament stood out: Michael Jones, the forthright flanker who is as modest as he is successful. A year before, Jones, twenty-two, was an Auckland reserve at Province level and in New Zealand terms had played only a handful of first-class or senior matches. His displays during this tournament have been masterly, the epitome of power, pace and perception.

Fox put New Zealand ahead with a dropped goal from a free-kick after France had withdrawn too late from a formed line-out. The pressure never eased and when Lagisquet fumbled another Fox attempt, Jones swept aside Blanco's tackle for the try. The painstaking Fox carefully converted and New Zealand turned round to face the breeze and the setting sun 9–0 ahead. Still the locals were apprehensive.

Those fears did not slacken when Camberabero, from far out on the left, struck a perfect goal after the All Blacks for once had poured over the top of the ball instead of remaining on their feet. Two swift penalty goals rattled the French. Jones added to their misery in sterling support of Fox, and Kirk, avoiding three tackles, scored the try. Immediately Kirk, always elusive at scrum-half, broke away again attacking the short side. When the tackle came, Shelford, the No. 8, picked up at full tilt and Kirwan, at fire-engine speed, was alongside for the try. At 19–3 the final was over.

The gallant Berbizier did get across the New Zealand line at the whistle and Camberabero converted, but Fox had already kicked two more penalty goals, both for offside. New Zealand, unfussed, unscathed, were the world champions.

23 JUNE

WHY RUGBY'S WORLD CUP IS HERE TO STAY
John Mason

The voyage through previously uncharted water is over. The dreaded unknown of rugby union's first World Cup, its threat to the ideals and attitudes of conservative administrators among the Home Unions, has proved harmless in reality. International Board members from Britain and Ireland, the areas where there has been most reticence, appreciate far better than previously a variety of rugby issues in New Zealand and Australia. They have studied at first hand the problems that Australia have in promoting rugby union – and the immense progress that has been made irrespective of indifferent public support in Sydney.

There will be a greater awareness, too, of the part that rugby plays in New Zealand's life and why the commercial world there sees rugby, and its stars, as highly desirable vehicles for media and television advertising. In a salubrious Auckland watering hole the company was asked who the most popular man in New Zealand was at present. The only doubt was which All Black it should be – David Kirk, the captain, or Michael Jones, the World Cup's leading player.

Rugby's first world tournament (less South Africa), which yielded four weeks of intense competition between sixteen nations, was a resounding success in all practical terms except, conceivably, financial. Every unofficial estimate points to a surplus of £1.2 million, if not more. The formula for cutting the financial cake is complicated, nor are the divisions equal. New Zealand will receive twenty-three per cent, Australia, as co-hosts, seventeen and the International Board ten. The remaining fifty per cent will be split fourteen ways. John Kendall-Carpenter, chairman of the World Cup organising committee, was not joking when he said that the money could never be enough. The Board are mandated to establish a permanent secretariat as well as promoting the game worldwide.

In theory no decision about another World Cup will be taken until the Board meet in Agen, home of Albert Ferrasse, the chairman and president of the French Federation, this November. But while the niceties of procedure and protocol have to be observed, nothing is more certain than that there will be a second tournament in 1991. The venue and timing (probably autumn) will be subject to Olympic-style lobbying. Had France beaten New Zealand in the final, Monsieur Ferrasse could have presented an unassailable case for staging the next World Cup. Defeat, though, meant that the four Home Unions must remain as equal contenders.

The withering snorts of disapproval in the Northern Hemisphere that have greeted New Zealand's methods to secure victory at Eden Park I find puzzling. France were not allowed to spread themselves, New Zealand did not need to. As a means of ensuring possession of a sport's first World Cup, the match plan was less than riveting. As an example of forthright single-mindedness, efficiency and physical fitness, it was an exercise beyond compare.

France could not compete in that arena, the stranglehold exerted by the back row squeezing every attacking idea from their system. Containment, and destruction, are not pretty to watch but they brought the sweetest victory of all. France fell bravely, as did Scotland in the quarter-finals against the same opponents. Both restricted New Zealand to fewer tries than usual; both conceded a succession of penalties that Grant Fox (126 points) put away for breakfast, lunch and dinner.

Wales, aglow with pride at third place, deserved everything they got, a sentiment which, the deliberate ambiguity notwithstanding, must be taken at face value. In most respects they did well, despite difficulties because of injuries. The trouncing Wales received in the semi-final when New Zealand scored eight tries will have left scars that may never heal. Huw Richards, who was sent off, will never forget that afternoon, that is for sure.

28 JUNE
LETTERS TO THE EDITOR
ALL-CONQUERING ALL BLACKS

SIR – The All Blacks won fairly and in my view could have given any of the other competing teams a ten-point start and still have won the cup.

J.R. Waldron
Henley-on-Thames
Oxfordshire

1987 RESULTS – Quarter-finals: New Zealand 30, Scotland 3; Wales 16, England 3; France 31, Fiji 16; Australia 33, Ireland 15. Semi-finals: New Zealand 49, Wales 6; France 30, Australia 24. Third-place: Wales 22, Australia 21. Final: New Zealand 29, France 9.

CHAPTER TWO: 1991

HOSTED BY ENGLAND, FRANCE, IRELAND, SCOTLAND & WALES

3 OCTOBER
A MINORITY SPORT OUT TO CONVERT A GLOBAL AUDIENCE
John Mason

The Rugby World Cup, the tournament which was born of a fear that outside commercial interests might hijack the sport, begins an operation to persuade a sceptical public world-wide that the game does have a popular appeal. A programme of thirty-two matches in five countries in little more than a month will delight the devoted. The RWC organisers, though, have targeted a far wider audience in the hope that rugby union, a minority sport in most countries, can establish a higher profile.

For once, England, who can reasonably lay claim to have fostered if not founded the game, and New Zealand, the world champions, must take a back seat. Instead, the sport's emerging nations, those without funds or a rugby tradition, stand to derive most benefit, financial and in kind. Appetites, it is felt, will be whetted by the televising of the tournament to an audience said to be two billion in more than sixty countries, ranging from China to Chile.

Though RWC is a £24 million venture it has not attracted anything like the amount of sponsorship money originally expected. Instead of companies queueing up to be part of the event, the arms of the accountants and the marketing managers have had to be twisted. Another setback, in addition to worldwide economic recession, has been an indifferent response overseas to supporter packages. Add in the collapse of the Keith Prowse Agency, who had the hospitality contract, and the returns have been substantially below the sums budgeted for initially. There has been a knock-on effect for the ticket touts, too. Black-market prices for England versus New Zealand tickets have dropped sharply. A pair of tickets previously on offer at £400 were available for £150. One London travel agent was able to purchase fifty cheaper tickets at face value for use by an overseas rugby club. They had travelled with tickets for matches in other pools and had expected to watch the Twickenham game on television.

Yet whatever the arguments about the business side, to say nothing of the calamities and the possibility of much smaller surpluses than had been bargained for, the World Cup will stand as the sport's prodigal son, sired by New Zealand and Australia. Even England and Ireland, the two countries most alarmed initially at the implications of such a tournament, which has been set up on a four-year cycle, accept that the future worldwide development of the game – playing, coaching, refereeing, administering – cannot be paid for in any other way.

England, the Grand Slam champions, and New Zealand, who won the inaugural competition, are two of the five countries regarded as possible winners. The absence of South Africa is regretted, though the principal wish in this respect is that their Springbok officials get their house in order as soon as possible. New Zealand, who openly acknowledge the forthright challenge of Australia, believe that they will beat England here – a conclusion which is not easily disputed. Scotland, with the prospect of five matches at Murrayfield for as long as they go on winning, have a heaven-sent opportunity to reach the final. Recent stumbles by them can, I think, be discounted, though a lack of reserve strength among the tight five forwards could be their undoing.

4 OCTOBER
HARD TRUTHS RAMMED HOME BY POWER OF THE ALL BLEAK ALL BLACKS
Michael Calvin

Perhaps it is as well there were no New Zealanders around in 1823 when William Webb Ellis had the bright idea of picking up a rugby ball and running with it. One would not only have feared for the schoolboy's health. The game he created, with an inspired gesture of non-conformity, would have been stillborn as a spectacle. The launch of rugby union's second World Cup at Twickenham was a time for hard, unpalatable truth. The wolf pack espousing professionalism remains at the door and multi-national sponsors will expect their global audience to be maximised here.

There was much for the initiated to admire in the intensity of commitment that marked England's 18–12 defeat by the All Blacks. But the sport has to come to terms with the fact that New

Zealand, its best team, are also its worst advertisement. They are functional rather than the stuff of fantasy, and instinctively strangle important matches by playing result rugby. To those outsiders whom the game wishes to woo in this World Cup, they are as inviting as a Pythagorean puzzle.

'They're fast, physical, fit and durable,' said a notably low-key Will Carling, England's captain. 'There's not a lot of thrills when they play, but not many mistakes either.' Geoff Cooke, the England manager, said: 'New Zealand are very predictable, but difficult to stop. They're very good at putting sides under pressure. They just turn the screw.' Even Brian Moore, the hooker who continues to be the most overtly emotional of England players, reflected the grey mood of the day. 'They are the best at ensuring an advantage is pressed home,' he admitted.

Something, clearly, was missing. Someone forgot to invite the founding spirit of rugby to the party, which promptly fell flat. As if to prove amateurism is alive and well in at least one area of the game, the organisers produced an opening ceremony that merely highlighted the competition's pretensions. It had the patronage of Prince Edward, whose speech fell foul of the rugby fan's endless search for double entendre, and a nostalgic parade featuring such legends as Colin Meads, Gerald Davies and Bill Beaumont. Yet it had the razzmatazz of a Rotarians' annual meeting and generated the sense of occasion of a village bring-and-buy sale. It was as inappropriate as Arnold Schwarzenegger addressing a feminists' convention.

Twickenham, on a day for the ages, is not about a prim singer, Michael Ball, fresh from Broadway, delivering an instantly forgettable made-for-TV anthem, available immediately in all good record shops. It is about the camaraderie of the car park, old friends sharing a sense of anticipation that simmers gently until an explosion of enthusiasm greets the players who trot out from beneath the West Stand. Those traditions, and not sideshows such as sky-divers, whose attempts to deliver the match ball are vulnerable to the vagaries of the English climate, make the Five Nations Championship so special.

The car parks were a sorry sight, even before the rains came and ruined the big moment of the RAF's Falcon precision-parachuting team. The nanny state had banned barbecues and the impromptu picnics were regarded with suspicion. To pass the time, all the spectators had were tawdry concession stands and the full, mind-numbing scope of the World Cup merchandising catalogue to contemplate. This ranges from ladies' knickers to a portrait of the sixteen World Cup captains, endorsed by Carling, and hardly a snip at £250. The captain was quoted in the programme advertisement as saying: 'The portrait, like the finals, is unique, an outstanding memento of a great event and something to treasure and enjoy for years to come.'

The hard sell fell on deaf ears. The Grand Slam decider against France was a vibrant, theatrical occasion. The opening match of the World Cup had the dour air of a report on tractor production, undertaken by pre-*perestroika* Soviet TV. It had all the failings of similar occasions in the soccer World Cup, which also tend to be decided by penalties. New Zealand played the percentages and showed no inclination to refute the modern gospel of avoidance of risk.

It is one of the afternoon's ironies that Michael Jones, one of the few All Blacks capable of capturing the imagination with his speed and athleticism, reaffirmed his determination to miss the quarter- and semi-finals because of his Christian beliefs. That will not matter while the indiscipline of opposing sides enables Grant Fox, the stand-off with the *joie de vivre* of a mathematician, to maintain his assault on the records with his right boot.

Thankfully, the game is not so enmeshed in the barbed wire of cynicism that the rather convenient theory that defeat suited England appears plausible. A quarter-final win at the Parc des Princes may, indeed, be within their scope, but there was a convincing air of disappointment as they left. John Hart, co-coach of the All Blacks, put his finger on it when he observed: 'England had been building up to that match for months.' The England players will be taunted by the fact that the All Blacks are not invincible. The problem was that the public expected the world champions merely to be better than they needed to be.

7 OCTOBER
WORLD CUP EXIT DOOR BECKONS WALES DESPITE FIGHT TO SALVAGE PRIDE
John Mason

The ten-year humiliating descent of Wales to the lower reaches of the world game is almost complete. The once proudest rugby nation in the world, the winners of five Triple Crowns and three Grand Slams in the 1970s, are set to be among the also-rans of the 1990s. Defeat, by 16–13, to Western Samoa at the Arms Park, Cardiff, in their opening match in the World Cup was the unkindest, harshest blow of all in what has been a decade of dithering in the committee room and disgrace on the field.

But, unlike in Australia in July 1991, at least this Welsh team, though beaten by a goal, try and two penalty goals to a goal, try and penalty goal, went down honourably. Emyr

Lewis battled mightily throughout, refusing to be intimidated in a match of resounding physical commitment. The tireless, forthright Lewis, who moved from flanker to No. 8 after Phil Davies had gone to lock in place of May, who dislocated a shoulder, stirred his colleagues into a sort of Dunkirk rearguard. They responded boldly in the final quarter, by which time Rayer had replaced full-back Clement (hip) and Jenkins, the reserve hooker, was in the back row in place of Collins (shoulder).

The Western Samoans tackled with a clattering relish that not only stopped opponents in their tracks. Time after time players in possession, or circling for a high ball, were knocked back yards, the ball spilling loose as the unfortunate recipient of the tackle attempted to get breath back into a bruised body.

That this was the greatest day in the history of the game in the Islands, there can be no doubt – it is their first win over an International Rugby Board country. Yet, amid all the deserved congratulations and resounding back-slapping for a famous victory, Wales were fiendishly unlucky. The try that, in all probability, has consigned them to the pre-qualifying section of the 1995 World Cup, should not have been awarded. French referee Patrick Robin was unsighted when awarding a try to To'o Vaege, Western Samao's centre, thirty-six seconds into the second half. In fact, Robert Jones, the Wales scrum-half, was first to the ball over the line to deny the score.

The conversion took Western Samoa, a dozen of whose team live and work in New Zealand, to 9–3, and a sigh of sadness at the demise of the men in red enveloped a ground barely two-thirds full. Either the absentee Welshmen knew something in advance or had no heart for a wake. As, eleven minutes later,

Wales were also a man short when Western Samoa scored their second try to make it 13–3, there appeared to be fertile ground for reasonable complaint. The try, beginning on the left-hand touch, involved five players and was completed by the flanker Vaifale, who crossed in the right-hand corner.

The embers of the fire of the Welsh dragon were sufficient to warm even the coldest heart, though. From 13–3 down, plus the need for three replacements because of injuries, Wales managed two tries in a catching-up exercise that would not have been possible a couple of months before. Inevitably Welsh heads did go down, and for a period the jarring tackles took such a toll that some hasty shifting of responsibility left Wales with an often shaky defence. Lewis, helped by Hall and, later, the coolness of Rayer, brought everyone back on course.

The final attacks were more than spirited ripostes from fallen heroes. Though victory was always an unlikely outcome once Western Samoa had built their lead, Wales did match them try for try, Evans scoring in the second minute of time added for injuries and stoppages. Vaea, the scrum-half, had a hand or foot, or both, in most of the better attacks that brought Wales to the brink of the precipice. He kicked the opening penalty goal when Griffiths came tumbling over the top, besides converting the try awarded to Vaega, whose co-centre, Bunce, was the game's outstanding back. The sturdy scrum-half also put over the penalty kick on the right-hand touch late in the second half, a well-judged effort which, in effect, won the match for a team who, as Bob Dwyer, Australia's coach, suggested, would be the surprise package of the tournament.

Hints of Welsh back play of previous years allowed Emyr and Evans, the wings, to score worthy tries. Ring, always willing to test the reflexes of opposition and colleagues alike, converted

Emyr's try, which owed much to Lewis and Hall, and kicked a penalty goal. The points were not enough to stop Welsh Rugby Union officials, whose team finished third in the 1987 World Cup, calling for the timetables and training grounds of the pre-qualifiers for 1995: Belgium, Holland, Spain and Italy. A case of see Naples and die.

10 OCTOBER
SAMOANS USE POWER TO PROVE POINT
Michael Calvin

Welcome to the World Cup, in Pontypool on the proverbial wet Wednesday. Dusk has fallen before lunchtime at the people's park and rain permeates every pore. Just when you think things cannot get any worse, you glance downfield and see Fats and his boys glaring at you, silently promising an afternoon of mayhem. As an Australian forward, you know that the Western Samoan pack, led by captain Peter Fatialofa, one of Auckland's more celebrated piano shifters, have the capacity to live up to their threat.

The walking wounded in the Wales squad, Phil May, Tony Clement and Richie Collins, will testify that these boys are fair, but play rugby hard. As Peter Schuster, the Samoan coach, confirms with a slow, wide smile: 'Fats certainly gets his boys psyched up.' Bob Dwyer, Australia's coach, unwittingly challenged them by suggesting Argentina would accompany his side into the quarter-finals from Pool Three. In such circumstances his revised verdict, which was given a clarity by a narrow 9–3 victory that ensured the Wallabies' qualification for the last eight, came too late. 'As a race, like most islanders, the Samoans have great explosive power,' Dwyer said post-match. 'I don't think they are scared of anything. Add those two things together and you've got a pretty lethal sort of weapon. They've drawn great benefit from their New Zealand experience. It has added to the side, given them another dimension. If you can sidestep them, then you do.'

Nick Farr-Jones, as a solicitor, is accustomed to the power of logic and sweet reason. But here he fell victim to an altogether more elemental force. One could not help but admire his courage in hanging on to the ball in midfield, ten minutes into the match. But, as the Australian captain was engulfed by Samoan forwards and driven backwards like a bottle top on an outgoing wave, it was cruelly counter-productive. As Farr-Jones was twisted, and then folded to the ground in a calamitous tangle of limbs, he damaged the medial ligaments of his right knee. Television cameras captured his face, contorted by pain. Teams reveal much of themselves in adversity and it speaks volumes for the Australians that, obliged to rally around outside-half Michael Lynagh, they managed to shrug off the loss of such an influential player.

The intensity of the physical confrontation they endured cannot be overstated. Forwards inhabit rugby's private world. Its violent, unseen rituals remain at odds with the current glamorisation of their game, typified by the unprecedented attention this World Cup is receiving. Some of the tackles here prompted even Pontypool's seasoned spectators to laugh nervously, like cinema-goers attempting to disguise that they have been frightened by a horror movie.

The rain fell so relentlessly, pavement entrepreneurs were doing a roaring trade in black dustbin liners, sold as impromptu raincoats, for 50p each. The lucky ones sheltered beneath golf umbrellas, which added a splash of colour to the scene. The ground, centrepiece of the 158-acre park, was bathed in an eerie light, which lent a soft focus to proceedings. When the rival sets of forwards came together steam rose gently from their straining bodies. At the end, when the players completed the time-honoured ritual of swapping sodden shirts, they had the look of racehorses who had just negotiated Aintree on Grand National day.

The mutual respect, rugby's saving grace, was total. The pride in the voice of Bryan Williams, the former All Black who is mentor of Samoan rugby, was fully justified. 'We're not smiling as much today,' he insisted as Fatialofa, sitting beside him, gestured, unsuccessfully, in the press room for a bottle of beer. 'But we have sustained our credibility. We might not have played Australia before, but we are used to measuring ourselves as individuals against the Wallabies and All Blacks. I tend to think we compare pretty favourably with everyone else here.'

Fatialofa, who appeared entirely suited to his trade, hit on a key point when he said later, in a gentle tone of voice: 'We are gaining experience all the time.' Whatever the evidence of the scoreboard, which referred to them as the visitors because the signs did not arrive in time, they are the surprise package of this World Cup. They fulfil sport's need for an underdog and generate awe with their physical power. The poodle show, the next major event to be staged at the people's park, has got something to live up to.

21 OCTOBER
RESOLUTE ENGLAND HOLD FIRM
John Mason

Not even lurid tales of assaults on the referee as the teams left the field could spoil England's moment of triumph in a match in which victory was everything. Whatever reservations there might be about the way in which it was done, the incontrovertible fact is that resolute, single-minded England beat nervy, inefficient France on every count. The reward for playing the percentages successfully, as well as recognising scoring opportunities, was a World Cup semi-final with Scotland.

For France, at odds with themselves let alone England, there was little but disarray, dissension and, for coach Daniel Dubroca and prop Pascal Ondarts, disgrace. Nor did Serge Blanco, a pale, irritable imitation of a marvellously gifted player, endear himself in what presumably was his farewell match. Either the occasion or the cares of office got to him because, sad to relate, Blanco's shortcomings helped to establish the foundations for England's rough-hewn victory by a goal, try and three penalty goals to a try and two penalty goals, 19–10.

England, understandably, were well pleased with themselves. The forwards cleared the trail, captain Carling had an outstanding match in every respect, and with a touch of class at the precise moment from Guscott, England had won a prize which I, for one, believed to be beyond their reach. Skinner, who should have a gold medal for one tackle alone on Cécillon, did exactly as the selectors required in his roving blindside flank role and, in the last quarter, Ackford ruled the line-out in a way which will have set the alarms ringing north of the border.

Manager Geoff Cooke could not resist a dig – ridiculous was the word he used – at the team's critics, conveniently forgetting that before the game he, too, had spoken less than enthusiastically about England's performances over the preceding months. It is right and proper that mother hen should bridle. It has been a hard road and until around about tea-time in Paris, not even those directly involved could be certain that they had been travelling in the right direction. Cooke told the RFU in his post-Australia summer 1991 tour report that England's minimum World Cup target was a semi-final place. That ambition achieved, the immediate future is tantalising, daunting and intriguing.

The tattoo that French fists beat on Heslop's chin in the opening minutes, after he had pursued his own high kick, set unenviable standards. Blanco, piqued at being challenged after calling a mark, joined in vigorously after Champ had let fly. The Bishop lectures began early. That was penalty goal number one to Webb, and when another short-arm came piling in three minutes later on Teague, England were six points up and France had scarcely set foot outside their territory.

The extremely bothered Lacroix, after dropping the ball initially, was in much better heart after kicking a penalty goal when England were offside. Flanker Cabannes had a strong influence on the proceedings that followed, though it was England who stated the next definitive case with a fine try. England won a two-man line-out, and with the ball being quickly worked to the left, Carling timed his pass acutely. Guscott straightened, showed Blanco the ball, and shuffled, at speed, either way. In the last stride Guscott decided not to take on the full-back and unleashed the ball to Underwood for the try – a flat, sharp pass that some of the opposition claimed was forward. I doubt it.

Lacroix's second penalty goal – offside again – took the score to 6–10 at half-time, and eleven minutes into the second half Lafond scored the try that gave France hope. It stemmed from a free-kick, the ball rebounding off Webb's shoulder. Galthié kept moving to the left and, though almost running out of space, was able to present Lafond with the scoring pass. The score was locked at 10–10 for twenty-four minutes, and with extra time looming fast, Webb's third penalty goal crept over the bar after Ondarts, to his fury, had been penalised for seeking the ball illegally. He was not happy, especially after England had offered him a few words, none of them consoling. With Ackford in command of his kingdom in the final minutes, England were safe. Hill made quite sure with another high, hanging kick. Lafond was beneath the ball and, for his pains, was driven over the line. Carling, as ever, was first up and his try, converted by Webb, was entirely appropriate.

24 OCTOBER
LETTERS TO THE EDITOR
TIRED AT THE TOP

SIR – I watched the last few minutes of the France versus England Rugby World Cup quarter-final in the lounge of a hotel in Dieppe, in the company of some French supporters and in an atmosphere of much good humour and sportsmanship. I was the only English person present.

When Webb's fine penalty kick just cleared the bar to break the 10–10 deadlock, I suggested that God must be an Englishman. '*Non,*' a charming Frenchman replied. 'He is French – but he is tired.'

Martin Middlebrook

Boston

Lincolnshire

21 OCTOBER
AUSTRALIANS COUNT COST OF LAST-GASP WIN AGAINST IRISH
Charles Randall

The genius of David Campese lit up this magnificent quarter-final at Lansdowne Road, which Australia won 19–18 with a try four minutes from time. However, doubts surround the winger's fitness for the semi-final. Campese finished the match limping and is due to have tests on his right ankle, raising fears that he has suffered another stress fracture similar to the one to his left ankle in 1987. If Campese's injury proves to be serious and Farr-Jones's fitness remains suspect, Australia will struggle to reach the final on this showing.

Ireland, beaten cruelly by Lynagh's late try, could take credit in defeat for whipping up the best contest of the tournament, helping to soothe memories of that televised chessboard violence between France and England the previous day. The Dublin game proved to the armchair millions that rugby football can offer more than wall-to-wall Garryowens and a hit record for Dame Kiri.

The start was not exactly auspicious. Within seconds, as soon as Lynagh's kick-off had descended, a mass punch-up erupted

among the forwards. Calm, though never fully restored, tip-
toed along anxiously until the pace of the game sucked the
tension out of the players. Ireland might have felt a burden of
non-expectancy, but they matched this gifted Australian team
in the set-scrums and in the loose. Even in the line-outs, where
Australia had superior forces, Ireland won fifty-five per cent, a
respectable return bearing in mind Australia were throwing in
twice as often.

Francis was again the key man in the Irish line-out, and
Smith, at hooker, could hardly have had a more effective all-
round match for his country. It was Australia's backs who
shaded the game, making every attack count, and the try
tally of three to one suggested, rightly, that many people's
favourites deserved their success. Australia, the 'home' side
in the semi-final, will probably have the Irish crowd behind
them against New Zealand after their display of resilience and
skill. It is almost unthinkable that Australia could take the field
without 'Campo' against the All Blacks. As it is, Farr-Jones,
their influential captain and scrum-half, had to be helped off
after only eighteen minutes, having aggravated his knee injury.

Campese, in his sixty-second international, emphasised his
value by scoring two lovely tries and gave Lynagh the chance
to snatch the late winner in the corner. For his first try, after
sixteen minutes, he popped up in midfield and side-stepped
his way to the posts from a long way out for the best solo try
of the tournament. In the second half, he added his second
try, his forty-fifth for Australia, after Little and Roebuck had
looped in midfield.

Australia's injury problems were nearly made hypothetical by
Ireland's committed performance which, with seven minutes
remaining, seemed to have brought about the upset of the

tournament. That was when Hamilton sprinted forty-five yards for an extraordinary try. Ireland trailed 15–12 when Staples put through a grubber kick on halfway. Clarke collected and managed to slip a pass to Hamilton on a burst which took him clear of the cover defence, Keyes converting from wide out. In the few minutes remaining, Australia forced a set-scrum back upfield and Horan and Little cut through. Campese was caught, but Lynagh followed up to break a thousand Irish hearts.

27 OCTOBER
ANDREW DROPS ENGLAND INTO THE FINAL
John Reason

A dropped goal by Rob Andrew gave England their ticket to the World Cup final after a dreadful error by Scottish full-back Gavin Hastings. With the scores level at 6–6 midway through the second half at Murrayfield, Hastings missed a penalty kick in front of the England posts. Hastings had kicked so well throughout the World Cup, and in this match, that it seemed inconceivable that he could miss. But the ball flew dramatically wide.

England then squared their shoulders and their forwards took such relentless control in the last twenty minutes that Scotland spent the whole time fighting for their lives. If they had not done it so effectively, England would have pulled clear away. Rory Underwood nearly squirmed in for a try on England's left, and half a dozen times the England scrum looked to be on the verge of scoring a push-over try. The scrum collapsed as often as not, but the referee looked no more likely to award England a penalty try than he had earlier in the half when the Scotland pack was broken just to the left of their post and pulled the scrum down as a last resort. England were given a penalty kick on that occasion and Jon Webb brought some comfort to what had been a miserable afternoon for him by kicking the goal from point-blank range.

But that only brought the scores level. England still needed another score to win. They got it from the last of a series of attacking scrums, two of which collapsed with no more stringent award than another put-in to England. From that final scrum Andrew dropped the goal. The England supporters erupted with joy and England led – by 9–6 – for the first time in the match. All England had to do then was spend what was left of the match in the Scotland half of the field and keep the same iron clamp on possession.

England were never threatened. The only inconvenience they suffered was when Skinner predictably had his white-socked toes trodden on after losing a boot and finishing the match without it. Quite properly he did not dare go off the field to put it back on. Scotland were forced to run the ball from suicidally deep positions and sometimes from behind their own line. They have nothing like enough pace to attack from a hole as deep as that, and when Tukalo on their left wing was driven into touch just short of halfway, England settled themselves comfortably to the task of winning the last line-out.

They did that with some style. Dooley caught the ball cleanly in the middle of the line-out and the England forwards wrapped themselves around him. Moore had time to peep round the maul to see if something more ambitious than a shut-out might be attempted. England thought better of it and the referee blew his whistle for the last time. As he did, Gavin Hastings's head went down. It was cruel that he should feel Scotland's defeat so personally because he, above all others, had stood between England and a more decisive victory.

He had started by kicking two penalty goals from two attempts to give Scotland a 6–0 lead, whereas Webb had kicked only one from five and was looking more and more anxious. This meant that the marked periods of the England forwards' superiority were not reflected by the scoreboard. Hastings always looked as if he was the one man who could win the match for Scotland. His tactical kicking was so much more powerful than England's and so much better placed, and his high kicks soared so far into the lowering, grey sky that for a long time it seemed as if Scotland might yet again scrape a victory out of nothing much. With a stringbean-like Weir in their second row and a crucial lack of weight and power at tight-head, Scotland were always under pressure in the scrums, but they did not fall apart in the way that many English sceptics expected. What killed Scotland in the end, as it has so many teams in this tournament, was domination of the scrummage put-in.

New Zealand shut England out of the first match of the tournament by winning twelve successive scrums in the second half and gaining total control both of possession and field position. To a lesser extent, England did the same to France in Paris with eight scrums in succession. Against Scotland, when the whips were really cracking, England put the ball into eleven scrums in a row. Scotland huffed and they puffed, they wheeled and they collapsed, but they simply could not break the grip which England held.

Scotland had started the match with the sensible objective of keeping the ball on the field as much as possible to play away from the strength of the England line-out, and they also took quick penalty kicks and switched drop-outs to keep England on the move. Initially, those switched drop-outs were aimed at embarrassing Underwood on England's left. Stanger, Scotland's burly right-wing, was the man whose physical presence was aimed at doing some bullying and harassing.

England, though, soon saw what Scotland were trying to do and split their field to cover it. Scotland also split a two-man line-out and sent flanker Jeffrey surging through it with great success – shades of Dave Gallaher and the 1905 All Blacks. Scotland were fortunate not only to escape at least one penalty try being awarded against them, but also escape punishment when their dogged little scrum-half, Armstrong, blatantly late-tackled Webb. The referee missed it completely.

Hastings kicked Scotland's first penalty goal the first time his team battled their way out of defence. Sole, Hastings and Armstrong had set up a loose ball but when it was moved out to Jeffrey in midfield, Winterbottom was penalised for falling over him. That really was an aberration by the England flanker and Hastings cashed in. He took some more profit late in the first half when Probyn, the England tight-head, and Sole, the Scotland captain, were involved in a scuffle on the ground at the front of the line-out. Sole, with his sleeves cut to his shoulders to follow the example of New Zealand's McDowell, was bowled over backwards. Hastings had no trouble kicking the goal. England did get three points back before half-time when Webb kicked a penalty goal for a scrummage collapse, and they drew level midway through the second half when he kicked another goal for a similar offence, when Scotland were going backwards.

It was yet another game that was paralysed by the fear of making a mistake. There was hardly any back play in the whole match and once again we had to endure an almost ceaseless succession of up-and-under kicks. The match was also played in an atmosphere of such rabid nationalism as to be thoroughly unhealthy, but happily the players congratulated each other and exchanged shirts with such good feeling at the end of the match that fears of another Bannockburn were dissipated, at least temporarily.

28 OCTOBER
WALTZING CAMPESE LEADS NEW ZEALAND MERRY OLD DANCE
John Mason

David Campese, eagerly aided and abetted by fourteen other Australians, brought a sparkle back to rugby in the twinkling of a few star-studded strides in Dublin. In routing the pedlars of caution, the purveyors of the unimaginative and second rate, the extraordinary Campese also brought down New Zealand, the world champions, 16–6. Victory by a goal, try and two penalty goals to two penalty goals took Australia storming through to the Twickenham final, where England will resolutely guard their territory.

If Campese, international rugby's record try scorer with forty-six, strikes only a fraction of the form that humbled the All Blacks, England will have immense problems. Ways of keeping him away from the ball will test the ingenuity of all concerned. Nor will England fool themselves that Australia cannot function without a sequence of match-winning contributions from the most talented running three-quarter in the world. They are far from being a one-man band, not the least of their abilities being the defensive barrier they erect in midfield. New Zealand could find no way through.

While Campese's skilled contributions were essential to the Wallaby cause, victory was a well-organised, spirited team effort, so competently carried out that against the All Blacks, of all teams, Australia could afford to coast a shade in the second half. New Zealand, who beat England in the opening match of the tournament, were despatched to the third-place play-off with scant ceremony. So rattled were they in the opening period that it was difficult to believe that here was the nucleus of a squad who have ruled the world for the better part of four years. Since beating France to win the inaugural World Cup, New Zealand have dealt summarily with all other opposition. Only Australia have challenged them consistently of late, winning two and drawing one of the ten matches since 1987.

The statistics, though, are austere. I am not even sure that mere words can convey the shimmering skills of Campese, who pursues magical paths of his own making. The opening try was sufficient to titillate the palate. Quite what Campese, nominally right wing, was doing far out on the left, goodness knows. It would, I suppose, have been sacrilege for an Englishman to have attempted so daring a course. There was a line-out, Australia's throw on the left midway into New Zealand territory. Away went Lynagh, searching for a gap well to his right. He got a double sandwich tackle for his pains and was submerged by wave upon wave of black shirts. Yet ball retention is second nature to these well-drilled Wallabies. Back the ball came at speed with scrum-half Farr-Jones, his right knee heavily protected, rifling the ball fast and low to his left. Campese reached for the pass at pace, attacking the ball with gusto. That took him beyond the first line of defence, and with the adrenalin pumping and the try-line in his sights, Campese pinned back his ears and went. The crowd, even some of those sporting black favours, erupted.

A Lynagh penalty goal (offside) took Australia to 7–0, and just as it seemed that the All Blacks had escaped lightly from a prolonged period of concentrated Wallaby attacks, Campese struck again. So relaxed and assured was he against some of the better players in the world, he might have been on a training run. Poidevin, a great source of comfort for Australia in the close-quarters work, re-won the ball in midfield. Farr-Jones smartly attended to the preliminaries, and with Lynagh chipping deep to his right, full-back Crowley, hastily summoned from New Zealand for this match because of injuries, moved in for the ball as it bounced at thigh height.

Even as Crowley swung in for the ball, Campese, leaning forward, swept it up without breaking stride. Horan came tearing up on Campese's left, and though spaces were being created, there was still plenty of work to be done. Campese, swaying one way and then the other, sensed that Horan had switched outside him. Still he leaned inwards, as if making for the posts at a diagonal. Then came the cheekiest of flips over his right shoulder, the ball hanging in the air for a fraction as if willing Horan to run on to it. He did – at speed again – and though there was one more challenge to come, that was a try close to the posts for Lynagh to convert.

There was a semblance of known All Black form to end the half. But Australia met every defensive demand and already it looked as if the Wallaby management could decently begin to make arrangements for a London hotel stay. Fox did not have a kick at goal throughout the half, and though he was on target in the first minute after the break, there was a lack of conviction about much of what New Zealand attempted.

Scrum-half Bachop did steal away at times and, in due course, Kirwan, the right wing, made in-roads when in possession. But everything was untidy, rushed, even inefficient. The All Black machine had met its match against a team who sought to use the ball at all times.

Lynagh's second penalty goal (early tackle on Farr-Jones when he was in mid-air) settled the match, despite some twenty minutes remaining. It was an uncanny feeling to see the men in black reduced to states of panic that I, for one, have not previously seen in a New Zealand representative team. What with Campese deciding he would do some defending for a change, Timu could not escape at any stage. If the wing stepped inside, Campese was there, and once, when trying his formidable opponent on the outside, he ended up being clattered into the advertising boards.

New Zealand decided to try the right-hand side of the pitch and there the run of play often meant that Crowley, no longer in the first flush of youth, was the extra man in support. He had neither the legs nor the match fitness to get away, so New Zealand went back to their forwards. A late penalty goal by Fox brought an edge of respectability to the fallen champions and there were a couple of mighty lunges by lock Gary Whetton, the captain, and his twin, Alan. How the Whettons must have wished that New Zealand's silver-tongued management could have persuaded Michael Jones to take part. Such are his religious beliefs that Jones, the world's most astute flank forward, will not play on Sundays.

This convincing defeat was the end of an era in New Zealand rugby, a time for reassessment and recruitment. They will not be in the doldrums for long. Australia's march to Twickenham, which has included that resounding shock they had against Ireland in the quarter-final, has been a just reward for a team who believe in the virtues of attacking rugby which, properly played, requires all fifteen players to be involved. That Australia should convey that message with such lightness of touch and sharpness of attitude must be the Rugby World Cup's continuing testament.

31 OCTOBER

NEW ZEALAND PERSISTENCE EARNS THEM CONSOLATION
John Mason

New Zealand, for the present, must reluctantly settle for third place in the world rankings. The evidence in Cardiff suggested that an improvement will not be long delayed. Victory by 13–6 against Scotland, thanks to a try and three penalty goals to two penalty goals, did a little to boost All Black morale after defeat by Australia in the semi-final. Scotland, too, made life difficult for a much-changed New Zealand team, without ever indicating that they could raise their game sufficiently to force a second helping of humble pie upon players not accustomed to defeat.

Though New Zealand's try did not come until the final seconds of a hard-fought match in which Scotland defended mightily, the contest was an impressive display of thrust and counter-thrust by both teams. Do not be misguided by the crop of penalty goals, two to Scotland, three to New Zealand. If one's heart warms to the Scots, it is because all fifteen were involved in the clattering semi-final with England, a bruising experience mentally and physically. In comparison, half-a-dozen New

Zealanders had the day off, as it were. Scotland's management can be justly proud of their part in the preparations for a competition which makes harsh demands on players. Rugby is a fierce, physical contact sport and it is well that a wider audience than previously is now aware of that.

Walter Little, paired again with Craig Innes in New Zealand's midfield, all but took charge of a match which, considering the flak it attracts, was far from being an anti-climax. While none of the top nations ever want to be involved, here both countries presented a cross-section of skills and commitment worthy of the best. That the All Blacks were a shadow of recent all-conquering teams cannot be in question. But for sheer persistence, ball-winning and ball retention, the example set throughout a fierce eighty minutes played at a demanding pace, New Zealand still managed most of the answers.

Even when the bone-shaking tackling of Scott Hastings, Jeffrey or Lineen interrupted the All Black flow, the ball rarely went astray. Back it came and off Little went again. He alone found gaps, helped by a deceptive change of pace, body swerve and sheer strength. Amid all of this, full-back Gavin Hastings prowled hungrily, secure beneath the high ball, swift to counter-attack. This, praise be, was not the player who finished the England match head down, distraught at having missed a relatively straightforward penalty goal at 6–6. Here Hastings began with a penalty goal in the fourth minute (offside) and already Little, for New Zealand, and Armstrong, for Scotland, were making their mark. So, too, was the tidy Preston at outside-half for New Zealand, who had won a World Cup place as a utility back. The points had to come, though, and Preston, in his second match for his country, was the scorer. Penalty goals in the thirteenth, thirty-fourth and forty-eighth minutes took

New Zealand to 9–3, a grip that was more secure than might appear apparent. One of those All Black raids, surely, would succeed.

Wright, still an attacking threat even after a thunderous, jarring collision with Gavin Hastings, linked left and right from full-back. At that stage Scotland were relieved, probably, that Tuigamala, having torn a hamstring in the first half, could no longer add his weighty contribution to the game. New Zealand, too, were grateful for let-offs. Hastings did pull a penalty goal attempt at 3–9 to show that lightning can strike twice. Unnecessary stamping by Loe was suitably punished, though, and, at 9–6 with about three minutes remaining, lent hope to the gallant Scots.

But it was not to be. New Zealand attacked right and left, expertly keeping possession. Again the ball was moved left through several hands. Wright flicked the ball on and Little, straightening on the left-hand touch, accelerated to the line. The road back had begun. The last moments involved Calder, who at tea-time resumed a retirement he broke for the World Cup only. The ball came snaking over the top of a line-out and there was the grey-haired, craggy Calder reaching athletically for possession. He succeeded and away Scotland went, only for a knock-on in midfield. Calder, hands on hips, slowly followed the path of the ball and within seconds, amid the handshakes and embraces, he and John Jeffrey were former internationals. Both can look back, if not on victory, then on jobs well done. Scotland have cause to be infinitely grateful.

2 NOVEMBER
CUTTING THROUGH CONSTRAINTS
OF NORMALITY
Mark Bailey

The hype attached to the New Zealand haka has reached indecent proportions. Unable to gain any form of rugby ascendancy over the mighty All Blacks, opposition teams have taken to aggressive confrontations at this pre-match ritual. Hence it is all the more significant when, under all the pressure of a World Cup semi-final, one player prefers to stand on his own and juggle with the ball while his team-mates eyeball the haka. Australia's David Campese has always been a little different.

There are many kinds of wing three-quarter, each of whom present a particular set of problems to the opposition. But there is one style of winger who will always set crowds buzzing and other wingers trembling: the fast and unpredictable runner. The front-row union may mutter about strikes against the head, but – believe me – there is nothing in rugby more humbling than lying in the mud staring at the back of Chris Oti's knee-supports as they disappear down the touchline.

Elusiveness, pace and power are the main ingredients in the armoury of a great wing three-quarter. Rory Underwood has all these qualities, plus fine ball-handling ability to boot. Yet there have been times during his distinguished half-century of international caps when Underwood has languished forlornly on the England flank. Campese has done many things in his rugby career, but he has never languished.

The first time I faced Campese was for London against Australia in 1988. The game coincided with Dick Best's first major coaching assignment with London. At the Thursday night training session, I decided to seek technical advice from Best on how to play the great man. After the briefest pause for thought, Best said: 'Do you drink much vintage claret at that educational establishment of yours?' Thrown by the conversation's sudden change in direction, I stammered an affirmative. 'Right,' shouted Best, 'then your best hope is to get a couple of bottles and tie them around his legs before the game. It's the only way you'll ever keep him subdued.' I duly drank the two bottles of claret on the Friday night, but was unable to implement the second half of the plan.

Campese's main attacking strengths are his balance and acceleration. Acceleration is the key to penetrative running in international rugby, because gaps are closed down so rapidly. Balance enables him to follow defensive gaps as they appear, and to ride the half-knocks. Balance is nature's way of compensating Campese for any lack of raw power. For an international three-quarter there is no substitute for either of these qualities, though they alone are not sufficient to elevate a player to the heights of greatness. Campese's real assets are his nose for an opening, and his taste for the unexpected.

Much of Campese's contribution to the Australian effort is based less on instinct than on precise planning and training. Australia seldom look to pass the ball directly along the three-quarter line to Campese from scrums and line-outs. Instead, the midfield backs will employ a pre-set move designed to fix their opposite numbers into running a particular defensive line. Campese will then come off his wing at an angle of attack which cuts against the grain of the defence. Most international sides employ moves of this nature, but their objective is principally to get the ball-carrier in front of their forwards. Campese, however, is always looking to go further, as his quarter-final try against Ireland indicates. His ability to penetrate 'first-up' defence owes much to his precise and astute lines of running.

Of course, the real joy of watching Campese is his unpredictability. When a penalty is awarded, or a line-out signalled, players invariably relax their concentration; in contrast Campese comes alive at such moments, his instincts alert. A favourite ploy is to slip silently outside his winger (while the opposition argue with the referee over the penalty award), and to chase a quickly taken cross-kick by Lynagh. In this mood Campese is – in the words of Alan Black – 'a bloody nuisance'.

Campese's irreverence for the predictable is based on a deep confidence in his own ability, and a salutary disrespect for the consequences of a failed mission. Yet errors are the crumbs which can inevitably fall from such a high-risk diet. Indeed, some of his countrymen have not forgiven the blunder which gave the Lions their series victory in Australia in 1989. Despite such lapses, and contrary to popular opinion, Campese is not a poor defender. He is useful under the high ball, and possesses a monstrous boot. When asked about the running skills of Andrew Harriman, the England wing against Australia in 1988, Campese answered that any winger was good if given enough room. That reply is the heart of his defensive philosophy.

In the semi-final, the New Zealand winger John Timu was unable to breach Campese's defence. None of those tackles would have passed close technical scrutiny, and if repeated on the training field would probably have earned Campese another half-hour on the tackle bags. But all were effective. The trick lay in his positioning. Whenever New Zealand ran the ball, Campese closed down Timu immediately.

The ball-carrier is most vulnerable immediately after taking a pass at pace, for the simple reason that the body position for catching is different from that for physical contact or side-stepping. Technically, Campese is an indifferent tackler, but he engages opponents at their weakest moment. This positioning also enables him to sneak the odd interception, such as the one that kept Australia in the game against England at Twickenham in 1988.

Campese's Achilles heel lies not in his defensive capacity, but in his selection of tactical options. Against Australia in 1988 London played the game at frenetic pace, rarely opting to kick the ball (these were the carefree days of 1988, remember, not 1991). Such a fluid style is meat and drink to Campese, but to Australia it was both unwelcome and unpalatable. An inexperienced Australian squad needed to establish control and stability in the early games of their tour, not to engage in shoot-and-run rugby. Here, a calming tactical influence in the Australian back division was crucially important, and Campese was the senior figure to whom the youngsters in the side should have turned. Yet his only offerings were an exotic mixture of quick throw-ins and mesmerising counter-attacks from his own try-line, most of which were too fast for his bemused colleagues.

To suggest that cool-headed decision-making is not Campese's strongest suit is scarcely original. But this observation misses the point. Campese is tactically aware, but he will occasionally choose not to be. Such is the privilege, and essence, of genius. But this means that someone else in the Australian camp must seek to balance Campese's creative ability against his potential liability. It is Farr-Jones and Lynagh, the Australian half-backs, who balance this equation, for it is their tactical control which reduces the risk factor inherent in Campese's free spirit.

It is also significant that Campese has been more effective when Australia have possessed a powerful pack. These factors prevent Campese's unpredictability from descending into desperation. Above all, Campese actually relishes playing rugby football, transcending the grind which accompanies the international game. He particularly enjoys playing on the European stage, where crowds appreciate his unique talents, and Twickenham provides the best possible forum for this mercurial winger who has provided enjoyment for countless spectators.

2 NOVEMBER
ENGLAND GET THEIR KICKS ON ROUTE '66
Ian Ridley

So the television slogans about this being the biggest sporting event in England since soccer's World Cup in 1966 have proved to have some justification. And indeed similarities, mainly that England have reached the final. There are even uncanny omens. On the way they were involved in an ill-tempered quarter-final and, twenty-five years later, the No. 8s – Jimmy Greaves and Dean Richards – were dropped in both cases.

Bobby Moore, etched into a nation's consciousness as the captain of 1966, has seen plenty of similarities as the memories of the progress of the tournament, the preparation for the final, the day itself, the aftermath and even the criticism endured by the players have come flooding back. 'It seems to have captured the nation's imagination the same way,' he said. In his role these days as a soccer summariser for London radio station Capital Gold, he was at the Crystal Palace versus Chelsea match a week ago, and the six rows in front of him were all facing away from the pitch towards the televised semi-final against Scotland in the executive boxes behind him.

'I'm certain that the whole country is looking forward to the final against Australia and hoping that England can pull it off,' he said. 'It has all developed the way it did then. Our group matches weren't particularly good and we struggled, especially in the opening group game against Uruguay, which we drew 0–0. We improved a little in the second game against Mexico and a little more in the third against France. And after we had beaten Argentina in the quarter-final, we gradually felt we were capable of beating anybody. I'm sure the English rugby boys felt the same way after beating France in Paris. I was at England's opening match against the All Blacks and I felt then that they would get stronger as the tournament progressed, the way we did, and that has definitely been the case. You can see that the momentum, spirit and morale have picked up as they have progressed and they've got keener with every new phase they've reached.'

What of the week leading up to the final? 'You have a lot of time to think and rest, but then you need it to prepare yourself mentally and physically, especially physically in rugby, I would think. You know everybody is willing you to win but you have to withdraw into your own cocoon collectively as a team. In fact, some individuals do – they're all different. But you want to feel the tension, you want a nervousness which makes you aware of the importance of the occasion and to bring you to the peak of your condition.'

And the day itself? 'You try to make it as near to a normal

match as you can but it's not really possible. The rugby boys just have to try and enjoy it because most of them are not going to experience anything like it again. Yes, it is possible to enjoy it, even though the day goes by so quickly. You think you're aware of everything going on but eventually you realise it has passed you by. You just have to make the most of what you can. I think you realise afterwards the importance of it all, how important it is to everyone else. When you have detached yourself from the tournament and you're back in your own environment you have time to think about it all. Then you get overwhelmed by all the invitations, requests and demands. When you are away from the hype, excitement and razzmatazz of it all you suddenly realise what you have achieved.'

And if England go behind, as the soccer team did against West Germany? 'By that time you believe in your game plan. You have to stick to it and believe in your own ability and confidence.' Ah, that game plan, the one that has spawned so much criticism. 'People were disappointed with our early performances,' said Moore, the team's 'wingless wonders' tag coming later. 'England played with wingers at first but because of injury and lack of form a certain style of play developed. Come the final Alf [Ramsey] couldn't make any changes. That's the way things have developed and evolved with the England rugby team. People may well have criticised the way they play but if they feel that their style of play is the best for the team then it would be foolish to play any other way.'

Had he considered the consequences of losing on that summer day? A puzzled look came over his face. 'No. It didn't come into it. No, no. Never.' There are, of course, many differences between now and 1966. To begin with, rugby union is not ingrained in the psyche of popular culture the way that soccer was and is. The television audience for this Rugby World Cup final will probably be somewhere between ten and fifteen million, whereas in 1966 an estimated twenty-five million tuned in. Now that viewing figures can be measured accurately, the television companies know that as many watched the 1990 World Cup semi-final between England and West Germany. In addition, there is no recorded recollection of any team containing Bobby Charlton being labelled boring. Nevertheless, Moore believes that on their home ground England can invoke the spirit of 1966. Should Will Carling then remember to wipe his hands before receiving the Webb Ellis trophy? 'Please God he gets his hands on it,' said Moore.

3 NOVEMBER
ENGLAND BANG HEADS AGAINST SOLID YELLOW BRICK WALL
John Reason

From the moment midway through the first half when Tony Daly scored a try which was converted by Michael Lynagh it always looked as if Australia would win the World Cup final. It has to be said, though, that the result would have been a lot closer than 12–6 if referee Derek Bevan had decided that a deliberate knock-on by David Campese late in the game was worth the award of a penalty try. Winterbottom's attempted pass to Underwood was knocked abruptly upfield. If the pass had been made there was not too much space between Underwood and the Australian line, and Campese has never been quick enough to catch England's left wing. The referee took a long time to make his decision. He ran a few yards and had a good long think. He then gave England a penalty, which Webb kicked, but Australia were fortunate. Even if the referee had awarded a penalty try and the try had been converted, England would still have been 12–9 down. At that stage, though, there was just enough time for England to have some prospect of making another score.

It was not a big prospect. Australia's defence was as aggressively determined as ever, and on those occasions when England did look as if they might create something they passed so badly that the ball ricocheted around as if bumping down a pin table. That was always the danger of England trying to play a game that they have not been practising. When they won in New Zealand in 1971 the British Lions did not try too much in the way of extravagance in the Test matches, but they did practise the alternative whenever they could and so they always had it as a second option. Wellington discovered that to their cost when the Lions scored nine tries.

England never remotely looked as if they might do anything like that. Apart from the possible overlap knocked away by Campese – and he cheerfully accepted the booing that followed – England found themselves frustrated at every turn. They tried a stream of switch moves but few of them reached the gain-line against such an uncompromising defence. When the ball was stopped Poidevin did some priceless retrieving for Australia. He has had a remarkable tour considering how long he has been in the game and how much punishment his style of play inflicts upon his body.

Australia had some sizeable problems of their own. Their line-out got into a real mess in the second half when they needed another score for insurance. Australia called a succession of five-, four- and three-man line-outs and did not win the ball from any of them. Despite his size, Coker found it difficult to make a useful contribution either as a line-out alternative or as a No. 8. The kicking of the Australian midfield did not enchant their forwards either. Admittedly, a blustery wind was difficult but they missed touch far too often when they really needed to make it, and for once Australia often finished up on the wrong end of the ground gained and lost equation in the various bouts of ping-pong kicking.

The line-out degenerated into such a mass of heaving bodies that it looked like a lump of six-month-old cheese. England did not win the war there, not by any means, but they did not lose it either. What they did lose was just about the most important line-out of the match. Horan, the Australian centre, broke out of defence with a loose ball and with Campese at his shoulder; England were casting round desperately for a few lifeboats, even though the Australians had seventy yards to run.

Campese decided to kick ahead and there is not much doubt that he would have scored if the ball had taken a kindly bounce. His progress, when he tried to regather, looked as if it was impeded by Guscott, but Australia held the attacking position and when Ofahengaue won the ball at the tail of a line-out a few yards from England's line, Australia's two props sandwiched the ball between them and drove over the line. Both were congratulated by their teammates, but it looked as if Daly had secured the touchdown and so eventually it was agreed after a prolonged debate. Lynagh converted.

Lynagh had already given Australia the lead after twenty-seven minutes when England were penalised at a line-out. It was a long kick in the wind, even though he was kicking from the slightly more sheltered side of the field, but he gave it a thoroughly good thump and saw it sail over from forty-five yards. Six minutes earlier he had missed an easier thirty-five-yard kick, awarded when Skinner went over the top in a ruck. Lynagh went for a flat draw to keep the ball under the wind, but the kick dived past the post.

England might have cut the deficit with the last kick of the first half, but Webb had the sort of day when kicking at goal against Scotland that would have required an intensive session with David Leadbetter if he had been a golfer, and his problems here were rather similar. He seemed to be getting over the top of the ball and smothering it. This shook his confidence and so the kick he had against Australia was a real knee-trembler. He missed it.

England badly needed to make a strong start playing into the wind in the second half, but Ofahengaue went storming away from the kick-off and achieved a field position which Egerton squandered with a lamentable kick. England then had their best spell of the match as Dooley won a succession of line-outs and Australia's problems in that area multiplied. Probyn, the England tight-head, caught Australia's captain Farr-Jones behind a line-out and the England forwards smashed into the Australian twenty-two. They rolled back a good ball, too, but Andrew's drop at goal was snatchy and badly directed.

At least England never conceded the attacking scrummage positions from which Australia devastated them when England conceded forty points in Sydney four months earlier. England also succeeded in denying Australia the sort of loose possession with which they can be so dangerous. This forced Australia to try to exist on rather less than half rations. It was a pity England could not do more with the lion's share of the nourishment.

Midway through the second half Webb kicked a penalty goal to the enormous relief of the crowd, but before England had time to let the possible threat sink in, Dooley was penalised after a line-out and, kicking down the wind, Lynagh drove home a superb penalty goal from fifty yards. That was effectively game, set, match and World Cup. Australia led 12–3 and not much more than ten minutes remained.

England did manage one late flurry, but they needed to advance in sixes rather than threes and when they were rewarded with only one more penalty goal by Webb after Campese's deliberate knock-on, they still had to score twice to win. They were given a mite of encouragement by Roebuck, Australia's full-back. He made some mistakes with his kicking which might have been expensive, and a huge spiralling kick by Webb drove Australia deep into their half. Then Lynagh, trying to run the ball, was caught by Underwood with a most tenacious tackle. Some continuity there and England might have snatched the brand from the burning. As it was, they knocked on when they tried to develop the attacking position. Somehow that was entirely appropriate.

4 NOVEMBER

COMMISERATIONS, MOTHER COUNTRY: YOU MUST FEEL AS GHASTLY AS A SICK OYSTER AT LOW TIDE
Peter FitzSimons

Aw, come on now. No need to feel so bad. You may not have won the Rugby World Cup. You may not now have the symbol of world rugby supremacy just sitting proudly right up there on your mantelpiece for all to see. You may not now be able to strut the world stage as possessors of the finest rugby team in captivity.

You may indeed have narrowly missed out on a victory of truly Churchillian proportions. You may . . . oh forget it.

Actually, you have every right to feel quite as ghastly as a sick oyster at low tide. Your guys did you proud. Instead of the litany of up-and-unders the world was expecting, instead of ye olde stodgy style of carefully calibrated rugby for which you have on occasion become renowned ('Two degrees to port if you will, Mr Briggs'), you played with the commendable bravado of the Light Brigade. Cannon to the left of them, cannon to the right of them, cannon in front of them, volleyed and thundered . . . but England kept coming and, as we say in Australia, went for the throat. At 9–0, there were shouts heard all over Australia to the effect of 'We want fifty!' But of course it never happened. Just when Australia thought it was safe to play the ball wide, the English back row knocked them over. Just when they thought it was safe to send up the middle, the English tight five stood like a wall.

In the coming days there will no doubt be endless analysis made of why Australia won and England lost, ranging from luck through to personnel, from defensive patterns to the prodigious kicking game of Michael Lynagh. But from this end of the planet, and viewed from the perspective of one raised in the current Australian coaching ethos, one particular English fault stands out like Everest: turn-overs. How many times did we see England, commendably throwing caution to the wind, sending the ball out wide for a bit of back-line razzle-dazzle, which more often than not rattled the Australian defence, only to then see the ball be jolted loose from English hands in the tackle?

Or how many times, after a fearsome English forward rush, when the Australian defence seemed to be just barely holding on, did one or other of the English forwards lose control of the ball in the maul to see Australia awarded a scrum? By my own admittedly inexact count, on seventeen occasions England lost control of ball they were clearly in possession of, against three occasions for Australia . . .

As this was a victorious World Cup final, there is some chance that the three transgressors for Australia escaped with only mild castigation from Australian coach Bob Dwyer, but under normal circumstances there would be no such luck. A bare minimum would be a public whipping; a maximum being dropped from the team. In Dwyer's list of Cardinal Sins for his players to commit, the first of ten thou shalt nots is: 'Thou Shalt Not Lose the Ball in the Tackle.'

To ensure that this does not happen, a significant part of Australian training is taken up with practising that very skill. Time and again, till their noses bleed, Australian players practise going into a tackle and laying the ball back so there can be absolutely no chance of losing control of it. It seems like one of the more basic skills, sure, but one would have to say that if England had been imbued with the same philosophy they would almost certainly have come away with the Cup. But the Cup has found a good home. And it will change significantly our sporting landscape.

For decades, the Wallabies have been the poor relations of the All Blacks, just as rugby union has been the poor relation of rugby league. With the completion of the World Cup, though, the poor relations have just taken rightful possession of the best mansion on the block, while the All Blacks have been evicted to some rather more modest dwellings down the road. As to the league boys, if they are still to get to live in the same neon-lighted extravaganza of before, they must now look with some envy at the stylish residence of the Wallabies, built with a *genuinely* international touch.

The William Webb Ellis trophy might not look quite so fantastically gleaming on our mantelpiece as the America's Cup once did, but in many ways it is more impressive. For while the yachting cup was mostly a victory of money and technology, this was a victory of men and spirit. Playing in the style of the nation from which sprung – 'Have a go, you mug' . . . 'Damn the torpedoes, full speed ahead' – the Wallabies took on the best the world could throw at them and won. Bravo, and so say all of us. (You'll forgive us if we preen ourselves a little. Curious colonists that we are, no victory sits so well with us as one over what used to be our mother country.)

The only trouble for coach Bob Dwyer has got to be the impending decimation of the finest side he has ever put together. It is the back-line who most risk being wiped out. In those august ranks, there is only one man whose presence next year you would feel totally confident in wagering the sheep station upon: full-back Marty Roebuck. For the rest, captain and half-back Nick Farr-Jones keeps making worryingly persistent noises that he will retire; Michael Lynagh has accepted an invitation to go to Italy for the next eight months; the two centres, Little and Horan, are surely the primest of all prime rugby league targets; Campese says he has had enough, thanks, and the other winger, Rob Egerton, will be going to America. Which leaves Australia rugby where, precisely? Still in the nicest sporting house on the international block, though we might have to fight hard to keep it. Still, you will excuse us if we savour it for a while.

1991 RESULTS – Quarter-finals: Scotland 28, Western Samoa 6; England 19, France 10; New Zealand 29, Canada 13; Australia 19, Ireland 18. Semi-finals: England 9, Scotland 6; Australia 16, New Zealand 6. Third-place: New Zealand 13, Scotland 6. Final: Australia 12, England 6.

CHAPTER THREE: 1995

HOSTED BY SOUTH AFRICA

22 MAY
WATERSHED FOR RUGBY
John Mason

Whatever happens on the field, the arrival of sixteen twenty-six-strong squads of international rugby players is of huge significance to South Africa's self-esteem. Sporting isolation hurt badly, the wounds of ten years beginning only now to heal. As a further restorative pick-me-up, the Rugby World Cup, in which South Africa are competing for the first time, is the best possible tonic. Whether the quirky patient, some of whose long-standing complaints attracted little sympathy worldwide, will be rid of all ills need not be debated here. But if rugby, whose record in the bad old apartheid days did not always bear close scrutiny, does help, that must be a bonus, a year on since the accession of Nelson Mandela. May rugby union, the sport currently confronted around the world less by a crossroads than a six-lane motorway interchange sign-posted filthy lucre, benefit too.

The World Cup, now about to be staged for the third time, has revolutionised the sport, its attitudes, its commercial capabilities and its praiseworthy, if dated, concepts of amateurism. Mammon has struck, leaving the ideals of the game's unpaid administrators in mortal danger.

There will be no Dunkirk this time. A professional game is at hand and, at rarefied level only, will be fully in place come the 1999 World Cup. Of that, I am regrettably sure. The King Canutes, much as I sympathise, have had their day. The flow of the tide towards contract and match fee is inexorable; the ebb in the direction of leisure pursuit for amateurs will continue, thank goodness, the important difference being that there will be a choice of which canoe those concerned wish to paddle. I would like to think that the present administrators, and their elected successors, will remain in charge of the sport while being mindful of change and deeply hostile to the takeover merchants. Unhappily, some of the enemies are within, and when serious money is involved, principles, it seems, can be accommodating. Should you wish, take rugby league's abject surrender as an example.

Rugby World Cup itself has not been particularly profitable. But it has sharpened the image of the game, especially so since the 1991 tournament in Britain, Ireland and France. Without being the financial bonanza promised *ad nauseam* by over-confident marketers, the competition itself grabbed the imagination of even the previously lukewarm follower. To rugby's lasting shame, World Cup accounts have become an endangered species, as elusive as compliments from David Campese about English back play. Rank incompetence, not fraudulent intent, has been responsible – to such an extent that Louis Luyt, South Africa's Mr Rugby, in reply to a mumbled question from me at a press conference in Edinburgh in November 1994, has promised categorically that the 1995 accounts will be available within a month of the tournament ending. In 1987 the profits were about £1 million, and in 1991, depending which limited sums the organisers cared to do, in excess of £10 million. This time round, quoted with a splendid Gallic shrug of the shoulders by Marcel Martin, the France-based bilingual RWC finance chief, it's £20 million.

The powerful Luyt, chairman of the organising committee, does not disagree. As at times it has been difficult to determine whether he works for RWC, or the other way about, it is probably fair to say that – at last – this competition will make money that can assist sensibly in the development of the game in the under-developed rugby nations. The sport, in fact, cannot sustain a World Cup in competitive terms. The gulfs are too large, the interest lacking, the cost, not only financial, excessive. The International Board proudly speaks of sixty-seven members, or whatever. Fine. Good show, chaps. Got to make a start, of course. But there will be more absurd mismatches in the two weeks that follow which will do no one the slightest good.

In 1999 the intention, apparently, is to widen the finals to twenty nations – five groups of four, though precise details have still to be agreed. That makes little sense, bearing in mind the already increasing gaps between the top half-dozen and the next ten. A two-tier competition is the answer, each involving eight nations linked by a promotion-relegation system. In that way the ambitions of the emerging rugby nations would be accommodated at World Cup time without the trauma of conceding mountains of points to the big boys. But then, as a total reactionary, I consider the World Cup has quickened the demise of the principles of a sport which, to its lasting credit, used to allow the better practitioners to meet every demand, be it career, family or the game.

It follows that as an old wind-bag of ample years, I readily acknowledge the general good of the stewardship of the Rugby Football Union on behalf of all their members, irrespective of playing standards. In the public relations field, where in most respects they have served as a role model for other administrations in dispensing information to the media, there has been one enormous blind-spot. The RFU appear oblivious to likely public reaction when restrictions of personal freedom are involved – the right to criticise, the dismissal of Carling, the reluctance to permit women members, the continuing opposition to the full reinstatement of former league players. Happily, second thoughts tend to prevail – eventually.

The often parrot-like demands of the players for financial recognition remain an irritation, not least because of genuine and acceptable progress in that area. The irritation is as good a reason as any for wanting to return in due course to the cheerful anonymity of the grass-roots, from whence I came. That said, countless others like me will delight in applauding long and loud the skills of those who secure the World Cup in Johannesburg, irrespective of nationality – just as long as they are English.

27 MAY
ELEPHANTS ARE UNLIKELY TO FORGET HASTINGS
Brendan Gallagher

Gavin Hastings broke every record in the rugby book except one as he amassed forty-four points in Scotland's crushing 89–0 victory over the World Cup minnows Ivory

Coast. Incredibly, Hastings's effort does not constitute an individual scoring record in international rugby. Ashley Billington, the former Loughborough University captain, scored ten tries to total fifty points in Hong Kong's 164–13 World Cup qualifying win against Singapore in Kuala Lumpur in October 1994. That contest was probably as valid as this gross mismatch, so Billington's record must be left intact. Among senior international matches, the thirty points claimed by France's Didier Camberabero against Zimbabwe in 1987 and Rob Andrew's identical total against Canada in November 1994 were generally recognised as the record.

But every other landmark fell to Hastings and Scotland, whose score and margin of victory was the biggest in the World Cup finals. Scotland's thirteen tries equals France's achievement against Zimbabwe in the inaugural World Cup of 1987 and Hastings's individual haul of four equals that of Ieuan Evans, Craig Green and John Gallagher in 1987 and Brian Robinson in 1991. 'I've never been particularly interested in individual records in a team game, but I was lucky the ball came my way,' the ever self-effacing Hastings said afterwards.

A capacity 20,000 crowd, basking in late-evening sunshine, enjoyed the command performance, though exactly how relevant the result is to Scotland's World Cup chances is debatable. What was encouraging was the ruthless way in which Scotland pursued their biggest victory. British sides are often accused of lacking the hard edge to destroy – and, yes, humiliate – manifestly inferior opponents. Ivory Coast, known as the Elephants, froze horribly on the biggest day in their history and one can imagine the depths of despair as they contemplate further carnage against Tonga and France.

Their misery was compounded by a knee injury to their

popular captain Athanase Dali after twenty minutes when the score was a comparatively respectable 13–0. Indeed, Scotland made a poor start, appearing as nervous as the West Africans, and it needed a typically forthright burst from Hastings to open the scoring after ten minutes, though he benefited from a lucky bounce that cruelly deceived Victor Kouassi. Scotland continued to splutter during the opening thirty minutes, but Hastings hit top gear as half-time approached, gathering twenty-nine points before the break with two further tries, two penalties and four conversions. Only Peter Walton's touchdown threatened his monopoly. The flood of points continued unabated during the second half with a fourth try for Hastings, two for Kenny Logan, a second for Walton, and single scores for Tony Stanger, Paul Burnell, Peter Wright, Craig Chalmers and, most deserving of all, the outstanding Graham Shiel.

Dali, happily recovered, was a graceful figure at the post-match press conference and at least he managed to find consolation in the fact that 'Scotland and Gavin Hastings had not underestimated us, which must be a compliment'. Such obtuse logic could not disguise the massive contrast with the vibrant and competitive contest between South Africa and Australia on the opening day. On this evidence, rugby union still struggles to validate its claim to be a world game at the top level. That should not concern Scotland as they justifiably celebrate. The Elephants, meanwhile, can only ruminate on a day they will never forget.

5 JUNE
BRITO PARALYSED IN 'FREAK' ACCIDENT
Rupert Bates

Ivory Coast left-wing Max Brito was left paralysed with spinal injuries after the game against Tonga in Rustenburg. Brito, twenty-four, is in the intensive care unit of the Unitas Hospital in Pretoria, but hospital spokesperson Magdel du Preez would not confirm whether the electrician was still paralysed in his legs and left arm as announced by the hospital straight after the match. 'Brito's condition is stable and he is breathing on his own,' said Du Preez, adding that an operation to defuse the vertebrae was planned.

The game was three minutes old when Brito, running out of defence, was tackled by Inoke Afeaki, the Tonga flanker, before several players fell on top of Brito, leaving him prone and motionless on the ground. The dreadlocked Brito, who is married with two children, plays his club rugby for Biscarosse in France and his fearless tackling has been one of the Ivorian highlights of the World Cup.

Etienne Hugo, the Pool D doctor and an orthopaedic surgeon who treated Brito in Pretoria, said it was too early to say if paralysis would be permanent. 'This was a tragic and freak accident, but we were very concerned about spinal injuries in rugby. Law changes have depowered the scrum but the tackle is still a major problem,' said Hugo, chairman of the South African rugby medical committee. The game itself was rendered meaningless after the Brito incident. Three players from each side were replaced before Tonga, with four tries to one, ran out 29–11 winners of a scrappy affair.

12 JUNE
LETTER TO THE SPORTS EDITOR
RUGBY 'SMALL FRY' IN DANGER

SIR – Tremendous interest and excitement has been generated by the Rugby World Cup. It is appropriate that your articles should direct attention to the dangers of spinal injury. Unfortunately the Ivory Coast winger, Max Brito, sustained such an injury. He was said to have been trapped at the bottom of a maul. An important issue has to be addressed. Accidents in rugby can be caused as a result of a mismatch of abilities.

I drew attention in the *British Medical Journal* eleven years ago to the effect of fitness, both general and specific, in the cause of injuries and to the dangers of mismatches of strength and skill. 'Some injuries occurred where there was a discrepancy of strength and skill, particularly in the front rows of the scrum. On four occasions there was a discrepancy of skills, and on seven occasions schoolboys were playing with adults: they were unable to match them in strength, and so on three occasions the scrum collapsed. On another occasion a fifteen-year-old boy turned up at the local club, played for the third team and was pushed in the back while stooping for the ball. A sixteen-year-old boy playing for a local club's second team broke his neck in a ruck and maul.' As a result of this research, the English RFU addressed this issue and tried to eliminate the mismatch of strength and skills by stopping the game between schoolboys and adults, and it is notable that when a front-row forward goes off, he must be replaced by another front row.

On a recent phone-in on BBC Radio 5 a caller referred to the mismatch of skills in the World Cup. Ivory Coast, who by all accounts have only a small number of clubs and were not particularly fit, lost 89–0 to Scotland, 54–18 to France and 29–11 to Tonga. Such scores would suggest that there was indeed a mismatch. While the actual injury that occurred to Brito may well have been an accident, were the Ivory Coast players adequately prepared for the competition, both physically and mentally? Should Ivory Coast have been on the field at all in competition with more powerful opponents? While I realise that they did qualify for the tournament by beating other sides such as Namibia, and the World Cup is a means of encouraging the game throughout the world, if such a mismatch of skills did occur, perhaps Brito is paying too high a price and the organisers of the next World Cup, to be held in the United Kingdom and France, should address this problem.

J.R. Silver

National Spinal Injuries Centre
Stoke Mandeville Hospital

11 JUNE
WILLIAMS SHINES OVER RAINBOW NATION
Kate Battersby

'Chester, Chester,' bellowed the vocal might of sixty-five thousand voices at Johannesburg's Ellis Park as the giant screen showed their idol waiting patiently in the tunnel. 'Not even Nando's make wings like Chester,' read one banner in the stand, in a reference to a local fast-food chain. Four tries for Chester Williams later, it was difficult to argue. The crowd could hardly be blamed for their joy at the 42–14 quarter-final victory over Western Samoa. After the shameful brawling in Port Elizabeth the week before, the South Africans might have spent the days since hanging their heads. But the absurd loophole in the tournament rules which allowed the Springboks to benefit from their indiscipline brought about Williams's return. With that, sunlight shone through the dark clouds and the much-vaunted Rainbow Nation was restored.

South Africa is fortunate indeed that the man whose lot it is to personify so much burdensome symbolism is the person he is. So much rides on him. His twenty-four-year-old face has become the embodiment of the spirit South African rugby wishes to project. President Nelson Mandela – himself a universal symbol of hope and freedom – has publicly described Williams as a hero. But what if Williams, rather than Pieter Hendriks or James Dalton, were the sort to bring shame on his country? It is only by the goodness of fate that he is anything but.

Certainly the colour of his skin played a huge role in getting his face on all those posters, but Williams has earned his place as the living embodiment of what is good about Springboks rugby because of his extraordinary modesty. It has to be experienced to be believed. 'It is an honour for me to be my country's totem for change,' he says. 'There is no burden. I know everyone looks up to me, but I can manage. I just take things as they come. I still find it surprising that someone like President Mandela should talk about someone like me. I was honoured when he recognised me and spoke publicly about his regret that I was injured. That he should call me a hero is a great honour for me.' If his words appear cloying on the page, in person his unassuming sincerity cannot be doubted. If you have witnessed at first hand Williams's sweetness of manner, his utter lack of self-importance, his unsophisticated simplicity, it is impossible to interpret the marketing of his image as an exercise in cynicism.

Marketing is part and parcel of modern sport, and any promotions executive would be glad to work with Williams. The irony is that the common reason for the attention he generates – the colour of his skin – is so often wrongly described. No black player wore a Springbok shirt here. Williams is Coloured, a term which in this sense is not pejorative, as it would be in Britain. As a racial group, Coloureds are far more in line with the white population than the black majority. It is the whites among whom Williams is especially popular. The distinction between black and Coloured is important, perhaps best illustrated by the fact that as a person of mixed race, Williams is far more likely to have voted for F.W. de Klerk's Nationalist Party in the 1994 elections than Nelson Mandela's ANC. The Western Cape, where Williams was born and lives, is predominantly Coloured. It was the only area of the country where the ANC failed to triumph. The Nationalists took it on the Coloured vote. Like the whites, Williams's first language is Afrikaans rather than Xhosa, the tongue of the black majority. When Western Samoa played South Africa, television cameras focused on Williams during the playing of the national anthem, leaving no doubt as to his unfamiliarity with the Xhosa words to 'Nkosi Sikelel' iAfrika'. His teammates were equally at sea, though here Williams had devised a diplomatic middle way by remaining mute throughout.

That match against these Samoans in April 1995 produced a scoreline of 60–8 in the Boks' favour. It was in that match that Williams sustained the hamstring injury which kept him out of South Africa's World Cup pool games. This then was an altogether happier occasion. It was inevitable that the first time Williams got the ball in his hands, he sprinted through for his eighth try in a dozen Tests. His next was not long coming, though the fact that it came from a forward pass by Ruben Kruger escaped official eyes. But there was no doubting his third of the day, South Africa's fourth. In accepting Christiaan Scholtz's high overhead pass, Williams leapt into the air as if in celebration of his hat-trick some twenty metres short of the line.

His mis-tackle on Shem Tatupu which resulted in Western Samoa's second try blemished his performance, and was probably welcomed by those determined to see Williams's presence in the Springboks line-up as a token. But he made brilliant amends minutes later by picking the ball out of the back of the ruck and darting over for his fourth; and if he hadn't stumbled on a thrilling sprint two minutes after that he would have bagged his fifth. In any case, even before this performance, Williams's awareness in defence and attack, his way of coming inside to make tackles and his sheer speed would have made him an automatic selection for practically anybody's World XV. It's plain to see – a matter of black and white.

11 JUNE
ENGLAND RETAIN FOCUS TO LOOK BEYOND THE GHOSTS OF '91
Paul Ackford

Rory Underwood was in tears; the rest of us just slumped on the wooden benches in the dressing room at Twickenham. We had lost the most important game of our lives, the most important game in the history of England rugby. World Cup 1991: England 6, Australia 12. There were no recriminations. No one spoke, no one looked at anyone else. Fifteen men alone with the realisation that the chance of sporting immortality had passed them by. Then, out of the blue, there was a knock on the door and in walked the Prime Minister, John Major, flanked by two protection officers. It was an unreal moment. Still frozen by the enormity of failure, no one moved a muscle in acknowledgement. As the situation threatened to become acutely embarrassing, eyes turned to Will Carling for a lead. Still nothing. Then Micky Skinner took charge. Slowly he rose to his feet and walked across the dressing-room floor, a towel covering his nakedness. Hand extended, he smiled and said: 'Nice to meet you, fat boy.'

The spell was broken and it was time to get on with the rest of our lives. Yet there are those who remain from that grey November day, still playing rugby, still unable to erase that awful memory. Now Jason Leonard, Brian Moore, Jeremy Guscott, Rob Andrew, Carling and Underwood have a chance to set the record straight. In press conferences and one-to-one interviews, the tabloid newspapers have been trying to build the quarter-final encounter with Australia into the ultimate grudge match. 'What you goin' to do to Campo, then Mooro? Knock 'is block off?' Captain Carling has played it all down. 'I'd like to think we have evolved as a team,' he said. 'There are always bits and pieces you can pull out of previous games, but very few from that one. Revenge is a powerful force if it's still alive within you, but four years is a long time.' And he is right. The last thing England want is for their experienced players to run on to the pitch yelling 'payback time'.

Nevertheless, the match is still significant. It is the reason why Andrew continues to play international rugby and why he believes England can go one better in this tournament. For others the memories are more specific. Leonard still draws confidence from the successful forward effort on that day. 'We took them to the cleaners up front,' he said, fully aware that five of that Australian pack are still playing, as are four of the backs. 'We also made mistakes. All that ball which we won but which we didn't use terribly well. The Australians defended superbly but we didn't really test them.' Guscott refuses even to acknowledge the significance of history. Like Leonard, he has never watched a tape of the match and will not draw any parallels. 'Two years ago I was contacted by a journalist and asked about an incident in the final,' Guscott said. 'I didn't have a clue what he was on about. That's how much thinking I've done about the match.'

It is left to Mr Motivator himself to put the experience into context. 'I suppose it remains the one that got away but I won't mention it in the team talks,' Moore said. 'For half the side it doesn't mean a thing. If anything, it will be more significant for the Australians. Having won the tournament once, I don't think there will be the same desire to achieve. It takes a very special team to re-achieve.'

The game of rugby has changed a great deal in four years, and so have the men who played in that final and are still turning out at the highest level. World Cup '91 is only really poignant for the nine England players who are not around any longer, who sit powerless at home or in the stands, having forfeited the opportunity to make amends. Do it for us, guys. Please.

12 JUNE
ANDREW KICKS ENGLAND TO DREAM FINISH
John Mason

Rob Andrew's soaring, sweetly struck dropped goal allowed England to squeeze past world champions Australia in the final minute of a tense, nerve-jangling World Cup quarter-final. An English dream for which everyone had been working for four years had come true. Andrew was offered the freedom of Cape Town by delighted colleagues: modestly, he declined. England's victory in injury time at Newlands was, Andrew insisted, a team effort which would not have been possible without the massive contribution of the forwards. Then, practical soul that he is, the outside-half, who kicked twenty of England's points in the 25–22 victory, reminded all concerned that there was another big match, the semi-final against New Zealand, to come in Cape Town. A battle had been won but not the war.

Here, England, having started splendidly, played ducks and drakes with the nerves of the most devoted followers. A relatively comfortable 13–3 lead after twenty minutes, control fore and aft a positive and recurring feature, subsided to 13–13 in the opening minute of the second half. No praise can be too high for the work of scrum-half Dewi Morris, whose enthusiasm and refusal to concede an inch was a glowing example of everything that a competitor should present in this arena. He, Andrew, of course, and Martin Bayfield ensured that the Newlands shoot-out went England's way – bull's-eye and bulldog.

No one in the England camp spoke of revenge, though plainly an element of England's joy was the knowledge they had overcome by a whisker the nation who beat them in the 1991 Twickenham final. That mighty contest, goal-kicking apart, had much in common with this bruising encounter in which inherent skills had to play second fiddle to the need to win. Such pressures do not make for epic running and handling, nor for a match of unsurpassed quality. But it was a gripping struggle of stomach-churning excitement, a form of muscular chess in which the result might have gone either way, even after Andrew's long, long goal from way out on the left.

The tactical schemes on these occasions, especially when England are involved, demand a shutting down of the opposition, denying possession and using the driving, rolling maul relentlessly. Thereafter the bottom line, in these days of the siege-gun kickers, is to wait patiently for the referee to punish opposition error. All laudable, legal but hardly lovely. It was enough to bring England a win they dearly wanted and, on the day, it was everything they deserved. Bob Dwyer, Australia's briskly articulate coach, agreed politely that it was not a style he favoured personally. He sought, he said, a broader game by preference, though it was never his intention to tell opponents how they might play. England had controlled two-thirds of the match and Australia had been shut out. England's manager, Jack Rowell, was content to say: 'It was one of the matches of all time.'

Michael Lynagh kicked the first of his five penalty goals in the second minute. Andrew followed suit in the sixth and ninth minutes – line-out offences, offside and obstruction attracting the attention of the referee. England's try came from a long way back and, ironically, Australia were attacking, ball in hand. Sport being a cruel taskmaster, it was Lynagh who dropped the ball. Eager English hands seized upon it, Andrew to the fore.

The raid swung to the right: Andrew to Will Carling to Jeremy Guscott. At that point the midfield was blocked and Guscott delayed his pass to the last possible moment. By then, right wing Tony Underwood was in full stride, running on to a flicked pass that may have been forward. Head back, knees pumping, he stepped up a gear to sweep round the cover and there was time and room to finish close to the posts. Andrew converted.

English nerves were sorely tried, not least by lock John Eales, who had a remarkable match – a true athlete and competitor. Lynagh kicked a late penalty goal to end the half and immediately afterwards it was his chip high to the left-hand corner that, for the first time, exposed an English defensive frailty. Mike Catt, making his only mistake, and Tony Underwood attempted to cover, but Damian Smith, Australia's large left wing, was quicker and stronger. As he reached for the ball, Smith turned and rolled through the tackle, landing over the goal-line for Lynagh to convert from touch

Suddenly English roses were not in bloom. Two more penalty goals by Lynagh put Australia ahead only for Andrew to peg back the Wallabies: 13–16; 16–16; 19–16; 19–19; 22–19 and, in the seventy-sixth minute, 22–22. Andrew's fifth penalty squared matters again; extra time loomed. Lynagh twice ran the ball when a dropped goal might have been the better option. Another penalty award, this time on England's left. Up stepped Catt to drill the ball to touch; England's throw at the line-out. The telescopic reach of middle jumper Bayfield, the RFU's player of the year, plucked the ball out of the air. His colleagues converged and England's pack rumbled downfield. At scrum-half Morris's barked command, the release was swiftly efficient. The ball thumped into Andrew's cricketer hands and back went the right foot, some forty metres from goal and two minutes and thirty-six seconds into time added on. The rest is history.

12 JUNE

INSPIRATIONAL CAPTAIN'S FAREWELL AS SCOTS GO DOWN ALL GUNS FIRING
Brendan Gallagher

Scotland, determined that Gavin Hastings should not be embarrassed on his farewell to international rugby, dug deep into reserves of pride and courage before finally conceding a gloriously entertaining quarter-final to New Zealand. Only Australia have scored thirty points against the All Blacks before, and no side has achieved that total and still lost to New Zealand. Scotland went down 48–30, but with all guns firing, as you would expect from any side with Hastings at the helm. After the inevitable dressing-room television interview, the loyal Scottish supporters demanded that the Scotland captain re-emerge after his sixty-first and final appearance. An impromptu lap of honour followed, ending with Hastings being chaired off to thunderous applause.

At one stage, midway through the second half, Scotland trailed 45–16 and humiliation seemed one step away. But this essentially young side have character in abundance and retaliated with two late tries. The All Black class of '95 have many attributes – power, pace and opportunism – but their forwards are not the awesome force of old, and they are prone to inexplicable lapses in defence.

Scotland had worked hard during three days of closed training to prepare a package of surprises, and unveiled their first immediately from the kick-off, a sevens-style grubber which Rob Wainwright bravely gathered before Chalmers's dropped pass saw the attack fizzle out. The game exploded into life when the incomparable Jonah Lomu created a try, the like of which is rarely seen in international rugby. Collecting the ball sixty-five yards out, he cruised around Craig Joiner, a former Scottish schools sprint champion, and dismissed the challenges of Scott and Gavin Hastings before gifting a try to Walter Little. Andrew Mehrtens converted before Hastings reduced the deficit with two well-struck penalties. But the relief was only temporary, Lomu again making a mockery of Scotland's defence, this time to score a converted try himself

Mehrtens, exuding remarkable confidence for a twenty-two-year-old playing only his fourth Test, swapped a penalty apiece with Hastings before half-time. At 17–9 down, dreams of a first Scotland win were still permissible. These were effectively dashed in an astonishing orgy of points – twenty-eight in eight minutes – immediately after the break. It began from the restart, Gavin Hastings untypically spilling a high ball from Mehrtens for the ever-present Little to pounce for a converted try. Scotland were shell-shocked, but worse was to follow as Mehrtens seized on a loose ball and sprinted seventy yards to score a fine individual try, which he improved with the conversion.

Scotland hit back through the industrious Doddie Weir, a major success on hard South African grounds, who boosted morale by barging over for Hastings to convert. The torrent of points continued, this time from the most unlikely of quarters. New Zealand captain Sean Fitzpatrick crossed after an attack initiated by Marc Ellis and Jeff Wilson. From that low point, Scotland climbed back, Weir scoring a second try after Graham Bachop had fumbled while trying to clear his lines.

New Zealand, sensing the danger, were concerned enough to ask Mehrtens to kick a second penalty, a sensible precaution as it proved because Scotland came hammering back, Scott Hastings diving over for a well-deserved score. Brother Gavin converted magnificently from the touchline, the last two points of his memorable international career. During the match, in which by his own high standards he occasionally struggled, Scotland's captain led by example, refusing to duck the challenge. Nothing has changed in that respect since he made his debut against France in 1986. Scotland will miss him dreadfully, and judging from the crowd's ovation after the game, so will world rugby. Opposing captain Fitzpatrick, who started his international career in the same year, summed it up when he said afterwards: 'Gavin has been a fantastic ambassador for the game. He is a great credit to rugby union and has proved in this World Cup that he is the best full-back in the world.'

19 JUNE
LOMU LAYS DOWN THE LAW TO SHATTER ENGLAND'S DREAMS
John Mason

Everything the rugby world warned that Jonah Lomu would do to England, he did. He began with a try after seventy seconds, followed with three more and at all times had seasoned opponents in a state of impotence, if not panic. It was a hair-raising marvel of a performance from this six-foot, five-inch giant of a man, blessed with a strength and physical presence way beyond his twenty years. From the kick-off it was: 'Good afternoon, Tony Underwood. Here I am to make your life a misery for the next seventy-nine minutes, fifty seconds.'

At the start, a dummy line-up by the All Blacks on the right had England covering in the wrong places. Lomu, the lay preacher's son from Tonga via South Auckland, was in business instantly, thundering in pursuit of a soaring ball well to New Zealand's left, England's right. The alarm bells were at full decibel even before the opening try. But it was not just the youngest Underwood who had a recurring nightmare in attempting to stop the eighteen-stone, eight-pound Lomu, a runaway potting shed in boots. Will Carling, Mike Catt, Tim Rodber, Dewi Morris and Dean Richards discovered that the genuine, well-timed tackle was not sufficient to do more than momentarily slow an athletic mountain.

The sorry outcome was that in losing 45–29, England conceded more points than they have ever done previously. There have been a couple of worse defeats, including one by New Zealand, in Wellington, in 1985, when they scored forty-two points. The try-count finished at 6–4 to New Zealand. For England it was not much of a consolation for a team striving to lead the world. They knew, best of all, that they had been well beaten. Whenever in that opening twenty minutes of ice-cool, calculating rugby New Zealand cared to employ Lomu, England were in trouble. Perhaps not paralysed, they were Lomu-lised, well and truly. If New Zealand do not win the World Cup, there will have to be a stewards' inquiry.

In defying all the tenets of a team game, here was one player who spent the semi-final of the 1995 World Cup reducing a previously competent, well-drilled England team, seeking an eleventh consecutive victory, to bedraggled also-rans. It was embarrassing; it was also inspiring, a sporting occasion to treasure, to remember fondly the next time a tedious Courage League One game devoid of imagination and inspiration has to be witnessed. During that opening quarter New Zealand scored three tries, kicked a penalty goal and, in a kind of sporting leg-pull, as if for a dare, No. 8 Zinzan Brooke dropped a long goal, the first by a forward in international history, from the range that allowed Rob Andrew to topple Australia in the quarter-final. If it had not added so much to English doom and despondency, it would have been permissible to laugh.

Andrew Mehrtens, the outside-half, controlled distribution and the midfield in equal measure. Flanker Josh Kronfeld was in support of everyone everywhere and when, by chance, he was not immediately next in line, Glen Osborne, the full-back, was. All this spelt out an exhilarating team performance by the All Blacks. Sadly, too, it was in utter contrast to the pudding form of the game favoured by England.

Lomu, so superior at one stage that he could afford to dawdle against a defence in tatters, added tries in the twenty-sixth, forty-second and seventy-first minutes, all of which required a helping hand in preparation by his colleagues. Graeme Bachop, the scrum-half, was important, though few ran better than either Kronfeld or Walter Little. There was also a slide-rule chip over the top by Mehrtens. Little ran on to it and Lomu had time to look around to see what remained of the defence. Not much.

England, 35–3 down in the twelfth minute of the second half, turned corners of sorts thereafter, desperately running every penalty. For a while they looked good, worthy of sharing the pitch with the best team in the world. But, in truth, the damage had been done. This was frantic catch-up rugby which ensured only that in defeat there was a degree of honour. Four second-half tries, three of which Andrew converted, guaranteed that.

In this period Morris did not stop in rallying the cause. Carling snapped into action, too, and with the back row driving and driving, the All Blacks started grumbling. Ben Clarke, Victor Ubogu and Rodber can look back on a tolerable second half and Martin Bayfield proved that he has few peers at the line-out. England's forwards did themselves proud throughout this recovery and they, above all, were primarily responsible for the brace of tries apiece scored by Rory Underwood and Carling.

Even then Lomu got into the act, Bachop seizing on a stray ball. As Lomu moved up a gear, Tony Underwood got the hand-off and Catt the brush-off. The crowd loved it and though England, Morris in the lead, did have the last word with a second try by Rory Underwood, this was, I fear, in world terms, men against boys.

19 JUNE
MANAGEMENT CLOSE RANKS TO GUARD THEIR 'CROWN JEWEL'
Michael Calvin

Jonah Lomu stood over the stricken figure of Tony Underwood, whom he had tossed into touch with the casual disdain of a child discarding a sweet wrapper. Then he laughed, with icy-eyed contempt. David Campese is the only other international of recent memory to taunt his victims in such a fashion. He takes an obsessive pride in being able to think faster, react quicker, than any lunging tackler. Lomu's arrogance is the manifestation of his physical superiority rather than any mental dexterity. He finds succour in the all-enveloping All Blacks culture and it was no coincidence that the legends of the Silver Fern stood four-square around him when, much to the consternation of the world's media, Lomu refused to discuss his domination of a semi-final that exposed the fragile inner core of the English game.

'You don't become a great player in one game or one year,' intoned Colin Meads, the fabled manager and former captain. 'We can start calling Jonah great in a couple of years' time.' Brian Lochore, fellow manager and another gnarled figure hewn from the granite of Kiwi folklore, stressed: 'Jonah doesn't want all this furore. He just wants to get on with playing.' Current captain Sean Fitzpatrick insisted: 'He's got a bit of work to do,' before he realised he had taken circumspection a little too far. He added hastily: 'What impressed me was the way he used his brain, his wit, for the whole eighty minutes. That's fantastic for a twenty-year-old.'

Little by little, the facade of caution crumbled. Laurie Mains, a coach with an undertaker's demeanour and a poker professional's restraint, was moved to suggest 'the Crown Jewels should be put up to ensure Jonah stays in rugby union'. There was an irresistible logic to the statement. The only way to prevent Lomu from dominating the fifteen-man code up to and beyond the millennium is to bring him down with a siege gun or a scout's cheque book. He tackles with the force of an artillery shell, gathers pace with the inevitability of a missile and exudes the invincibility of a tank. To put such military analogies into perspective, he also has an almost balletic sidestep.

'He's amazing, a freak,' mourned Will Carling. 'The sooner he goes away, the better. I never want to see that man again. They were amazing, but the difference between the sides appeared on the left wing. When you have someone like that you are in a different league. Without being funny, if you take

him out of the game it would have made a huge, huge difference.' Jack Rowell, the England manager, sitting beside his
captain, nodded in assent. 'He's a phenomenon. Someone
should have bought him up before this World Cup.'

The bidding for Lomu's services will become all the more
frantic after a performance that became increasingly ominous
once he ran straight through full-back Mike Catt to score the first
of his four tries. His individual contest against Tony Underwood
contained all the absurdities of the lurid mismatches for which
professional boxing is rightly notorious. It was akin to matching
Mike Tyson against Chris Eubank, a contest in which there was
always going to be one winner. The younger of the Underwood
brothers did not deserve to be treated with contempt. Though
he looked an especially forlorn figure at the interval, when
he squatted abjectly between Rowell's long legs in the team
huddle, he refused to be intimidated.

It is inherently unfair, unforgivably one-dimensional, to view
his inferiority in isolation. Rugby prides itself on being a game
of evolution and these All Blacks, infused with young talent, are
taking it into a different orbit. They are bigger, faster than their
forebears. They move the ball with the speed and smoothness of an
NBA basketball team. They ally physical power with artistic flair. If
England's disappointments are to have any long-term relevance,
English rugby must distance itself from the introspective attitude
which dictates that the Five Nations game has real worth in a
global context. Rowell suggested that the championship of the
Northern Hemisphere remains 'a cracking competition'. Yet he
added, tellingly: 'We have to interact more readily, more regularly,
with the Southern Hemisphere countries.'

The most valuable underlying lesson of the game is contained in the New Zealanders' faith in collective will and

ambition. They are consciously protecting Lomu from himself. Mains acknowledged that he harboured doubts about Lomu's capacity to cope with the magnitude of his talent. 'Before this World Cup, we didn't know him as a person. We needed to get inside his head to get the best out of him,' he said. The All Blacks no longer need such tokens of theatricality as the haka. That is not to say they no longer have the need of legends. The supporters who spilled on to the streets to slake their thirst after a warm afternoon had only one name on their lips. 'Hey you. Hey you. What you gonna do,' they chanted. 'When Jonah Lomu gets the ball he'll run right over you.'

26 JUNE

LETTERS TO THE EDITOR

ENGLAND MUST SEE PAST LOMU

SIR – It is important that the extraordinary performance of Jonah Lomu in the Rugby World Cup semi-final is not seen as the only reason for England's humiliation in the first hour of that match. The key to the match was the difference in attitude. England's forays into the fifteen-man game have so far only happened in press conferences and even then we are told the more expansive approach will be considered after we have 'established a platform'. Unfortunately the platform never seems quite strong enough.

The All Blacks, on the other hand, had the courage to play 'total rugby' from the very first minute of the game. The risks involved were high – the switch kick-off from Mehrtens had to be accurate and the decision to run the ball from their own twenty-two a couple of minutes later had obvious inherent dangers. The risks were ignored and the game was won inside ten minutes.

The strength of will shown by the All Blacks is not developed on the training ground, it comes from the heart. Jeremy Guscott is a world-class player with a rugby ball in his hands but is reduced to mediocrity when asked to chase one all day – it is only when we have the arrogance of the All Blacks that we will see the full potential of this England team.

Ant Salmon
London

JONAH OR JESSIE?

SIR – I should like to know if Mick Skinner regards Jonah Lomu as one of 'the Jessies in the backs'. And, if so, would he be prepared to say it to his face?

Patricia Hennessy
Woodcote
Reading

THE WHALE IN THE ROOM

SIR – My dictionary defines 'Jonah' as: 'Person who brings, or is believed to bring, bad luck.' The writing was on the wall.

Gareth Jones
Bradford-on-Avon
Wiltshire

19 JUNE
SPRINGBOK DEFENDERS KEEP TEAM ON COURSE
Brendan Gallagher

The South African miracle continues but the waiting, despite thousands of posters to the contrary, is not yet over. The Rainbow Nation faces a week of growing anxiety and excitement before discovering if a pot of gold can be unearthed at Ellis Park. The 58,000 spectators at this extraordinary semi-final might have cursed the tropical downpour and moaned when Derek Bevan delayed the kick-off, but this was a contest that will live in their memories.

South Africa, defending desperately during the last five minutes, clung on as France mounted a final assault that resembled their remarkable comeback against Scotland earlier in the tournament. The outstanding Abdelatif Benazzi was chopped down by Hennie Le Roux inches short and then the Springboks somehow survived an excruciating series of four scrums on their own line without buckling. The tension was unbearable – even for the neutrals – and only dissipated when Joel Stransky cleared his lines in the third minute of injury time and the final whistle sounded at 19–15. The Springboks, drained of emotion, rushed straight off while the French huddled together on the halfway line before receiving a tremendous ovation.

It never rains in Durban in June – so the locals kept telling us – but the weather was quite appalling, with squalls of Biblical intensity reducing King's Park to a paddy field. The original decision, taken by the Rugby World Cup directors in consultation with Bevan and the ground authorities, to delay the kick-off by sixty minutes was probably correct but badly undermined by the subsequent amateurish efforts to mop up. Some twenty-three kitchen attendants and a solitary child, all armed with brooms, splashed around in uncoordinated fashion, doing more harm than good. At 3.45 p.m. the word came that the game would be delayed a further half-hour, which only allowed more rain to fall on the unprotected surface. The effect on thirty players, each preparing for one of the biggest games of his career, can only be imagined and it is to their credit that they still managed to present the game as a spectacle.

The match finally started ninety-five minutes late, with the spotlight firmly on Bevan. Tournament rules meant if he had abandoned the match in the first half the contest would have been decided on tries scored in the game. If no tries had been registered then the tie would have been settled on the disciplinary record of the teams during the tournament. All this placed added pressure on Bevan, as South Africa would have lost by virtue of their poor disciplinary record, having had James Dalton sent off against Canada and Pieter Hendriks cited. If the match had been stopped in the second half the result would have stood. Conditions throughout were just about playable, and while there were mistakes aplenty, these were balanced by moments of sublime skill – notably from Jean-Luc Sadourny, Benazzi, Andre Joubert and Stransky.

The game started predictably with South Africa applying the early pressure. Stransky kicked a penalty goal and Ruben Kruger was adjudged to have wriggled over after twenty-five minutes. The French remained cool and Thierry Lacroix, striking the ball magnificently, bagged two penalty goals to narrow the gap by half-time. A further storm arrived shortly after the break, but so absorbed were the combatants they scarcely noticed.

Stransky and Lacroix swapped two penalty goals, Joost van der Westhuizen departed with damaged ribs and then finally French discipline cracked. The volatile Olivier Merle drove into Francois Pienaar unnecessarily on the blindside and conceded a crucial penalty after his forwards had worked wonders to win a defensive ruck. The impressive Stransky made no mistake and bought his side valuable breathing space. Lacroix kicked a fifth penalty goal to post a tournament total of 102 points as France rallied with great spirit. But South Africa, not for the first time, showed much courage and organisation in defence.

23 JUNE
ENGLAND FOUND WANTING AGAIN IN THE BIG LEAGUE
John Mason

Erratic England, infuriating experts at flattering only to deceive, flopped again. A 19–9 defeat by France in the World Cup third-place play-off means that England, who removed Australia, the 1991 champions, a fortnight before, will have to pre-qualify for the 1999 tournament. Being beaten is one thing. Being openly derided – justly so – as England were by a cosmopolitan crowd, mostly without a definitive allegiance, is another. England must stop talking a good game because when it matters in the world league, they cannot deliver the goods.

Grand Slam England must get rid of their semi-static, stop-start, kicking-for-position version of rugby football – the sooner the better. What is suitable to rule the Five Nations competition has no place on the world stage. Against the big boys it is, ultimately, self-defeating, deflating besides being way, way off the pace. Remember New Zealand, 18 June, 1995. In this third-place match, with the honourable and sustained exception of scrum-half Dewi Morris, there was little about which to cheer. The tiny crumbs of comfort were that France, in beating England for the first time in nine matches since 1988, did score a couple of tries after the compulsory exchange of penalty goals between Rob Andrew and Thierry Lacroix, this time three each.

The points by the admirable Lacroix, who also often split the midfield on telling counter-attacks late on, took him to 112 and top place in the 1995 competition. His total put him eight points ahead of Gavin Hastings, Scotland's inspiring captain and full-back. Hastings, as it happens, is now enjoying the first few days of retirement from international rugby. May several England players now feel that a similar course would benefit them – Dean Richards, Andrew, Brian Moore, Jeremy Guscott, Victor Ubogu for starters. It is time for young England to take the field.

While France could not impose themselves until midway through the second half, they finished worthy winners, primarily because even in the darker moments, thcy subdued England when it mattered most at scrum and line-out in attacking situations. England, despite overall winning sixty-one per cent of the line-outs and fifty-eight per cent of the scrums, had gone a match too far. Those statistics do not indicate in what part of the pitch the match was being played or what the attacking opportunities were. England looked jaded and dispirited from an early point. Maybe this was because, having been at sea level for five matches, they were playing for the first time at six thousand feet. More likely, I think, it was the scars of that 45–29 mauling by New Zealand in the semi-final that hurt most.

Sadly, France, too, took their time in using the quality possession they won in a match which, though attracting 44,000 to Loftus Versfeld, a record for World Cup matches in Pretoria, was a gloomy, low-key affair – a grey, colourless advertisement for the state of the game in the Northern Hemisphere. Should such an opinion grate with an England squad who have worked unceasingly for two years, the comment is not new. After England's 1994 Cape Town defeat by South Africa, I wrote in the *Daily Telegraph* that England were not in division one of a world league and that success in the World Cup was unlikely. Nothing that has happened here, victory over Australia included, has changed that view, especially after this latest dreary offering.

Andrew struck first with a penalty goal in the twenty-seventh minute – barging at the line-out. Seconds before half-time Lacroix levelled the score – backs offside. Immediately after the break, his second penalty (backs offside again) put France ahead. Andrew pulled that back in the forty-ninth minute (6–6), Lacroix making it 9–6 in the fifty-seventh minute – not releasing. Indeed the only release was a sporadic Mexican wave and prolonged chants of 'boring'. It was difficult not to agree.

A glorious midfield break from a long way back involving the complete French back division turned the jeers to cheers. England scrambled the ball to touch. Olivier Merle won the line-out and the pack drove on the ball carrier, who, by now, was Olivier Roumat. That was the first try, the second coming only seventeen seconds before injury time. Andrew, whose precision kicking for position was expertly done, as ever, kicked a third penalty goal between the tries. All his efforts to run the ball came to naught: wrong options, clumsy approach work, poor passing. England's backs could not create anything decently resembling a threat. If France contained Morris, the danger was over. France finished with a flourish when scrum-half Fabien Galthié fed Émile Ntamack on the short-side. Tackles by Morris, Rory Underwood and Mike Catt did not register as the speeding Ntamack stepped gracefully inside, the goal-line and victory his destination. No wonder John Major has resigned.

25 JUNE

EXTRA-SPECIAL SPRINGBOKS WIN IT FOR RAINBOW NATION
Paul Ackford

South Africa were destined to win this World Cup; it was written in the stars. No side could have had a harder path to tread. They faced the world champions in their first match, overcame floodlight failure, the sending-off of James Dalton and the citing of Pieter Hendriks at Port Elizabeth, and played a semi-final in Durban in torrential rain. Nothing disturbed their momentum and even the best team in the competition by far, New Zealand, were unable to deny them the celebrations which a country craved. After the final whistle their hugely impressive and modest captain, Francois Pienaar, said: 'We did not have sixty-three thousand fans behind us, we had forty-three million South Africans.' He was right, and the memories of President Nelson Mandela dancing a jig before the first game of the competition and waving his Springbok cap after the last match will live with me for the rest of my life.

Joel Stransky won it for them. Eighty minutes could not settle the match, neither could the first period of extra time, but Stransky gave South Africa a crucial three-point winning margin three minutes into the final period of drama. From a scrum he hoisted a huge up-and-under which Zinzan Brooke knocked on. The position was on the twenty-two slightly to the right of the posts, and all of South Africa knew what Stransky was going to attempt. On the first occasion the scrum slewed sideways, but the Springbok pack regrouped and managed to provide a stable platform for Stransky to attempt the dropped goal. Graeme Bachop tried to intercept the path of the ball, Andrew Mehrtens raced up to block the kick, but Stransky ignored everyone and struck the ball cleanly between the posts to leave a nation delirious.

It was a compulsive match, rarely living up to the expectations of free-flowing rugby, but of its kind it was a classic. Neither side managed to get more than three points ahead. The tension as the game built towards its memorable climax was unbearable. That South Africa were able to keep the lid on an astonishingly talented All Black team is a tribute to the resolve and courage of the entire team. They tackled like demons and the All Blacks were never able to create the space and continuity to launch their dangerous backs. Jonah Lomu was the name on everyone's lips before the game, but he rarely had the opportunity to get out of the starting blocks, faced as he was with two or three pumped-up Springbok defenders. In the end the All Blacks asked too much of Lomu; he was given the ball and told to work a miracle, and in the biggest game of his life he could not deliver.

Aside from their defence, the Springbok pack had a wonderful match. They shared the line-outs but held a discernible edge in

the scrums, and the work of Pienaar, Ruben Kruger and Mark
Andrews was compulsive. Time and again the back-row trio
killed All Black attacks or started some of their own, and when
they appeared to falter there was always the massive presence
of Kobus Wiese and Balie Swart to add weight to the move.
The other impressive figure in the Springbok pack was Chris
Rossouw, who played like a man possessed and suffered nothing
in comparison with the All Black captain, Sean Fitzpatrick. Bolt
on to this display the phenomenal kicking of Stransky, who
slotted three penalty goals and two dropped goals, the midfield
tenacity of Japie Mulder and Hennie le Roux – who snuffed
out the All Black centres – and the inevitable peerless display
of Andre Joubert at full-back, and you get some idea of why the
Springboks edged home.

Although no tries were scored, South Africa had the satisfaction of getting a player across the line when Kruger was driven
over by his colleagues but could not ground the ball because
Olo Brown dived in underneath to stop the try. It was typical
of the backs-to-the-wall effort which the All Blacks put up. Ian
Jones had a memorable match in the line-out, appearing to
win the ball at will, and there were some delightful kicks put in
by Mehrtens, but the All Blacks never hit top gear. Even Josh
Kronfeld, the best forward in the tournament, had a quiet
game, knocking the ball on twice when a safe pair of hands
could have changed the course of the game.

Nevertheless, the All Blacks nearly pinched the match three
minutes from the end of normal time. Ian Jones won a line-
out, Frank Bunce set up the ruck and Mehrtens let fly with a
dropped goal in front of the posts which missed. He is young
enough and talented enough to recover, but the memory will
be with him for a very long time. For much of the game the

match was a form of muscular chess. Each time one side set up an attacking position the other team defended their line, and for long periods neither side could gain a decisive advantage. Bachop would roll a long kick into the corner to set up an attacking line-out only for Mark Andrews or Hannes Strydom to steal the crucial ball. Minutes later, at the other end of the pitch, it was the same old story, the Springboks would threaten near the All Black line, only for Ian Jones to rescue the situation for New Zealand.

After Stransky had kicked that crucial dropped goal the All Blacks did their level best to come back. But the confusion in their last attacks echoed the uncertainty which enveloped them throughout the match. Bunce burst up the right-hand side and called for Marc Ellis to come in off his wing to confuse the defence. Ellis came late and put down the pass as the Springbok defence threatened to crumble. Moments later Ellis was unable to hang on to the ball as Bunce again tried to set him free. It was untidy and careless and so unlike the style of rugby which we have seen from the All Blacks throughout this tournament. They have set new standards of creativity, but this final also proved that the old virtues are still sacred. Get a side together, tell them to do the basics well, get them fit and inculcate a spirit which carries them through difficult moments and they will be an impossibly difficult team to conquer. That was the story of the Springboks in this World Cup and on the back of it they have stormed the world of rugby.

26 JUNE
MANDELA'S STATESMANSHIP
LEAVES INDELIBLE MARK
Michael Calvin

The World Cup began and ended with an old man, who pledged his allegiance by wearing a Springbok shirt, tightly buttoned at the collar and hanging loosely over his trousers. The Ellis Park crowd chanted his Christian name, where they once murmured his surname with the fear and loathing reserved for public enemies. He punched the air with both fists, in utter abandon rather than studied defiance. The symbolism of a new nation, renewing its vow of reconciliation beneath cloudless skies, was perfect. The sight of Nelson Mandela, the people's president, presenting the William Webb Ellis trophy to Francois Pienaar, the icon of white youth, was uniquely moving.

There were so many incongruous images on a day when sport allowed South Africa to ease towards peace with itself. The sound of a white crowd singing a Zulu anthem framed on the chain gangs was strange, even to those accustomed to Twickenham resounding to a Negro spiritual. The Springboks – the Amabokoboko to black Africans, die Bokke to Afrikaners – celebrated in the very hotel where, five years earlier, Mike Gatting's rebel England cricketers had provoked a sit-down strike by staff because they had allied themselves to an abhorrent regime. Roads were blocked by revellers, of all races. Traffic was reduced to a cacophonous crawl. The minority who attempted to flaunt the old flag, the emblem of apartheid, were derided, isolated.

A camouflaged police van, synonymous with suppression, toured the suburbs bedecked with flags and banners. Pienaar's white tribe of Africa once demonised Mandela. Yet he was driven to the point of tears by the memory of his president, wearing his No. 6 jersey, visiting the dressing room. 'You have done more for our country than we can ever do,' the captain told him. 'You wearing my shirt is an honour I cannot express. It is one of the biggest thank yous I have received in my life.' Morne du Plessis, the Springboks' equally impressive manager, spoke with an air of awe, about 'the surge of this nation, the unbelievable emotional force that carried us through'.

It would, of course, be unforgivably naive to suggest that attitudes changed overnight. There are still too many apologists for the old ways, too many men who talk glibly of a new South Africa without believing it. The black sporting majority remain isolated by economic reality. Development programmes are at an embryonic stage, despite increasing support from major companies. One leading South African sports administrator, in sombre mood, suggested: 'We have a problem because, after the success of this World Cup, certain people will now think everything we do is perfect, faultless.'

He was referring, obliquely, to the ludicrous figure of Louis Luyt, president of the South African RFU, who acted totally in character when he soured the official dinner with the most inane and insensitive speech [claiming that 1995 was the first 'genuine' World Cup because of South Africa's return to the international fold]. He embodies the lack of sophistication that is the legacy of South Africa's international isolation. He can be crass, condescending, and has an unchallenged reputation as an autocratic bully. His saving grace is popularly assumed to be his astuteness as a businessman. However, intriguingly, some suggest that Southern Hemisphere rugby might have been undersold by the ten-year £342 million television deal Luyt helped broker with Rupert Murdoch's News Corporation.

The worth of sport, as a commodity in the satellite age, is only just beginning to be appreciated. Some analysts, for instance, estimate that the commercial value of the rugby union agreement to Murdoch is in the region of £1.3 billion.

The game reached a watershed in Johannesburg. It must now be judged as a professional entity, whatever the increasingly peripheral figures of the International Rugby Board decide at their next meeting. Amateurism is the ultimate diversion which, among other things, deflects from the RFU's establishment of a modern, well-structured sport in England. Current international players, fated to emerge when the game is on the verge of historic change, do not deserve to be regarded as blinkered mercenaries. They are intelligent products of the existing system, who understand its ethos. Their supposed sin, of demanding adequate financial reward for their commitment, is begrudged by the reactionary few rather than the vast majority of ordinary followers.

Domestic rugby now has a great opportunity to take a quantum leap forward, if it can bridge the generations and seal its future in a positive, decisive fashion. Vernon Pugh, the IRB's most credible official, was correct when he observed that the Southern Hemisphere deal will help European rugby because 'they have upped the stakes'. A different game will emerge. Club loyalties will be stretched even further. Television, the paymaster, will expect its pound of flesh. Subtle changes will signal a shift in momentum. The incorporation of Italy into an extended European championship will offer greater commercial scope. The current television contract, with the BBC as a primary outlet for the Five Nations Championship, will be infinitely more lucrative when it expires in two years. It seems inevitable that an agreement in line with that just reached with

South Africa, Australia and New Zealand will be concluded with Murdoch. This will appal many, given that terrestrial television will be obliged to accept a secondary role. Change will be traumatic. It will require foresight and a fair degree of good fortune. But it can be done. Just ask Nelson Mandela, the old man in the Springbok shirt.

1995 RESULTS – Quarter-finals: South Africa 42, Western Samoa 14; France 36, Ireland 12; England 25, Australia 22; New Zealand 48, Scotland 30. Semi-finals: South Africa 19, France 15; New Zealand 45, England 29. Third-place: France 19, England 9. Final: South Africa 15, New Zealand 12 (aet).

CHAPTER FOUR: 1999

HOSTED BY WALES, ENGLAND, FRANCE, IRELAND & SCOTLAND

26 SEPTEMBER
IT'S TIME FOR ENGLAND
Paul Ackford

Time to put up or shut up. Ever since the inaugural Rugby World Cup in 1987, the Northern Hemisphere have been playing catch-up with the Southern Hemisphere. New Zealand won that first tournament, Australia the next and South Africa the last. Sure, there were decent performances from France in 1987 and England in 1991 when those two countries contested the final, but that was about it. The European challenge simply was not good enough. But that was then. When Rugby World Cup 1999 kicks off, England and Wales especially, Scotland and France possibly, and Ireland, if they get ridiculously lucky, might go all the way. Rugby World Cup 1999 could, indeed should, signal a fundamental shift in the balance of power and an end to Southern Hemisphere supremacy.

The host unions will never have a better chance. All will be playing their pool matches on home turf, in familiar surroundings, roared on by a supportive and expectant public.

All have had the benefit of a lengthy close season to reach the peak of physical conditioning without the interruption of a domestic league programme, and all will have taken comfort from the evidence of the Tri-Nations series where the standard of play was decidedly ordinary. But those factors are nothing compared to the most significant change to hit rugby in the last four years. For the first time all the major teams will enter the competition on an equal footing. The decision to usher in professionalism, taken weeks after the last World Cup, has levelled the playing field. The inequality which existed in the old days of shamateurism, exploited by South Africa and New Zealand, in particular, has been eroded. Money is legitimately available to all and standards have risen across the board.

The bad news is that the democratisation of the sport has done away with the excuses. If the Northern Hemisphere teams come a cropper, they will do so on the quality of their players, their coaching and their preparation. Rugby's oldest and most enduring truth will have been confirmed: that the men of Australia, New Zealand and South Africa are somehow culturally, mentally and athletically superior.

I can't subscribe to that. No one can tell me that Martin Johnson, Keith Wood, Gregor Townsend or Rob Howley have anything to fear from their Southern Hemisphere counterparts. All British and Irish rugby has lacked in the past is strength in depth and the organisation and direction which has under-pinned the success of the three previous Cup holders. The 1997 British Lions showed what was possible when they humbled the Springboks two years into the professional cycle. Now it is up to one of those four countries to complete the job. And if rugby on these islands has had to go cap in hand to the very nations they wish to dethrone to become competitive; if the influence of New Zealand coaches Graham Henry, Warren Gatland and John Mitchell has turned Wales, Ireland and England respectively; if the artistry of the imported Leslie brothers proves significant for Scotland, so what? These people have enriched, not diluted their sport, and to question their allegiance or motivation is to risk a lynch mob from their adopted countries.

But enough of the big boys and the big challenge. The Rugby World Cup is far more than a showdown between the superpowers. Sixty-five nations have played a total of 133 matches to reach the final stages, a significant improvement from forty-three in 1995 and thirty-two in 1991. The range of interest in the international game is now massive and truly global. Latvia beat Norway 44–6 in the first of the qualifiers in September 1996 and since then players from Israel, Moldova, Lithuania, Guyana, Chinese Taipei, Papua New Guinea, Botswana and Kenya have fought for the right to rub shoulders with the likes of Jonah Lomu. Spain and Uruguay have actually qualified and their game at Galashiels will provide one of the more charming moments of the competition. Figures from the world of commerce and television are equally astonishing. The tournament will be broadcast to more than 140 countries worldwide, with a likely cumulative audience in excess of three billion viewers. The commercial programme will net £50 million and, with the 2.2 million tickets expected to generate another £20–25 million, the chances are that Rugby World Cup Ltd will have a surplus of £70–75 million to play with, a large lump of which is pledged to the emerging nations to promote and develop the sport.

And yet proliferation brings its accompanying dangers. Twenty teams will contest the final stages instead of sixteen in South Africa. The increase to five pools of four, politically expedient in that each of the Five Nations is guaranteed an equal share of World Cup revenue, has provoked fears of mismatches such as the 145–17 hammering the All Blacks dished out to Japan in South Africa. Or, worse, a serious injury caused by the gulf in technique and fitness between the professional athletes of the major nations and the well-intentioned amateurs of the chasing pack.

Then there are the usual gripes about ticket availability and allocation. When surplus tickets went on sale all prospective purchasers could find was the engaged tone of a hopelessly submerged sales and distribution network. It did not help that France initially refused to hand over tickets because of an argument with Wales over the non-payment of an old invoice, or that the tickets for the opening game were wrongly dated and had to be re-issued. The message was of a sport unable to market itself properly.

That theme has dogged the development of the Millennium Stadium. When Wales played France recently, it resembled a television studio, alluring and magical when viewed from the outside but disappointingly tacky and insubstantial within. Doors lacked panes of glass and builders' dust clogged the corridors. Wales versus Argentina, the opening fixture of the third-biggest sporting event behind the football World Cup and the Olympic Games, will be the first time the Millennium Stadium is used at capacity. The place has every chance of becoming the most emotionally charged and vibrant theatre in European sport, but why attract all the negative publicity by leaving it so late?

And so to the battles and the questions ahead. What will replace the image of Lomu thundering over the prostrate bodies of Englishmen in the Cape Town semi-final in 1995?

Can Rob Howley or Graham Henry, captain and coach of the host nation, fan the flames as Nelson Mandela and Francois Pienaar did at Ellis Park, Johannesburg? Pienaar and Mandela were erasing a divisive and shameful past; Howley and Henry may just be on the verge of rediscovering a glorious one. Or is it Australia's destiny, sparked by the return of captain John Eales and the brilliance of their back line, to repeat their 1991 triumph and become the first side to win two World Cups? What about Tonga, Fiji and Samoa, the hard-hitting islanders? Can they recover from the leakage of their best players over the years to mount a credible campaign?

For me, the tournament comes down to one of two countries and a pool match played at Twickenham between England and New Zealand. If the form books are anything like reliable, the winner of that titanic contest will play Scotland and France en route to a final against Australia. The losers face a play-off game, two of the three Southern Hemisphere nations on consecutive weekends and then a rematch at the Millennium Stadium. The bookies favour the All Blacks; I'm going for England. North versus south, the old, old story, but this time with a different ending.

2 OCTOBER
THE HEARTBEAT OF A NATION
Paul Hayward

The people of Wales are understandably sensitive to condescending comment from across the border. But for now they would probably settle for an old portrait of the Welsh dug out by Jeremy Paxman for his book *The English*: 'A country of woodland and pasture, abounding in deer and fish, milk and herds, but breeding a bestial type of man.'

Tear-splashed, and with a Welsh roar at its back, the 1999 Rugby World Cup set off on its thirty-seven-day, five-nation journey with Graham Henry's stuttering side completing a ninth successive victory with a 23–18 win over Argentina. Celebs hang off the wagon as it departs. Gleam and glamour have come to the most elemental of team sports. But bestial man still leads the parade. There is no rugby without him. After a damp, nervy encounter with the Pumas at the new 72,500-seat Millennium Stadium, the Welsh are reminded that all the clever abstractions of modern coaching are only part of an equation that is completed by iron and blood.

When Shirley Bassey has tottered off in her high heels, rugby reaffirms itself as a wonderfully raw and courage-driven trade. At this level it is about men transcending their own physical and psychological limits. Next, at Twickenham, the Italians must stand up to a rampaging England pack. Then Scotland face the daunting might of South Africa up at Murrayfield. In Bristol the sky will go black on the gallant Tongans when Jonah Lomu begins to snort and run. Eventually the whole convoy will alight again in a stadium that is more California than Cardiff – 'a creative masterpiece, made possible by the skills of the people', according to the great Gerald Davies over the Tannoy. 'The story of a modern Wales.'

On this performance, the Welsh have some way to go before they match the splendour of their surroundings. Fire-breathing they were not. They scored fine tries through Colin Charvis and Mark Taylor but never imposed themselves fully on a persistent Argentina, whose stand-off, Gonzalo Quesada, kicked six penalties out of seven to keep Wales' first opponents naggingly close. If prevarication at the point of kicking was a bookable offence, then Quesada would already be out of the championship.

Though, logistically, this tournament is more of a European World Cup, with Edinburgh, Dublin, London and Paris drawn into the swirl, Wales are entitled to regard it as Cymru's championship. Dark, political horse-trading on bids and support forced the organisers to disperse the matches across two time zones. The English RFU demanded the right to stage both semi-finals as condition for supporting Wales' bid. Yet the Millennium Stadium itself acts as a kind of fortress behind which the Welsh can relish the sense of being the real hosts and spiritual guardians of a game that helped them measure their place in the world. Historians may trace the rebirth of Welshness not to the opening of a National Assembly, which only a minority of eligible voters turned out to endorse, but to the full unveiling of a stadium which claims to be the finest sporting arena on rugby's trampled earth. Such is the power of sport. Politics could never prompt the leader writers of the *South Wales Echo* to declare so rapturously: 'Now is the time to make friends. Now is the time to be proud. Now, above all, is the time to be Welsh.' Not a dry eye on the editorial floor.

Even the most doltish politician or businessman can see that sport on this scale has a dramatic oxygenating effect on the health of a nation. Like Manchester and Leeds, Cardiff feels like one of those corporate-driven British cities which are galloping away from their past. The mayor thinks the World Cup could be worth £12–20 million to the local economy. The real town criers for a timidly promoted tournament have been the media, local businesses and the city's 315,000 residents. Cardiff shops are awash with rugby memorabilia. Even the health-food shop, which sells soya sausages to vegetarians, has discovered a passion for the carnivorous business of rugby. Strange to relate, Cardiff's top attraction by a street is Harry Ramsden's, which receives twice as many visitors as the National Museum of Wales. But in Cardiff now, Harry has had his chips. The Millennium Stadium, which cost £125 million to build, becomes the architectural and cultural core of the town. Glanmor Griffiths, chairman of the Welsh union, reckons it is worth £250 million already (he should have been an estate agent).

The English, it has to be said, could never get away with such a polychromatic display of unabashed nationalism. They would be accused of imperial arrogance. Catatonia – good band, misleading name – set the tone: 'Every day when I wake up, I thank the Lord I'm Welsh.' It was less the reopening of a World Cup than the reinvention of Wales as a country no longer burdened by history. It was 2.59 p.m. before anyone mentioned the Argentines and then a Red Arrows fly-past bisected the playing of their national anthem. It was the day's tackiest moment.

A message from the Queen followed a 1,000-mile path through Wales before being read out by Prince Charles. The Manic Street Preachers interrupted a world tour to be back for the opening game. Many of the greats of Welsh rugby were paraded across the pitch to girder-rattling acclaim; immortal Welsh tries were replayed on two giant screens; there were male voice choirs and military bands and Shirley Bassey dressed in a Welsh flag. Max Boyce, 'the troubador of Wales', sang 'Hymns and Arias'. Reclaim the past, put in a bid for the future. Seldom has any nation of 2.8 million souls emerged so potently from the long slumber of seemingly inexorable decline.

There was a time, within the memory's touching distance,

when Welsh rugby seemed to be atrophying like the heavy industries that supplied it with bull-like men steeped in the romantic traditions of extravagant running and dexterous handling. Through much of the 1990s, Wales seemed to be on a long funeral march to obscurity. After the South Africa World Cup in 1995, where Wales failed to make it beyond the group stage, Vernon Pugh, then WRU president, said sorrowfully: 'Most people feel sorry for us and that is more painful than any other reaction.'

Pity has gone now, replaced, if anything, by an inflated sense of just how quickly Wales are escaping the bad old days. Eight consecutive victories were as intoxicating as eight pints of Brains. In the run-up to this match, Scott Gibbs recalled a scene from the team's long pageant through the Welsh provinces. 'Garin Jenkins was talking to a couple the other day and they burst into tears,' Gibbs said. 'They'd been married for twenty-five years and it was the first time the wife had seen her husband cry.' Front-row forwards have that effect on people.

To solidify team spirit, the Welsh squad headed to all points on the principality's compass. They climbed Snowdon – all 3,560 feet of it – and looked down on the land they hoped to conquer. Their odds came down even faster than a prop forward on a mountain descent: from 80–1 to 12–1. But the danger in the final hours was that both team and audience would submit to the nervous tension that invariably affects tournament hosts. So it looked here. Before the match the din was so ferocious that we were in danger of levitating. For long stretches of the game itself, the crowd fell sullen, angst-ridden, vulnerable to the kind of doubts that once accompanied every appearance of the scarlet jersey.

The bubble in the spirit level will settle where it belongs. The euphoria of an opening ceremony that could have been mistaken for a particularly lavish eisteddfod will give way to a more realistic appraisal of Wales' chance. Henry, who has preached sobriety of expectation throughout the last twelve months, may even be relieved that the scale of Wales' task has reasserted itself through the fog of firework smoke and the eddies of hymn and folk song. 'Land of my fathers? My fathers can keep it,' Dylan Thomas once said sourly. At the risk of taking a country's pulse from a ball game, it might not be stretching things too much to say that rugby has boosted the heartbeat of a nation that always regarded the oval-ball game as a powerful life-force. As Celtic revivalist festivals go, this might only be surpassed by a Welsh appearance in the final. The patriotism, chauvinism even, is already in danger of gushing over into the River Taff. Bestial man comes in twenty different jerseys, though from the opening ceremony, you would have thought that the only team worth mentioning was the one dressed in red.

11 OCTOBER

LETTER TO THE SPORTS EDITOR

PUT A LID ON IT

SIR – As an Englishman living in Wales I was fortunate enough to attend the opening match of the World Cup in what is clearly the best rugby stadium in the world. However, sitting in the rain in row seven my eyes wandered to the roof. Although I can understand why the preliminaries should be uncovered I do not see why the final should also be open to the elements. It is almost perverse that in 1999 we have the technology to ensure a dry showpiece final but choose to run the risk of letting the weather turn it into a lottery.

Keith Townrow

Whitebrook

Monmouthshire

10 OCTOBER

A NEVER-ENDING NIGHTMARE
Owen Slot

England's worst nightmare came back to haunt them. In 1995, Jonah Lomu wrecked England's dreams and here he did so again. Four years on, he remained unstoppable. Lomu's try in the fifty-eighth minute not only swung the group contest convincingly in New Zealand's favour, it also reopened a whole chapter of history that every Englishman would rather forget. Four years earlier, in that infamous World Cup semi-final in Cape Town, he blew England away with four tries. He only scored one this time in the All Blacks' 30–16 victory, but it was enough.

Lomu and the 1995 World Cup are synonymous. Images of South Africa are inseparable from memories of the flying Auckland giant blasting through defenders in a way that no other rugby player had done before. You could fill a book full of the theories, which, since then, have been dreamed up to stop him. Little by little, and also by dint of a severe health disorder, his aura has been eroded. We knew that he was back in form for this World Cup, but he proved once again that the danger he brings is as awesome as it ever was.

Whatever you do, you mustn't give him space on the ball. Everyone knew that. But on the occasions when England could not put theory into action they were made to pay for it. And in the fifty-eighth minute, they were put to the sword. It was uncanny, but a rerun of Lomu's famous first try against England in Cape Town could hardly have been more perfectly executed. The sequence of carnage he left behind him in his second-minute score that day has become famous in rugby lore. Tony Underwood was first to attempt to stop him and was brushed off with Lomu's fly-swat hand-off. Will Carling was second with a tap tackle that unbalanced him but could not stop him as he careered on, straight through Mike Catt, the third defender, and over for the try.

Here again a similar outcome – just different names strewn along Twickenham's green carpet as Lomu made his regal way to the try-line. First Jeremy Guscott, flicked off with the same fly-swat hand-off, then Austin Healey, who tried to grab him around the knees but could not break his stride. And then not one but two defenders blown away in the final few yards, Dan Luger and Matt Dawson, who succeeded in bringing him to ground but only with the ball grounded over the try-line. England will have kicked themselves for giving the huge man so much space in which to break into speed. This was indeed where they were at fault. But one day, probably a long way away, they will sit down and admire on video an athlete who is back to his supreme best.

Lomu had given indication of the threat he brought to this World Cup with two tries in New Zealand's 45–9 opening-game win against Tonga. He gave further proof of the possibilities in the twenty-fifth minute here when he brushed off two tackles, and he very nearly blew the whole team away again late on.

How had England prepared for him? On one occasion they put Healey into a scrum so that Lawrence Dallaglio could stand on the right wing and mark him. Generally, though, they believed in their tackling and the ability of the first man to slow him down in time for the rest to knock him over. Whatever the plans, they were inadequate. Four years on and England still had no answers.

His invincibility has already got to the stage where people are joking about it. Bob Dwyer, the former Australia coach, once said you needed an elephant gun to stop him. Will Carling said that a crowbar would do the job. When a huge creaking sound came from the direction of the changing rooms, Clive Woodward said it was probably Lomu getting out of the showers. Joking aside, the truth is that once again an enormous dark shadow looms over the Rugby World Cup. It is a magnificent sight and it is set to make an enormous impact on the rest of this tournament. This sport shuddered when Lomu arrived to reinvent the rules. Since then, we thought we had settled back down to normal. But suddenly he has upset the whole status quo again.

15 OCTOBER
SAMOANS RETURN TO HAUNT WALES
Mick Cleary

This time it will spawn no jokes, only heartfelt tribute. In 1991 little, unheralded Western Samoa caused the Rugby World Cup's first upset in beating Wales on home turf. The victory gave birth to a corny old line that it was as well Wales were not playing the whole of Samoa. Here they were, for the islanders are now known as Samoa. But this was no hollow triumph, no scraggy victory against ragbag opposition. Wales, though naive and careless here, are real contenders on recent form with ten successive wins. No longer should we give Samoa a patronising pat on the head for their exuberance and passion. Now we should salute them simply as damn fine rugby players. 'We were more under-puppies than underdogs,' said Bryan Williams, the Samoan coach, after the 38–31 success.

Samoa showed what a joyful experience this game can be. They played with enormous heart, no little skill through fly-half Stephen Bachop and the man of the match, full-back Silao Leaega, and deep self-belief that this could again be their day. They had to resist a furious last charge by Wales but resist they did. Samoa had already conceded two penalty tries at the scrummage and were on the rack once again as the clock ticked deep into injury time. Wales heaved, Samoa creaked only for Scott Quinnell, who had a poor afternoon, to lose control. Cue bedlam.

But let us luxuriate in what was a spellbinding occasion. The match was full of sound and fury. Samoa, eagle-eyed, pounced on every Welsh frailty, zipping clear for two interception tries during the match. Bachop romped in from fifty-two metres in the thirty-eighth minute, Pat Lam from even further, eighty metres, six minutes into the second half. Wales looked scatty and distracted. Their first penalty try for a popped scrummage in the thirteenth minute ought to have shown them that the path to victory lay in the midst of the heavyweight eight forwards. But no, Wales wanted to play loose, to put the ball through the hand rather than be creased downfield from Neil Jenkins's right toecap.

Wales fretted dreadfully at times despite having opened up

a 12–3 lead within seventeen minutes. Ed Morrison had given a penalty try and four minutes later right-wing Gareth Thomas secured a splendid one-handed touchdown in the corner. And then the mist descended. Wales lost their way, handing Samoa their first try in the twenty-second minute, a crooked throw only finding lock Lio Falaniko. Eight minutes later, Bachop, a canny, probing influence, scored two tries in the blink of a disbelieving Welsh eyelid. 'That was a hell of a scrap,' said Welsh coach Graham Henry. 'We've got to take it on the chin. We didn't kick for the simple reason that the Samoans all dropped deep waiting. Our players didn't really do the wrong thing. It was more a case that they didn't do the right things that well.'

The Samoans were more than happy to keep jabbing away at that glassy Welsh chin. They put pressure on the Welsh backline, had a terrier presence in their swarming forwards and waited for Wales to make mistakes. And they did. Four tries in all were due to error, but credit to Samoa for their anticipation and alertness. 'We had our backs to the wall,' said their impressive captain, Pat Lam, a former pupil of the one-time school-teaching Welsh coach. 'We put together the big plays when they mattered.'

The ginger Messiah, Neil Jenkins, was off-beam with his kicking but still kept Wales in the hunt, his three penalty goals and a conversion pushing Wales to within three points at 24–21. A fourth penalty goal shortly after the restart tied the scores. Lam's breakaway try dashed those hopes. The game blazed onwards. Another scrum near the Samoan line in the sixty-second minute, another desperate scramble to keep Wales out, infringement, penalty try. Scores tied again at 31–31. Samoa finished in style, full-back Leaega rounding off a fabulous move by taking a pop pass from Brian Lima to score in the corner. There was still a quarter of an hour to go. But Samoa knew that destiny was on their side.

21 OCTOBER
PUMA POWER JUST TOO MUCH FOR THE IRISH
Brendan Gallagher

The extraordinary goalkicking of Gonzalo Quesada, a well-taken try from Diego Albanese, and a courageous last-ditch defensive effort saw Argentina reach the World Cup quarter-finals for the first time. During an agonising eight minutes of injury time, Ireland stormed the Argentine line in a series of fourteen-man line-outs and thirteen-man scrums. Incredibly, the tiring Pumas held firm and a famous victory was theirs.

Their triumph was deserved and just. Ireland, ill-disciplined and lacking the killer instinct, squandered a twelve-point lead midway through the second half and Argentina responded by playing the best rugby of the game, a game that only properly ignited in the final hectic quarter. Prompted by their inspirational captain, Lisandro Arbizu, and the well-honed attacking instincts of their scrum-half, Agustin Pichot, it was Argentina who showed the greater desire for victory. When their try came in the seventy-fifth minute, it felt like the decisive moment and so it proved. The remarkable Quesada, so painstaking and unflappable in pursuit of perfection, responded by kicking his first conversion of the tournament, a magnificent effort from wide out, and later added further gloss to Argentina's 28–24 triumph with a seventh penalty.

Until the final exchanges, the match had revolved around a high-quality penalty shoot-out between David Humphreys and Quesada – hardly surprising given referee Stuart Dickinson's track record in this tournament, a lung-busting sixty-seven penalties awarded in his two previous games. Discipline, then, was paramount. Some hope. Instead, after a lively opening ten minutes from Ireland which hinted at a more expansive game plan, the first half quickly disintegrated into a battle of the boot.

The Ireland pack partially redeemed themselves approaching half-time as they pounded the Argentine line and created the platform for Humphreys to land another brace of kicks. Such pressure, however, demanded tries not penalties. Nothing much changed immediately after the break. Humphreys stroked over his sixth successful kick of a chilly evening and then added a smartly taken dropped goal before Queseda, laborious but so meticulous, opened his second-half account. Finally, Ireland threatened to pull away decisively during a burst of positive rugby. Centre Brian O'Driscoll was nearly through and an opportunist counter-attack from Humphreys could have brought dividends. However, Argentina, as they have done throughout the competition, clung on and waited for the next penalty to come along.

Quesada duly obliged with two more kicks as Argentina enjoyed their best spell. Ireland, though, could have put the game beyond doubt when Humphreys hit the post with another dropped goal attempt. From the resulting five-metre scrum, a cast-iron scoring position, Ireland predictably gave away another penalty for a needless technical offence. Argentina rallied gloriously and the most unlikely of semi-final places could yet be theirs. As Alex Wyllie said: 'It was the longest eight minutes of my life. As coach, I might have to get used to this.'

25 OCTOBER
DIAMONDS ON SOLES OF HIS BOOTS
Mick Cleary

The right leg of Springbok outside-half Jannie de Beer swung back five times in the second half. And five times the ball sailed between the posts. He might as well have planted his boot in the English crotch, for with each kick they sank further to their knees. By the time his fifth and final dropped goal went over six minutes from the end, England knew that the World Cup dream was no more than dust.

There was more to come from the diamond boot of this de Beer. Two more penalty goals as well as the conversion of Pieter Rossouw's try to round off an extraordinary afternoon. De Beer, who is normally second choice behind the injury-plagued Henry Honiball, finished with thirty-four points in all, a South African record. 'It was definitely supernatural out there,' said the deeply religious former London Scottish and Sale player. 'God gave us this victory.'

By the time the quarter-final matches drew to a close the home union flag lay limp and at half-mast. The Southern Hemisphere will play out its games in our backyard. England were not beaten solely by de Beer's virtuoso kicking performance. South Africa had a key edge in every phase of play. Their scrum was always on the front foot, their kicking from hand was long and well-directed while their tackling was mean and sustained. They gave one of the great swarming offensive defence displays of this or any other World Cup.

The depth and intensity of the Springboks' tackling, with flanker Andre Venter and centre Pieter Muller outstanding, evoked memories of the day they beat the All Blacks in 1995 to win the Webb Ellis trophy. They seethed with desire and stayed in England's faces from first until last. England simply could not shake them off. They only rarely got in behind the South Africans, and on the few occasions they did, they could not sustain momentum. South Africa had more power and drive through the middle and were more precise in the execution of almost everything they did. England, willing but limited, turned the ball over eighteen times, a flagrant waste of precious possession. They also played into South African hands by kicking badly and too shallow.

England succeeded only in drawing de Beer and Percy Montgomery into the game. They really ought to have varied their options. Matt Dawson tried midway through the second half to inject some zip into proceedings but it was too little too late. England's attack lacked a punishing edge on the few times they did break downfield. Centres Phil de Glanville and Will Greenwood were rocked back while wing Dan Luger was shepherded superbly. With the Springboks also doing a number on the scrum, England's half-backs were in retreat.

South Africa also read England so well. They nullified the potential threat of Lawrence Dallaglio's thrusts by cutting him off at source. In the end Dallaglio spent most of the afternoon out wide. There was huge passion in the South African performance but there was also clinical, dead-eyed efficiency. Heart and head in perfect harmony. The moment was there for England but they could not seize it. What is it about these Southern Hemisphere sides? They are so crisp, so forceful, so decisive when the big occasion comes knocking.

Coach Clive Woodward, whose contract runs out in summer 2000, was understandably subdued after the 44–21 defeat. 'It's so disappointing for the players who have put so much into it,' he said. 'What happens to me now is irrelevant. I'm big enough to look after myself.' Martin Johnson paid tribute to the Springbok defence and their kicking. 'That is what made the difference,' said the England captain, who rejected any notion that South Africa were fresher because they avoided a play-off. 'We didn't lose because we were tired. It wasn't a factor.'

South Africa, anticipating a tight game, had trained to put de Beer in position for a drop at goal. 'We didn't think he'd get five out of five, though,' coach Nick Mallett said. 'The scoreline flattered us. We studied England closely. South Africans are pretty useful tacklers. So once we figured where to stand it came together. The spirit in the squad now is special. We now believe we can win the World Cup.'

The first half was tense, with the kickers holding sway. Paul Grayson had belted over four penalties by the seventeenth minute, two from within his own half. De Beer was up to pace, stroking three in reply. The Springboks edged in front with a suspect try four minutes before the break. Rossouw ran back a skewed clearance. Montgomery and Muller took it on before the centre fed Joost van der Westhuizen. The Springboks captain appeared to make contact with the corner flag as he touched down but the try was given. De Beer did his stuff from the touchline and South Africa turned round with a 16–12 lead.

Two minutes after the restart Grayson had closed the gap to one point. Then came de Beer. Five dropped goals in a row, from the forty-third to the seventy-fourth minute, two of them towering efforts from over forty-five metres. The die was cast. The trigger looked cocked again in injury time, only for de Beer to hoist high to the corner. Dallaglio couldn't reach a ball that bounced infield and Rossouw gathered and dived over. One last kick for de Beer. One final nail to drive home. The lid duly slid into place and the death-knell sounded on England's World Cup.

SURVIVAL PROVES NAME OF GAME
Nick Farr-Jones

Winning World Cups is a game of survival. Australia proved that in 1991 when they were thrown a lifeline in the last minutes of the quarter-final against Ireland. And South Africa seemed to be aided by divine intervention as they clung to the smallest of margins against France in the 1995 semi-final, then somehow repelled the mighty All Blacks in the final. The most important thing that can be taken from the Wallabies' victory over Wales is that they too survived. And at 10–9 midway through the second half that victory was not always assured.

Wales bravely repelled the Wallabies' thrusts and enjoyed sufficient field possession to make it seem inevitable that the lethal boot of Neil Jenkins would rule the day. But Australia prevailed 24–9 and now know that only 160 minutes separates them from claiming rugby's greatest prize. Their performance was, again, not as polished as they would like and coach Rod Macqueen vented his frustration after the match at the inability of his team to achieve the multi-phased possession which is the essence of their game. He lamented infringing opponents and sub-standard refereeing, but he should be grateful for the win. In the six matches that it takes to win a World Cup it is unlikely that a team will be continually on song. Indeed, the past again reveals that teams who ultimately prevail can be downright dreadful in some matches. But building momentum is crucial and having the confidence to believe you can produce the clinical performance when needed most is what this tournament is about.

The Wallabies, while not firing on all cylinders, have the muscle and strike power to match anyone. Before the skies opened at Cardiff they had the Welsh defence stunned by the speed of their recycling and ease of transfer into space. Two early tries went begging, and had it remained dry, the Welsh may have been run ragged. The Wallabies will know they must focus on their ability to adapt to the varying playing conditions inevitably found in the United Kingdom. The Millennium Stadium may be the best rugby cauldron for spectators, but I would suggest the tournament organisers won't be publicly quizzing the players on the playing conditions. The surface is portable and, as such, patchy and prone to being ripped up under the weight of scrums and rucks. This makes for treacherous playing conditions which can be a great equaliser, as the Wallabies discovered.

But there were some jewels in this Wallabies performance. They were subjected to immense pressure in an atmosphere that will no doubt cause many a team to crumble. The Australians held firm and their patience and composure won the day. This composure will again be needed as the tournament heads for its climax. The Australian scrum also held firm. This was where Wales would have hoped to attack and, for me, the unsung heroes were the front three. In the absence of Phil Kearns, hooker Michael Foley again demonstrated his organising capacity to provide the Wallabies with a solid platform. This platform is so crucial that, should it buckle, they can forget booking a Qantas seat for the Webb Ellis trophy.

We also saw the continued progress of outside-half Stephen Larkham. He wasted the chance of an early try when he failed to draw full-back Shane Howarth, which would have given winger Joe Roff a clear run-in. But everything else bore the hallmark of a Larkham back to his best. This is a crucial position and, in Andrew Mehrtens, New Zealand have a general whose judgement and execution are at times almost faultless. In Larkham, the Wallabies, too, have someone who gives them direction and structure, but he adds even more than Mehrtens. His speed and strength are underestimated, and as he showed in setting up Ben Tune's match-winning try, he can create out of nothing. The Wallabies defence again held solid. Wales never really threatened the Australian line. World Cups are largely won by repelling whatever the opposition throw at you. And here the Wallabies again demonstrated they stand as tall as anyone in this tournament.

1 NOVEMBER
ONLY FABULOUS FRENCH CAN DO THIS
Mick Cleary

C'est fou. C'est incroyable. Yes, it was crazy. And it was most certainly incredible. As a bright autumnal afternoon turned to early winter dusk, the French supporters embraced each other in stunned disbelief outside Twickenham. For the many thousands of New Zealand supporters, there were no embraces, just a thunderbolt of shock to remove from between their eyes. For them the sky had turned dark long before Jim Fleming blew the final whistle on what was an upset on a colossal scale. France, wooden-spoonists in the Five Nations Championship, divided and bedraggled throughout this tournament, were outlandishly long odds in a two-horse race. But the deed of victory is only part of the story. The manner of it will warm many a night by the fireside to come.

After a lively opening by France, it looked as if the All Blacks were clicking into normal mode shortly after half-time. In the forty-fourth minute Jonah Lomu inflicted another bout of mayhem in smashing through several tackles for his second try. That took the score to 24–10 to New Zealand. Their thoughts must then have turned to Cardiff and a final against Australia. It was premature. France's thoughts turned to adventure and glorious resistance. '*Allez mes braves*' came the cry from the rear of the stand. And *allez* they did. France, in a tumultuous passage of play, scored twenty-six points in thirteen minutes. Christophe Lamaison dropped two goals (the fashionable way to get your points these days), then hit a penalty goal in the fifty-fourth minute. Still France trailed.

Not for much longer. A streak of blue, a flurry of hands, Christophe Dominici gathered Fabien Galthié's chip one-handed, slipped Andrew Mehrtens and flashed to the line in the fifty-fifth minute. Four minutes later, a beautiful fusion of brawn and brain saw Richard Dourthe over the line. The French forwards drove mercilessly from a line-out on the New Zealand twenty-two, recycled, Lamaison chipped delicately over the top and Dourthe timed his run and dive perfectly. The sensation was bubbling. It erupted in the seventy-third minute with Philippe Bernat-Salles's try, a length-of-the-field hack and chase which went the way of the Frenchman. As did almost everything else (excepting the penalty count) on this daft day of rare delights. Jeff Wilson scored for New Zealand in the final minute. The French barely noticed.

The whistle sounded at 43–31 and delirium ensued. Several players fell to the turf, others found flags to wave, while the prop, Franck Tournaire, emerged from the tunnel with his young daughter on his shoulders. Up in the press box, seasoned, sceptical hacks of all nationalities punched the air with joy. The mad cows had escaped. Only the French can do this. 'It was a big moment for us,' said Raphaël Ibañez, the French captain. 'If we made people cry in the crowd, then that makes us happy.'

France had no option but to give it a lash against these vaunted opponents. And lash they did, posting a record score by anyone against New Zealand. Never mind Aimé Jacquet's French side being written off prior to football's World Cup in 1998. They were mere sick notes compared to the obituaries served on Jean-Claude Skrela's men. Where did they find this from? From within their soul, that remote corner where only truth resides. They knew deep down that it was death or glory, oblivion or immortality.

Logic was given leave of absence. They played with the heart and with instinct. They cared not a jot about All Black reputation. They ripped into the opposition, detecting what few others had the nerve to suggest, that the All Blacks pack had a soft underbelly. Abdel Benazzi, restored to the colours, was a giant. So too was Fabien Pelous alongside him. Oliver Magne, the flanker, had the rare distinction of making the All Blacks' Josh Kronfeld look a mere mongrel in comparison to the Frenchman's greyhound darts. The half-back combination of Galthié and Lamaison, who scored twenty-eight points, formed reluctantly and in adversity, was calm and forceful in equal measure. Lamaison boomed the ball deep and knocked his goals over with aplomb. France worked the field superbly, taking the blindside when offered and time and again skinning New Zealand on the outside. Dominici was sharp and irrepressible. He sliced open New Zealand in the nineteenth minute with a break from halfway. Only Christian Cullen's despairing cover tackle prevented the French wing from scoring. Justice was done: Dourthe flipped the ball to Lamaison, who strolled over. It is not often the likes of Tana Umaga, Wilson and Lomu have been made to look ponderous and distracted.

The French were fired by self-belief. They were audacious as well as outrageous. In the sixty-seventh minute, they were awarded a penalty near the New Zealand line. They led 36–24. Three more points would have meant New Zealand needed to score more than two converted tries. Go for goal? Go to hell. They went for touch and seven points. They failed but they did not give a damn. God was wearing blue. Would New Zealand have been overwhelmed this way if playing Australia or South Africa? I doubt it. 'We are devastated,' said Wilson, the All Blacks' vice-captain. John Hart, the coach, put on as brave a face as he could muster. 'There are no excuses,' he said, bleeding inside. 'We should not have lost that game from 24–10 up. We made too many mistakes. We let ourselves down.'

Mehrtens kept his side on the move with three penalty goals before Lomu struck in the twenty-third minute. He bounced through six tackles (a normal day at the office) to touch down. Mehrtens kicked another goal to give New Zealand a 17–10 half-time advantage. Cue Lomu, cue another try. All seemed well with the world. And then the world tilted on its axis.

1 NOVEMBER
WAS THIS THE GREATEST GAME EVER PLAYED?
Paul Hayward

Until now the act of waving the Tricolour in an English suburban high street would have ended with the flag-bearer being locked in stocks and pelted with beef trimmings. Twickenham was probably the least likely venue on earth for the locals to proclaim the glory of French sport. This newspaper, in concert with all media outlets, would like to apologise if it gave the impression that the French were a bunch of mutinous wasters who had crept into a World Cup semi-final down a ludicrously easy route. We now accept unreservedly that scraped victories against Canada, Namibia, Fiji and Argentina were the perfect preparation for a 43–31 win over the mighty All Blacks. It was also careless of us not to predict that the French would come back from 24–10 down in the second half and score thirty-three points in twenty-seven minutes to take a 43–24 lead.

And while we're at it, we might as well withdraw the allegation that the gap between New Zealand, Australia, South Africa and the Europeans is now so large that the Southern Hemisphere countries must be doubting the wisdom of crossing the equator again. If the time had finally come to taunt the fallen All Blacks, it might have been with a football chant: 'Are you England in disguise?' New Zealand should be left alone to mourn. France were the real story of this almost absurdly exhilarating match.

In that wonderful documentary on Muhammad Ali, *When We Were Kings*, Norman Mailer describes the sensation of waiting for a big heavyweight fight to begin as 'physically almost unendurable'. By a tidy coincidence it was twenty-five years ago to the day when Ali flipped the world upside down by knocking out George Foreman in Zaire. Parts of this epic Twickenham match were also close to unendurable in the sense that France's improbable fightback opened up the possibility that we were watching one of sport's all-time greatest upsets. Could it yet be that something so magisterial could be spoiled?

Afterwards serious rugby men discussed the proposition that this was the greatest eighty minutes of international rugby ever seen. Into the sweep of these excited discussions came even the Barbarians versus All Blacks thriller of 1973. The rain-lashed, storm-driven Australia versus South Africa semi-final had raised this sometimes stuttering tournament on to an altogether higher level. But what followed when France burst out of their moodiness and introspection was pure epiphany. Nobody may ever be able to explain whether they played like men who believed they had no chance but were determined to enjoy it anyway, or warriors who had rediscovered their sacred connection with French rugby's exuberant and fearless past. After Jonah Lomu's second try, which helped cushion New Zealand with that fourteen-point lead, around 75,000 ultimately privileged souls inside the stadium sensed a black cloak being dragged across the match.

Plenty of valiant men have failed to stop Lomu on the hoof. France's full-back, Xavier Garbajosa, made history by dancing out of his way and almost waving him through. Ah, we thought, the stories of French capitulation were all true. Here was the wilting of the underdog spirit, the brutal laying bare of so much psychological frailty. You could almost hear the stonemasons chipping away at French rugby's tombstone. Defeat would be crushing, heads would roll. The whole neurotic debate about whether *Les Bleus* should be true to their romantic heritage or return to the bulldozer mentality would begin afresh. As it turned out, the most startling memories will be of Christophe Dominici zig-zagging his way through the New Zealand defence from an impossible starting position, and Richard Dourthe and Philippe Bernat-Salles charging on gloriously to slam down delicate chipped kicks ahead of poor Jeff Wilson. This was not some ground-out, percentage-driven, stick-it-up-your jumper reworking of the odds (New Zealand were 1–2 to win the World Cup before kick-off). It was a pageant, an exhibition, a video compilation of the best of French rugby. Even the watching English were drawn into an involuntary roar.

It is one thing to fight your way back into a semi-final, quite another to start picking up perfect tens for artistic impression. The questions came thicker than French points: where did this wonderful flourish come from, how did these apparently self-absorbed under-achievers summon the resilience, the energy, the unwavering skill not just to withstand the All Black counter-attack but actually increase the margin of superiority? At their worst French rugby teams can be craven, uninterested, narcissistic. At their best, they can wipe the word 'inhibition' from the dictionary and perform to a level that not even the rugby-obsessed New Zealanders can hope to attain.

World champions at football, World Cup finalists in rugby: the French are doing something right. Never mind the tales about disloyalty and disunity. On their lap of honour at the end, they looked like men who had all come from the same womb: brothers, inseparable, invincible. Franck Tournaire carried his young daughter on his shoulders. Lomu, who had smashed his way to two tries, waited, first in line, by the entrance to the tunnel to shake French hands. Stage left, Olivier

Magne, the openside flanker from southern sheep-farming stock, was parading his own little trophy, given to him by his opposite number, Josh Kronfeld, at the sounding of a whistle which confirmed the unlikeliest line-up for a third-place play-off – New Zealand against South Africa. At the dying of the storm, Kronfeld peeled off his scrum-cap and handed it to his conqueror. For Magne, it was like a scalp beautifully removed.

5 NOVEMBER
NOW IT REALLY IS ALL BLACK FOR THE ALL BLACKS
Martin Johnson

If there had to be a third-place match in this World Cup, then this was probably the only one worth having. Nothing stirs Southern Hemisphere passions more than the crunching collision of black and green, and two countries in which rugby is more of a religion than a sport never square up to each other with anything less than an equal mix of respect and dislike. Such are the passions involved that when this fixture was the All Blacks versus the No Blacks, even staid old New Zealand – where a honked horn in traffic qualifies as road rage – became embroiled in pavement punch-ups between rugby fanatics and the anti-apartheid lobby.

The way the studs went in at the rucks had people feeling queasy back in the twenty-fifth row of the stand, though ITV were a good deal less pumped up for it than the two teams – showing so little interest in the game that it was hidden away on cable, and not even considered worthy of a live afternoon slot, lest it interfere with more cerebral programming such as *The*

Jerry Springer Show. The old adage that sport and politics do not mix does not apply to All Black versus Springbok games. New Zealand's semi-final defeat may yet have serious repercussions for the incumbent government, and there was scarcely any less anguish in South Africa – at least in the Afrikaner strongholds – when their team lost to Australia. And the reason behind the thunderous commitment was the urge to fly home to be greeted with something other than national opprobrium.

The last instance of a New Zealand team not wanting to go home and face the music after a rugby match in Cardiff was in the 1960s, when their fiery prop forward Keith Murdoch was given an early plane ticket after chinning a doorman across the road at the Angel Hotel, and has never been seen since. Leastways, not in New Zealand. Rumour has it that he got off in Australia, made his way to the Northern Territory, and was last spotted skinning crocodiles in the bush by way of some *al fresco* dining. John Hart, the New Zealand coach, might not quite have been thinking of joining Murdoch for dinner on the way home, but he might have been considering a beard and dark glasses. Not even a victory in this game was guaranteed to save his skin, so fierce have been the shock waves after that French defeat, and losing to such deadly rivals may now make his position totally untenable. 'Let's keep things in perspective,' said Hart. 'There is more to life than rugby.' The problem is, and Hart knows it, that in New Zealand there is not.

Suddenly, the haka looks as intimidating as the hokey cokey, and it was South Africa who made all the early running here, after a competition in which running has rarely been in their game plan. For once, they decided to take the rapier to the opposition, as opposed to the previously preferred way of their coach, the Mallett. However, it still took an inspired piece of individual play to pierce the All Blacks' defence, and it came from their left winger Breyton Paulse, only the fourth non-white player to represent South Africa. By the time the next World Cup comes around, who knows how many that number may have increased by, or indeed whether the South Africans will still be singing 'Die Stem' before the kick-off. Paulse did not join in the Afrikaner anthem, either not knowing the words, or not liking them very much.

It was perhaps not surprising that South Africa seemed to have that extra bit of energy where it mattered, in that the All Blacks were the more devastated of the two by their semi-final defeats. Back at home, people thought the Springboks could retain the World Cup if everything went right, while in New Zealand everyone expected them to win. So revered are the All Blacks in their own country, that sales of their replica jerseys are lower there than almost anywhere else in the world. A lot of people simply won't wear them because of their almost religious connotations, a bit like the Turin shroud. And when New Zealand fail, as they did in this tournament, even losing this consolation match 22–18, people take to wearing black for altogether different reasons.

7 NOVEMBER
AUSTRALIAN DEFENCE HAS THE CUTTING EDGE TO LAND TROPHY
Paul Ackford

The match wasn't memorable but the result was. By beating France 35–12, Australia became the first team to win the World Cup twice and in the process have extended the Southern Hemisphere's dominance of this competition. Despite an occasion which was horribly flat, insipid and colourless, no one will begrudge Australia their moment of triumph. Somehow this sporting nation has a habit of producing winners. The rugby players join their cricketers in standing on top of the world, and for a nation which has a rugby-playing population of thirty thousand compared with France's one-hundred thousand, their triumph was an extraordinary achievement.

Australia also won this World Cup the hard way. Of all the pre-tournament favourites their route to the final has been the hardest. In winning the Webb Ellis trophy they have seen off Ireland, Wales, South Africa and now France. Only the Springboks stretched them, and their domination and professionalism has been complete. This was a match too far for France. They competed to the end but they were spent emotionally and they could not match the passion which drove them to that coruscating victory against the All Blacks in the semi-final. Many people thought that for France to repeat that performance within a week was asking too much and so it proved. They were unable to find their driving forwards and without that ascendancy the half-back pairing of Fabien Galthié and Christophe Lamaison was unable to stamp their authority on the game.

France were 12–6 down at half-time and struggling, and when Ben Tune scored Australia's first try after sixty-five minutes to stretch their lead to 26–12 it marked the end of France's faint chances of a revival. Émile Ntamack was unable to thrust himself into the game and both wingers struggled to outstrip the Australian defence. Without the adrenalin rush which fuelled their victory over New Zealand, France took on the appearance of a side lacking in ideas. Philippe Bernat-Salles came closest when he nearly recovered an intelligent kick from Lamaison, but Stephen Larkham beat him to the ball.

The last three Rugby World Cup finals had been disappointing matches. Only three tries have been scored in getting on for five hours of rugby and it is no surprise to discover that Australia have scored all three. Tony Daly crossed in 1991 against England and Tune and Owen Finegan picked up one apiece here. It is Australia's ability to deliver on the big occasion which sets them apart from other teams.

Australia had this match in control as early as the fourteenth minute when Matt Burke put over his second penalty to level the scores at 6–6. From that point on Burke's peerless goal-kicking, coupled with France's desperate knack of conceding penalties, kept Australia ahead. Burke ended the match with twenty-five points and he did as much as anyone to ensure that his country made rugby history. The other significant area for Australia was their defence. They had leaked only one try in this tournament, and that against the United States in one of their earlier pool matches. France never came close to scoring. Modern rugby might have overrated the importance of defence, but it is to Australia's credit that they have mastered the art of stopping opposition teams better than anyone else.

This was a great team effort from Australia. They have always possessed outstanding individuals but it is their organisation and willingness to work for each other which have underpinned their success. Having said that, Tim Horan had another marvellous match. While France could not recapture the excellence of their semi-final, Horan managed to hang on to his and it was the centre's explosive running out of the tackle and his swift-footedness which posed all sorts of problems to the French midfield. Equally important for Australia was the appetite for work from the two wings. Tune and Joe Roff came inside for work on numerous occasions and the power which they generated knocked the stuffing out of the French tacklers. Toutai Kefu, too, was effective in this regard. He was Australia's main ball carrier and he often dented the French defence.

Ultimately, France did not quite match up in these physical areas. Only when Abdel Benazzi and Olivier Magne reached deep inside themselves and ran at Australia did the side look incisive. But France's misfortune was that Benazzi could not raise himself often enough to carry his team to victory. At the end of the contest France went up to collect their losers' medals from the Queen and drew a large cheer from an appreciative crowd. But they knew they had lost a golden opportunity, as England had in 1991, to make a mark for the Northern Hemisphere, and their obligatory lap of the stadium was slightly apologetic.

Australia, too, did not greet the final whistle with the delirium expected of world champions. By that stage, after Finegan had driven through the remnants of a shattered French defence, Australia were twenty-three points to the good and the destiny of the trophy was not in doubt. Lock David Giffin, who in concert with his captain, John Eales, had a marvellous match at the line-out, jumped on the back of David Wilson to start the celebrations, but his was the only reaction of unbridled joy. The rest of Giffin's teammates were content with handshakes and hugs, and the theatrical and explosive fireworks which finally brought the curtain down on the 1999 Rugby World Cup were in stark contrast to the mood of the triumphant team.

This Australia team knew they had this match won very early on. Eales and a solid front row had established dominance in the tight phases and with David Wilson snaffling all the loose balls and making the big tackles wide out Australia were always in a position of superiority. George Gregan at scrum-half exuded composure and with Larkham mixing his game judiciously it was clear that France were going to struggle. And when Tune struck twenty-five minutes into the second half it finished France. Somehow Horan bounced out of the tackle of Benazzi and set off downfield. Matt Burke carried on the attack, driving in behind the French defenders, and when Horan took the ball up again France were in disarray. The killer blow came when Australia produced quick ball and Gregan, Horan and Finegan combined to send Tune through Xavier Garbajosa's tackle. With Burke's conversion it took Australia from a reasonably close 21–12 to a relaxed 28–12 and it tore the heart out of France.

Finegan's try right at the end of the match was merely icing on the cake. Australia knew then that they had achieved what no other side in world rugby has managed. World champions for the second time, they now have another four years to revel in that status, after which they will put their reputation on the line once more in 2003 in Australia itself. Only a fool would bet against them to make it three.

8 NOVEMBER
COURAGE TO ATTACK WAS LOST
Thierry Lacroix

So Twickenham was an illusion and Cardiff was reality. We have a saying in France that one tree can never hide a forest and unfortunately all the weaknesses visible before that amazing semi-final against New Zealand were again evident. I cannot fault the effort and commitment. Morale was high after the win over the All Blacks, and when I visited the team on the morning before the final they were relaxed and quietly confident. But what happened is that France lost the audacity and courage to attack. We became more cautious and allowed Australia – a very fine team indeed – to dictate and run the game at their pace. End of story.

The surging runs of Abdelatif Benazzi and Olivier Magne were gone, the Australian defence cutting them down swiftly. France failed to create openings – they have no player like Tim Horan whose first instinct is to avoid contact and create space – and from an early stage I could sense the game slipping away. France must not be deluded. We are not the second-best team in the world, nothing like it. Our tournament was saved by an extraordinary performance we will probably not see again. The problems still exist. There is too much dirty play – we saw that again here. Our discipline is very poor, we give too many penalties away. We must concentrate much more on playing rugby. We have shown that we have the ability. Why do we get diverted by this nonsense? We need better referees at home to start imposing discipline and we need an elite first division of just twelve teams to concentrate our talent.

But finally, to my abiding memory of RWC99. With five minutes to go of that incredible match between France and New Zealand, I looked around Twickenham to see a truly crazy sight: England supporters shouting and cheering for France, dancing jigs of joy, laughing and crying and letting all their emotion come out. Only sport can do this. I say to hell with politics, beef wars and so-called Anglo-French animosity. Our players and supporters share a passion for rugby. We can argue and debate great matches, play hard, drink together after games and enjoy the comradeship. We are getting to know each other better. We are privileged. Think how boring life would be without the rugby to bind us together. This goes for all the rugby world and the supporters who travelled to Wales and the other Five Nations. What a party they had. I hear that Cardiff never went to bed all week. People thought professionalism would change everything but I always knew that was wrong. Special people play and support rugby – people who want to get enjoyment out of life. Tens of thousands of people had a very good time, exactly how it should be. It is why we love sport, no?

7 NOVEMBER
ENOUGH MAGIC TO PAPER OVER THE CRACKS
Paul Ackford

So that's another World Cup over, then. Bigger commercially than the previous three tournaments and, with twenty nations competing instead of sixteen, more successful in terms of attendances at the live matches, but better? That's a difficult one. Any competition which produces occasions of the quality of the semi-finals cannot be dismissed lightly. The France versus New Zealand epic was the most glorious evocation of what rugby has to offer. Better than the celebrated Baa-Baas versus All Black encounter of 1973 because that game was essentially an end of tour frolic, while this one had enormous consequences for both teams. Better than the 1995 World Cup final because it created its own drama, whereas the emotional impact of that final had a lot to do with the social and political change taking place in South Africa at the time.

But if rugby wishes to continue to hang on to its claim that it is a global sport, it has to deliver more than the shuddering collisions of the major teams. Take both semi-finals out of the equation, together with England versus New Zealand, France versus Fiji, and Argentina versus Ireland, and the other forty-odd matches were not up to much. Even the quarter-finals, once you strip away the one-eyed nationalism which always adds allure to the knockout stages, were not particularly compelling.

And it is not good enough for Rugby World Cup to point to the achievements of Argentina and Samoa in beating more celebrated opponents, or the exploits of Japan, Spain and Uruguay who competed tolerably well in their groups, as justification for the twenty-team format. Over half the pool games were won by a margin of thirty points and matches on the world stage should be more than about not getting seriously injured or losing with dignity. The attendances in Scotland were shocking for much of the competition but, honestly, would you have fancied paying £30 for Spain versus South Africa at 5 p.m. on a Sunday?

But that gripe aside, plus the ridiculous five host-country arrangement, and the long midweek intervals with no matches followed by a torrent of eight over two days, Rugby World Cup '99 had much to commend it, not least the manner in which it exposed pundits like me. Never before have so many predictions proved wide of the mark and, if there was some consolation in the 'I was just one of many' excuse, there was considerably more satisfaction in what it said about the sport.

France did the rest of their Five Nations mates a real favour in beating the All Blacks because they raised two fingers to all of rugby's shibboleths. Deprived of their best back, Thomas Castaignède, and their best forward, Christian Califano, and playing the non-tackling Émile Ntamack at centre and Xavier Garbajosa at full-back, they nevertheless pulverised New Zealand. And this coming off one of the worst seasons in their history. France proved that all the training, preparation and coaching in the world counts for nothing provided you can find something from somewhere to make you believe in yourself and provided you have enough individuals with natural ability to put it all together. That's the glorious legacy of France's victory. And when in the future I try to make sense of rugby in any other way, which I will, please come to Canary Wharf and scream '*Allez les bleus*' at me until I stop.

1999 RESULTS – Quarter-finals: South Africa 44, England 21; Australia 24, Wales 9; New Zealand 30, Scotland 18; France 47, Argentina 26. Semi-finals: Australia 27, South Africa 21 (aet); France 43, New Zealand 31. Third-place: South Africa 22, New Zealand 18. Final: Australia 35, France 12.

CHAPTER FIVE: 2003

HOSTED BY AUSTRALIA

7 OCTOBER
AUSTRALIA'S CHOSEN DATES HAVE DILUTED RUGBY UNION PRESTIGE
Mick Cleary

Lovely to be here and all that. But why now? Why this time of year, wonderful as it is? The skies are clearing, the temperature is rising, and the city where Aussie Rules rules is getting in the mood for union party time. The blue and green World Cup flags fluttered along the Fremantle Highway, the busy road that flanks the Swan River as it heads out of Perth. The winds of sporting change may only be temporary in these parts, but rugby union should enjoy its moment in the Western Australia sun. The vibes are good. We have grown used to the Australians besting us at sport. Now they're showing us how to organise a major event. They'll be Trooping the Colour next . . . There have been cock-ups and glitches, primarily with ticketing and rogue hoteliers indulging in their latter-day impersonations of Ned Kelly by gouging room rates. But the general mood is bubbly.

But what are we doing here in October? The 1995 World Cup, the last to be held in the Southern Hemisphere, took place in June and early July, as did the 1987 World Cup. But now we have an autumn time slot, sneaked in almost unnoticed a few years ago when the planning for this particular tournament began. The reasoning was that it was the least disruptive period for rugby round the world and the most appealing to the commercial and broadcasting markets. Well, you can spin your tales and massage your figures to suit whatever purpose you fancy. The Rugby Football Union made an exhaustive study of this question in their bid to stage the 2007 World Cup, a proposal that eventually received a hefty kick into touch. France won the right to host Europe's next World Cup fling and have pencilled in a September slot.

I have no reason to dispute the RFU's research, but that is not the point. They can fight their own corner. But let us just ponder what a June–July slot would mean.

The run-up to this World Cup has been marked by concerns over player withdrawals and unavailability. Samoa, Tonga, Fiji, Canada and Namibia have all been emasculated. No Trevor Leota, no Epi Taione, no Jacob Rauluni, no Dan Baugh, no Lean van Dyk. All have stayed at home, all for different reasons, but all of which have money at their root. They cannot afford to participate. And the game cannot afford for them not to participate. Their absence will not ruin the World Cup, but it does undermine the competition's claim to be a prestigious world event.

The International Rugby Board acknowledge the problem, but feel powerless to take action unless they can prove that a club or province have deliberately prevented a player from playing at the World Cup. But if the World Cup were held in June, then the counter-attraction of a lucrative club contract would fade away. The big-money backers are in Europe, primarily in

England and France. The club season is done and dusted by early June. Remove the temptation to earn elsewhere and suddenly everyone is available. It is an issue that the IRB have to address. The need to underpin and re-galvanise these countries is a pressing, deep-rooted matter, and requires a much more profound solution than merely changing the time slot for the World Cup. That will rectify the cosmetic issue of having a full attendance roster. The desire not to see countries such as Samoa and Fiji slip off rugby's map requires more fundamental change.

So much for the long term. The short term is in good working order. There has been carping in some quarters that the Rugby World Cup is not all it is cracked up to be – that its appeal is limited when set up against football and even athletics. My heart sinks as deep as the next man's when pre-event claims are made of how many zillions will be tuning in on television. It is a hollow boast. Who cares if a hermit in a tree house is watching or not? Not many people care either that only one of a handful of countries such as New Zealand, France, England, Australia and possibly South Africa have a realistic chance of winning. Football is little different; the base may be far broader and tournament upsets more likely, but the final outcome of their World Cup has changed little in fifty years. The rich and mighty prosper there as well. So let us enjoy the spectacle for what it is – six hundred players of massively differing abilities going at it hammer and tongs. There may be punches thrown on the field, but it is an odds-on bet that there will not be many thrown off the field.

9 OCTOBER

SIT BACK AND ENJOY – THIS WORLD CUP IS GOING TO BE AWESOME
Matt Dawson

The clock is ticking and the excitement mounting. All the waiting will soon be over and we can get our 2003 World Cup campaign under way. Hopefully you are as excited as we are in the England camp. This is undoubtedly the most important rugby challenge of my career and I suspect everybody else in the squad is thinking along the same lines. In 1995 I thought I was ready for the big time and a World Cup trip, but in retrospect I wasn't and it was a wise decision by Jack Rowell not to take me. Instead I started the summer with an enjoyable tour of Australia with England A, then picked up an injury and had to head home early. I vividly remember watching the England quarter-final against Australia, when Rob Andrew dropped his famous goal, in the clubhouse at Northampton and vowing to be involved next time around.

But for all the build-up and hype, I'm afraid the 1999 World Cup hardly registers in my England memory bank at all, either good or bad. For me it just came and went. We played well against the 'lesser' opposition and pretty averagely in defeat against New Zealand and South Africa. I can't really explain it. I suppose it's just that I have known many highs with England, not to mention a fair few lows, and the 1999 World Cup sits somewhere in the middle. The Springboks closed us out so well in Paris that numbness was the thing we felt most in the changing room afterwards. Soundly beaten by a good side on the day, end of story. It was only as the days went by that the real disappointment sank home. Talking to England fans during that period I realised how hard they had taken defeat at the Stade de France, and how desperately they had hoped for an England appearance in a Twickenham semi-final.

I also pondered on the fact that sport is fickle and that might have been my first and last shot at a World Cup – and I hadn't remotely done myself justice. It was in those weeks, after losing in Paris, that I decided if it was humanly possible I was going to have one more shot at getting in an England World Cup squad. If I got to Australia I intended to play the best rugby of my life. Well, I'm here now. Some of you out there probably don't believe us when England say that Georgia is our sole focus at present, but seriously there is no mileage in trying to anticipate the next-but-one game, or beyond that, even. Yes, we have back-room and technical staff who have had a detailed look at all of England's opponents and that information will be invaluable on the day, but as a player you can't afford to be distracted. The next eighty minutes is all that counts. We have got to get our preparation right for every game and play every match as though it was a World Cup final. That's my approach anyway. If you let your standards slip, it is no easy matter trying to then hit top form against the supposedly 'better' sides. England have a fantastic squad and we intend to use it so there is no point in anybody holding back, even subconsciously.

Objectively New Zealand and ourselves are favourites – there's no point trying to be coy. The world rankings do not lie, and we are the two form sides over the past eighteen months or so. Next come Australia, who will be an altogether sharper outfit than the one we saw back in the summer. You can put your mortgage on that. South Africa have had their problems but nobody with an ounce of rugby sense ever underestimates a Springbok side, while despite their injury problems and the huge blow of losing Geordan Murphy, I still believe Ireland are capable of very good things.

So sit back and enjoy. Australia is a fantastic country and the World Cup is going to be awesome. Nobody organises and understands sport better than the Aussies. The travelling fans will enjoy the holiday of their lives, while Australia is full of expats from England, Ireland, Scotland, South Africa, Wales, Italy, New Zealand and the Pacific Islands, which will add to the atmosphere. As for everybody back home, it's time to get your mates round, crack open a few tinnies or perhaps even a nice bottle of red and fire up those barbies for a full-monty World Cup breakfast. I can smell it from here. You'll never have a better excuse for a liquid breakfast.

20 OCTOBER
ENGLAND SHOW MIGHT ON OFF-DAY
Stuart Barnes

As substandard efforts go, England's 25–6 win against South Africa was satisfactory enough. England may beat the Springboks with regularity but the World Cup is different. Until now, South African rugby supporters could boast that only Australia had beaten them in a World Cup match, and in a typically pugnacious manner remind you that, technically, that game was a draw – the teams being level after eighty minutes. That record has now evaporated along with any fleeting Southern Hemisphere hopes that England would freeze, as their predecessors have every four years at varying stages since 1987. The mediocrity of the effort is probably more a plus than a minus.

Any vestige of excessive self-confidence has disappeared. If anything, England started the match too well. Bar a sliced clearance kick from Jonny Wilkinson, the first ten minutes were textbook rugby. Twice England were within inches of crossing the South African line as characters as diverse as Wilkinson and Martin Johnson threw sharp miss-passes. Impassioned defence and Mike Tindall's schoolboy failure to tuck the ball under his outside arm kept the men in white at bay, with only a Wilkinson penalty to show for the slickest of starts. Too slick. It does not matter if English fans think a try is inevitable, but it does when that sense of inevitability envelops a team. England revealed all the necessary confidence to win a World Cup, yet it overflowed. When opponents as fierce as South Africa are on the attack, there is a time to compromise the set pattern, hoof the ball to safety and recommence the game with a line-out in opposition territory, beyond their kicker's range.

England were lucky here. Louis Koen is one of the best place-kickers in the game, but his four first-half misses offered an escape route to an England team who failed to realise a World match is a notch up from another Test. That lesson has been learnt without any lasting damage. Koen's failure was one reason, the ferocity and organisation of the England defence was another, but most of all there was Wilkinson. The best news of all for England is that he again demonstrated his ability to kick his team home regardless of his overall form.

In June 2003 he performed near his Test-match worst against the All Blacks in Wellington, but was the difference between the teams as he bisected the posts and dissected the opposition. He was not quite that poor here in Perth, but nor was he close to his best. His general game was riddled with nervous kicks, sliced or thumped out on the full, restarts that did not give his chasers a chance. All these usual areas of English strengths were weaknesses. If Australia, France or New Zealand expect a similar occurrence they will probably be disappointed. All that Wilkinson is likely to repeat is the metronomic goal-kicking that is akin to a six- or nine-point start for England. Considered like that, it will take a heck of a team to beat an England side with such a handicap advantage.

Hope that England's average performance is proof of peaking too soon is rife, from Sydney to Southland, but analysis of World Cup history does not make the theory an appealing one. True, the 1987 All Blacks were unchallenged, but they were the most dominant team in the Rugby World Cup's brief history. The 1991 Wallabies had an almighty struggle to dispatch little Western Samoa (as they were then) at Pontypool Park, not to mention a last-ditch win against Ireland in the quarter-finals. When it mattered they tore New Zealand to pieces behind the scrum in the semi-final and beat England at Twickenham.

The 1995 Springboks splashed their way to the most fortunate of semi-final victories against France in Durban, and in 1999 Australia made heavy weather of Wales at the quarter-final stage before needing extra time to beat the South Africans. New Zealand were again odds-on until their first blip at the semi-final stage – and that was that. In comparison, this victory against South Africa when so off-key is a chilling warning to the teams who would win the World Cup in 2003. England have proved they can win without performing well. Whether the other contenders can do likewise we are yet to discover. As bad days go, it was pretty good.

27 OCTOBER
DOZY ENGLAND'S WAKE-UP CALL
Mick Cleary

If the rugby world ever allows Samoa to disappear off the map then it should hang its head in shame. Just when this World Cup was in danger of subsiding into an embarrassing catalogue of pantomime matches, along come Samoa and with them, true drama. There was a tense narrative, complex character development and an outcome that was in doubt until the closing stages. England, who trailed 16–13 at the interval, only really wrapped the game up with Phil Vickery's try six minutes from time in a 35–22 scoreline. If all the games were like this, then the house-full notices would be posted all over Australia. Take a bow, Manu Samoa.

The upshot is that England's lofty ambitions to lift the Webb Ellis Cup have diminished in the eyes of several witnesses, notably the watching Australian and New Zealand camps, both of whom were in town. That view of things may suit England just fine. Mind you, Martin Johnson was nonc too impressed either. 'That was not good enough,' the captain said. 'Full credit to Samoa. They could have beaten us. We're not going to win anything if we play like that.'

Johnson has never traded in flim-flam. He did not on the night, either, producing one of the few England performances of note. Jonny Wilkinson proved a barometer of English fortunes. He rarely hit any meaningful rhythm, albeit he was scrabbling for decent possession for long stretches of the first half. But if that were worrying enough for the many thousands of England fans in the crowd of 50,647, then it was the sight of Mr Dead-Eye having an attack of the wobbles right in front of the posts that really set them on edge. Wilkinson missed one kick from point-blank range and only marginally off-centre, the ball striking the left upright. The resulting thud found a hollow echo in the pit of many England stomachs. In all, four kicks failed to find their target.

The half-back combinations have yet to strike the right chord. Here it was the turn of Matt Dawson to partner Wilkinson. For the second week in succession, England had to live off their wits when it came to reliable ball. Samoa never let them settle. England were discordant through the midfield and flustered in their control of the ball. Their penalty count was once again far higher than their usual single-figure target. England were lucky not to have a player yellow-carded. The ledger of negatives was substantial. Samoa rattled England, not just in the tackle but also at the breakdown. The English back row is not operating at full tilt. Lawrence Dallaglio knows that he is not reaching the standards he set on the summer tour to these parts. The return of the injured Richard Hill will bring more directness and precision to that area.

Samoa can consider themselves hard done by in the award of a penalty try against them for collapsing a scrum in the fifty-second minute. They had had no warning from referee Jonathan Kaplan, who otherwise had a fine evening. Semo Sititi, Samoa's captain and No. 8, scored one of the tries of this or any other World Cup. His touchdown in the sixth minute came at the end of an eleven-phase sequence in which the ball passed through forty pairs of Samoan hands. Do yourself a favour and catch it again somewhere. It will warm the cockles on the coldest day.

Let us not patronise Samoa with reference solely to their exuberance. They put together a mean game of rugby, too.

Sititi's back-row mates, Maurie Fa'asavalu and Peter Poulos, were prominent all over the field. Half-backs Steven So'oialo and Earl Va'a were sharp and authoritative in all that they did. Centre Brian Lima, in his record fifteenth successive World Cup game, never missed a beat. And all this from a scratch side. This is not a Samoan team of stars as it was in the early 1990s. They are an ad-hoc combination, drawn from the four corners, who play with one heart. Their coach, Joe Boe, has done a magnificent job. The cruellest cut of the night was that they did not gain a bonus point.

Samoa were ten points to the good within six minutes. Va'a's early penalty was followed by Sititi's try. It was a rich prelude, the move beginning within the Samoa twenty-two and zig-zagging across field with splendid assistance, notably from full-back Tanner Vili, wing Lome Fa'atau and prop Kas Lealamanua. England had to grind their way into contention and did so in faithful style, Neil Back touching down at the end of a line-out maul in the twenty-fifth minute. An exchange of penalty goals saw Samoa keep their nose in front. The penalty try sapped the first drops of Samoan morale, even though Va'a did manage to knock over two penalties in quick succession midway through the half. Wilkinson's smart dropped goal in the sixty-fourth minute triggered a sequence of uninterrupted England scoring. Iain Balshaw latched on to a pinpoint Wilkinson cross-field kick to run in unmolested. The arrival of Mike Catt on the field brought some width to movements, with the Bath centre involved three times in the build-up to Vickery's first try in an England shirt.

The relief was plain to see on England faces. There may be harder tests to come, but looking down on the Samoan warriors still lapping the field to warm acclaim quarter of an hour after the final whistle had sounded, it was hard to imagine how it could be so.

9 NOVEMBER
REFEREE PUTS THE LAST NAIL IN SCOTS' COFFIN
Mark Reason

Scotland gave it a go, but were worn down by a more gifted team and a scandalous refereeing performance. Australia weren't good, but they can at least get better. The real problem that this World Cup must face up to is the refereeing. Australia have played three big games in this World Cup so far and each time they have been assigned a New Zealand referee. That is unacceptable and fodder for conspiracy theorists. There was a moment in the first half of this match when the sequence of events defied belief.

Wendell Sailor, who had another wobbly game, had just knocked on and was extremely cross with himself. His reaction was to go and punch Nathan Hines on the nose. Gregor Townsend responded by sending out a wicked cross-field kick to the wing that Sailor had vacated. Kenny Logan could not believe the space in front of him and there was a very good chance that he would have scored. Instead referee Steve Walsh blew his whistle to penalise Sailor. The Scots were livid, but could at least console themselves with the thought of a one-man advantage while Sailor did his time in the bin. But all Sailor got was a talking to.

If this was an isolated incident you could just about forgive Walsh, but it wasn't. Australia's coach, Eddie Jones, whose neck is clearly made of brass, had said in the build-up to the match: 'Sides are now employing tactics [in the scrum] to gain favour with the person controlling the game. We were caught out a couple of times last week.' He didn't mention that Argentina's scrum was buried in the opening match against Australia by ludicrous penalties awarded against them. Sure enough, Australia were awarded a free-kick when Scotland had the put-in to the first scrummage of this game, and if Mat Rogers hadn't fumbled a perfect pass, they would have scored from it. Time and again in the match Australia didn't so much obstruct as run lead-blockers in front of the ball-carrier, but they weren't penalised for it.

With the game tied in the second half Australia won a turnover ball through Phil Waugh. It would be stretching the bounds of geometry to say that Waugh came in from the side of the maul, so far offside was he. But play was waved on and Australia scored. It was a crucial moment, but Scotland have to take their share of responsibility for that try. Scotland coach Ian McGeechan should have realised long ago that Glenn Metcalfe's non-tackling is a liability. But he has stuck with him and the decision cost Scotland any chance of reaching the semi-finals. Mortlock ran right over the top of the hapless full-back and Australia were away. So was Metcalfe, being replaced soon after.

Australia now had a seven-point lead, and minutes later Stephen Larkham took a speculative drop at goal that hit the bar. When Scotland went to clear the ball they were confronted by Justin Harrison, who was twenty metres in front of any other Australian. Penalty to Scotland for offside? No chance. Instead they missed touch, Australia countered and were awarded a penalty. They put away both the kick and Scotland. The most comical moment in the game came twenty minutes into the half when Walsh decided to have a word with Bryan Redpath, the Scottish captain. Redpath was so angry that he could not even bring himself to look Walsh in the eye for fear of completely losing it. The only thing to be said for this farce, decided 33–16, is that at least the only New Zealanders that Australia will meet in the semi-final will be on the opposition.

The host nation still have many flaws to sort out if they are to be competitive. Their line-out was blown away in the first half by Scotland's, though it did improve massively after Matt Cockbain came on at half-time. Lote Tuqiri was a big step forward in the back three – though there was one nasty moment when he charged Tom Smith in the back, unpenalised, of course – but Rogers and Sailor still look vulnerable. Rogers has now dropped too many easy passes at important moments and Joe Rokocoko will be rubbing his hands at the thought of running at Sailor again. Scotland wing Logan does not give Australia a chance against New Zealand.

Scotland are on their way home and the future looks pretty dreich. McGeechan is moving upstairs, Redpath retired from international rugby after the game and, perhaps less significantly, so did Logan. Townsend is now thirty and Smith is thirty-two. The only players of class who are facing in the right direction are Simon Taylor and Chris Paterson. They both stood out against Australia, even though Paterson almost managed to knock himself out in the warm-up before the game.

Jim Telfer, who now hands over the post of Scotland's director of rugby to McGeechan, said afterwards that his forwards had played as well as he had seen for a few years. But he was unhappy that Waugh was not penalised in the lead-up to Australia's opening try. McGeechan also rued the fact that

Logan had not been allowed his run-in near the end of the first half. These are not men who usually criticise referees. The authorities should listen to them or see the tournament become a lottery.

10 NOVEMBER

FIRED-UP WALES LEAVE ENGLAND FEELING THE HEAT

Mick Cleary

Never mind the land of their fathers being proud of them. The whole of planet rugby felt a warm afterglow following a swashbuckling match. And the men to thank were those from Wales. They brought colour and verve, wild fancy and unbreakable spirit to the occasion. They brought twinkling feet and flickering hands as well, scoring three tries to England's one. The Grand Slam champions were beaten senseless for long stretches of the first half by the Six Nations wooden-spoonists. The transformation in fortunes was scarcely credible. The Welsh Rugby Union may be fighting for financial survival. Their rugby team, however, once again look to be a going concern.

It was a game to treasure, won 28–17 through England's concerted drive and cussedness and, inevitably, the boot of Jonny Wilkinson. As Wales chased, so they infringed. Wilkinson took due retribution with six penalty goals, five of them in the second half. He also picked a ball off his toes in the final second to drop a forty-metre goal. The edgy, haunted first-half figure finished with a flourish. His first kick of the evening struck a post, his last hit the mark. The romantics may talk a good game: the pragmatists invariably have the last word.

One of the few good England calls was to bring on Mike Catt at half-time. The Bath old-stager stayed true to his roots, playing what was in front of him and not what was programmed into his head. He gave England much-needed craft and sharpness in midfield, also claiming valuable tracts of territory with his kicking from hand. Catt had recovered from a stiff neck in midweek. Wales caused several of his colleagues a similar ailment. Wales won the heart of every neutral, not that many were to be found among the colourful, raucous tribes of the Suncorp Stadium. Those watching round the world, though, will have sided with the unfancied Welsh. Unfortunately, the sympathy vote counts for nothing. Wales are heading home, while England pack their bags for Sydney and a final fortnight of testing competition. It was the underdog who was left howling at the full moon.

England arc not at their best. They know that and every team they have so far faced know that. They look pinched and stilted. Their first-half display saw them bunched time and again in a narrow-side channel, forcing passes under pressure and making little headway. There was no composure or thrust to their game in those periods. There was a catalogue of disturbing errors. Going walkabout is a cherished part of Aboriginal culture. They may have a couple of new recruits. Dan Luger, a late call-up after the double withdrawals of Josh Lewsey and Iain Balshaw, was jittery and off-key. He dropped balls and hit a horrendous sliced clearance just before the interval. It was no surprise when his place was taken by Catt in the second half.

Ben Cohen will also look back in horror at the video nasty of his cross-kick from a tap penalty under the Welsh posts in the twenty-fifth minute. England were guaranteed three points from that position, yet Cohen grabbed the ball and punted left. Small problem. Out there was the titch of the England team, Neil Back, up against the strapping Llanelli wing Mark Jones. 'No, I wouldn't have made that decision if I'd been on the pitch,' Clive Woodward, England's head coach, said. 'Ben wasn't thinking too cleverly.' Nor were many others. Mike Tindall's angled kick in the thirty-fifth minute pitted lock Ben Kay up against Shane Williams, the wispy Welsh wing. It was no contest. From just inside his own twenty-two, Williams backed himself. Quite right, too. He made serious ground, scrum-half Gareth Cooper took it on and found Gareth Thomas in support. From there, Williams got in on the act again, juggling the ball before flicking infield to Stephen Jones, who touched down. Marvellous stuff.

In that first half of English torment, the line-out was shaky and the decision-making flawed. Even though England had more possession, they were flagrant in turning over ball. They came out with fresh kit in the second half. They ought to have been wearing sackcloth and ashes. Wales played smart rugby. They had worked out England from long ago but had kept their thoughts to themselves. Their coach, Steve Hansen, knew that he had to put width on the ball and stretch England's defence, which tends to cluster in midfield. It worked a treat. Hansen had the personnel to make it happen, too, from the short but snappy Shane Williams to the tireless support workers in the pack, flanker Dafydd Jones and lock Robert Sidoli. How they ran. How they saw the gaps. How they took the game to England, not giving a tinker's cuss for reputation or percentage return. England were forced to scramble in defence as Wales targeted their big men in the middle and ran round them. They made clever use, too, of the slither kick in behind, turning England and then harrying them.

It was a downfield hoof from Cooper that led to the second Welsh try in the thirty-fifth minute. Cohen made the initial retrieve deep in his twenty-two but was then judged to have hung on to the ball. Wales kicked for touch rather than for the posts and were rewarded when Colin Charvis was driven over. Two tries in four minutes and England were reeling. It was 10–3 at the interval. But as England's cast list changed with the arrival of Catt, so did their fortunes. They were back on level terms within three minutes following a sensational sixty-metre break from Jason Robinson, who had fielded a clearance kick from Cooper. Robinson sliced through three attempted tackles and zipped outside two other defenders. The final pass to Will Greenwood was measured and the centre dived in at the corner for his thirtieth try for England.

Then Catt got to work and so, too, Wilkinson. Wales became reckless and ill-disciplined. They gave away seventeen penalties, a heinous figure when Old Dead-Eye is in opposition. By the sixty-fifth minute, Wilkinson had given England clear water on the scoreboard with five successive kicks. England ought to have closed out the game at that juncture. But where once they were mentally tough and settled, now they appear prone to feverish lapses. Hooker Steve Thompson conceded a daft, petulant penalty which allowed Wales to kick downfield. From the line-out, they attacked one way and then, when the ball was brought back, Ceri Sweeney's high kick to the left saw Lawrence Dallaglio clamber back alongside Shane Williams. The ball ricocheted backwards, where Martyn Williams was able to swoop and touch down. Wales were back at the races. They could not quite bring off the jackpot coup. Iestyn Harris scuffed a kickable penalty-goal attempt six minutes from time. Wilkinson was, by now, in his element. Fortune had favoured the hang-dogged.

12 NOVEMBER
WALLABIES CAN RISE TO OCCASION
Peter FitzSimons

I love this story. See, roughly this time in 1999, the Wallabies awoke on the morning of their World Cup semi-final against South Africa to the news that Tim Horan, the star back of the team, had fallen seriously ill overnight. In the breakfast room he looked like death warmed up. Having spent hours vomiting, Horan felt as weak as a sick rabbit on a hot day, and seriously wondered if he could even play.

John Eales, the Australia captain, took the matter in hand. Over breakfast – heaped fruit for John, delicate nibbles of dry toast for Tim – Eales told him not to worry, and that he might be able to do a 'Dean Jones' and play the game of his life. When Horan asked him what he meant, the captain told him the story of what had happened when the famous Australian batsman of the 1980s went out to bat during the famous tied Test of 1986 at Chidambaram Stadium, Madras, despite suffering from a combination of dysentery, vomiting and feeling faint. The temperature was simmering around the 40-degree Centigrade mark, the humidity in excess of ninety per cent, and at one point Jones thought he was going to collapse.

'Mate,' Jones had told his batting partner, Australian captain Allan Border, 'I'm going to have to go off. I just can't go on, I'm too crook.' You could have hit Border's eyes with a sledge-hammer right then, and it was the hammer which would have cracked. 'Sure, mate,' he said in reply, his voice dripping with sarcasm, 'and when you go back in, can you ask them to send an Australian back, because that's what we need out here.' Jones stayed and went on to register his highest Test score of 210 runs. And so did Horan, more or less. An hour later, he went on to play such an outstanding match against the South Africans in that semi-final that it is regarded as the game which cemented his place as the Most Valuable Player of the World Cup.

The point? As a group, at this moment – just days away from playing a semi-final against a rampant All Blacks team – the Wallabies are bearing a distinct resemblance to Horan on that fateful morning. With the exception of just a few passages of play in this World Cup, they have looked so crook that even we Australian rugby supporters have been feeling nauseous ourselves, merely from looking on. When the Wallabies played Scotland, it got so bad at some points there were even sections of the Australian crowd booing. But we haven't given up hope. Just as Horan rose to the occasion in 1999, so can the Wallabies of 2003 rise now and put those dastardly All Blacks to the sword they so desperately deserve. Let me count the ways:

Despite their ordinary performances the Wallabies do not lack talent. Players like Lote Tuqiri, Mat Rogers, Steve Larkham, Phil Waugh, George Smith and Brendan Cannon are genuinely world class – it is just that they haven't clicked yet. They fair dinkum have shown, in glimpses – OK, OK, short ones, but still – that they are capable of playing good rugby. If only they can find some way to stop dropping the ball or giving forward passes, it is conceivable that they can join all those glimpses together and call it 'terrific rugby'. Wales have already shown the way, when it comes to playing the All Blacks. Despite finishing last in the Six Nations, the Welsh put the fear of God into the All Blacks, simply by getting into their faces and pursuing the time-honoured policy of 'if-in-doubt-take-them-out'. And if Wales can do it, then so can we!

It's New Zealand. Our blokes always lift at least three notches when playing against our trans-Tasman brothers. It is written into our genealogical code that when playing against them in rugby, we must empty our tanks until our carburettors are running on fumes alone. Still don't believe me? All right, there is this, and it comes straight from the Bible. I quote Isaiah, Chapter 14, verse 12, lines 3–14: 'And yea, verily is it written, that in the future the weak shall be strong, the meek shall be bold, the poor will be rich, the rich will be poor and the All Blacks will miss out on winning four Rugby World Cups in a row.' (It is, admittedly, an Australian edition.) But you get the drift. As the semi-final against the All Blacks hoves into view, those aren't straws we Australians are grasping at, they're threads. And we're going to splice them into a cord and then we're going to whip the New Zealanders, but good. That's my story, and I'm sticking to it.

16 NOVEMBER
WALLABIES WALTZ ON
Paul Ackford

Bye-bye Blacks. On a night encased in searing intensity and dripping with emotion, the Wallabies confounded the rugby world by spilling New Zealand out of this World Cup. It was a wonderful match. The All Blacks battled and battled but they could not break down a ferociously organised Australian defence. Telstra Stadium went delirious at the end of the 22–10 win. 'Waltzing Matilda' boomed around the arena, followed by '(I Come from a Land) Down Under'. It was an orgy of Aussie blokeishness, and in the chaos of celebration few of the Australians in the crowd realised that their captain George Gregan had hurt an ankle in his side's last defensive play. Fewer still saw him limp towards Justin Marshall, his opposite number who had departed earlier with his rib cartilage banged up in the carnage of the contest. Gregan just wanted to congratulate a respected and worthy foe. It was that kind of night.

This was an absorbing contest. Australia jettisoned the baggage of mediocre performance that they had carried into the game. Like England, they have been iffy from the start. Like England, the media has hammered them. Blimey, even John O'Neill, the chief executive of the Australian Rugby Union, has had a pop in recent weeks. Yet Gregan's troops let none of that matter. They ripped into the All Blacks from the first minute, running the ball back from deep inside their twenty-two with conviction and energy. The Wallabies backed their ability to play the big one well. We on the outside might have legitimately doubted their control of the ball and their composure in the earlier rounds. We should never have questioned their character as individuals or their culture as winners.

Stirling Mortlock made the first significant move for his side. It was the centre's cute reading and interception of a Carlos Spencer long pass that got the Wallabies going. Mortlock dented the All Black midfield all night, bustling through the tackles of Aaron Mauger and Leon MacDonald, providing his forwards with a target to run on to. Other Wallabies also went well. Gregan was snappy at scrum-half, back to his busy best. George Smith and Phil Waugh dominated the contact areas. Lote Tuqiri was a livewire wide on the wing and Stephen Larkham made several telling breaks on the outside of Spencer. But none of that would have been possible without the work of the front five.

Sometimes people ask about pressure in rugby. What does it look like? How do you apply it? Well, this was it. The Australians competed at the line-out and the restart, closing New Zealand's space. They held up in the scrum, apart from one horrible reversal after which Ben Darwin was taken off on a stretcher, and they denied the All Blacks the momentum to launch their famed back three. The first half was a disaster for the All Blacks. Australia had twice as much possession and they forced New Zealand into making eighty-six tackles compared to their twenty-eight. Early on New Zealand did have two good chances to score but lucked out when Wendell Sailor hammered Joe Rokocoko into touch and then Tuqiri somehow flew across to frustrate Mils Muliaina as he tried to squeeze into the opposite corner. Those two early incidents set the benchmark and the tone for Australia's defence. They were able to gang-tackle All Black runners, forcing them back over the gain-line. On one occasion New Zealand went through seven phases of possession only to find themselves twenty metres behind where they started. It was not very All Black-like.

The deluge heading their way meant that Keven Mealamu and Jerry Collins, the runners who destroyed South Africa in the quarter-final, were unable to get in behind the Wallaby defence. And under pressure New Zealand conceded silly penalties. Chris Jack gave one at a line-out near Australia's goal-line on one of the few occasions when New Zealand were in a position to apply pressure. And Brad Thorn, a late substitute, had only just cantered into action before he handed Elton Flatley another shot at three points. It was headless, undisciplined rugby. Flatley finished with seventeen points. Like the rest of his mates, he barely put a foot wrong.

New Zealand's solitary try arrived from a turnover, a telling indication of the problems they had in creating openings when they were in possession. Larkham lost the ball in contact and Spencer jinked his way past Waugh and Mortlock, slanting his way in from the touchline before unloading to Reuben Thorne. Larkham did not shed many tears over that reversal. From then on in he came out well ahead in the battle of the two outside-halves.

So Australia sail on to a final the nation demanded. It is a wonderful lift for the tournament to have the home team still in the running. Wonderful, too, for Wallaby coach Eddie Jones, who prepared and motivated his side faultlessly against a background of harsh and barbed criticism. It will take a day at least to assess the medical fallout from the game but early signs are encouraging. Darwin, who lay disturbingly prone on the pitch for six minutes, was reporting full movement afterwards, and the other bumps and bruises, including Gregan's, do not appear as serious as first feared. If that is the case, Jones will have one more miracle to work. Sides that turn tables in World Cup semi-finals often struggle to repeat the feat. That was France's lot in 1999 when they came up against Australia.

17 NOVEMBER
ENGLAND CLEAR THE AIR AND BLOW FRANCE AWAY
Mick Cleary

England showed character and resolve to win through to their second final 24–7, while France all but disintegrated as the Sydney heavens opened on their World Cup parade. They had two men, Christophe Dominici and Serge Betsen, sent to the sin-bin and were ragged, off-key and ill-disciplined in equal measure. England may well have made them look a shadow of their former selves but France also need to look within. They had shown impressive form in the tournament, but when it came to the high-octane occasion they had no one to match the *sangfroid* of Jonny Wilkinson or the ferocious all-enveloping desire of Martin Johnson and his pack of forwards. Neil Back in particular gave tireless and intelligent support throughout, ensuring that England gained a decisive advantage at the breakdown. They did not waste that ball.

The contrast in fortunes was neatly captured just after the hour mark when a double substitution by France saw two of their key players, flanker Betsen and fly-half Frédéric Michalak, trudge off the field. These were the men who were supposed to haunt and taunt England, the former by suffocating Wilkinson at source, the latter by dancing through the English defence at will. Neither happened. Betsen was shown the yellow card for a late tackle on Wilkinson in the fifty-third minute, while Michalak showed the nerves of anxious youth, fluffing kicks at goal and under-clubbing several up-and-unders.

Creative tension proved to be the more productive means of preparation for this semi-final than designer chic harmony. While France unwound during the week at laid-back Bondi Beach, England had a clear-the-air meeting behind closed doors at their Manly training base and exposed a few home truths. The upshot was that England never appeared fazed or rattled when France went into an early lead, working their way back into contention by the time-honoured virtues of honest graft up front and well-marshalled play behind the scrum. France were too casual and disengaged for their own good. When the squeeze came on, they were jittery and out-of-sorts. They dropped balls, sliced clearance kicks and never established any sort of foothold in England's territory.

The dreadful conditions made it difficult for both sides to get a firm grip of things. There were errors on England's part, too, especially early on when their positional kicking was wayward. But once the radar got locked in, and once the forwards began to exert control, then it was France who found themselves continually on the back foot. England are masters at managing the moment. They have battled through all sorts of testing circumstances in this tournament, finding solutions as they go along. Betsen's try in the tenth minute might have frayed the nerves of a lesser side, but England rode that little squall to head into the break with a five-point advantage at 12–7. Referee Paddy O'Brien had to go to the television match official, Andrew Cole, to confirm Betsen's score, the flanker snaffling a ball at the tail of a line-out and haring towards the line. He was hauled down just short by Jason Robinson but slithered over on the greasy surface. Richard Hill managed to get an arm underneath the French flanker, but Cole adjudged that Betsen had managed to get proper downward pressure.

France failed to capitalise on that early advantage. England were fretful themselves in those early stages, but Michalak could not make it tell as he pushed two penalty kicks wide. The fault lines were already beginning to appear. Wing Dominici had a rush of blood in the twenty-third minute when he flicked out his right leg as Jason Robinson cut inside. The England wing went crashing to the turf as if he had been felled by Norman 'Bite Your Legs' Hunter. Dominici hurt himself in the process and was substituted after his ten minutes in the sin-bin. His reckless, rather than intentional, challenge was symptomatic of France's jumpy display.

'We were very edgy and fragile when it mattered,' Bernard Laporte, the French coach, said. 'The blame has to be at our own door. It's too easy to take refuge in the weather. It was the same for England. It was not them who knocked on several times and lost balls in their line-out. They showed flexibility and we did not. The better team won, that is for sure.'

There seems to be an inner assurance once again about England. Even though they are not sweeping past opponents, they dealt with this significant challenge with a great deal of authority. The value of being able to turn to such experienced campaigners as Johnson to lead the way was proven once again. Even though there had been some inner tension in the week before following the less-than-convincing quarter-final win over Wales, there is little doubt that by working through their difficulties, England have emerged the stronger for the experience. 'At the back of everyone's mind, this was the game that we had been waiting for,' Clive Woodward, the head coach, said. 'We had a meeting and there was a lot of bad-natured anger from the coaches and a lot of good-natured anger from the players when we saw the tape of that Wales game. We handled it all well.'

Mike Catt's recall to the front line eased some of the burden of responsibility from Wilkinson's shoulder. Catt did not settle immediately, miscuing some kicks. He is a very different player to the man he replaced, Mike Tindall, and though he does not punch his way across the gain-line in the same muscular manner that his Bath teammate does, Catt's ability to keep defences turning with his kicking game is a crucial addition to England's repertoire. Wilkinson seems more at ease with him alongside.

The England fly-half snapped over two dropped goals in the first half, making sure that his side took full advantage when they got within range. It was a similar story in the second half as Wilkinson landed two penalties and a dropped goal. 'They tell me that Wilkinson is dead,' Laporte said. 'He didn't look dead to me. He played a great match. You saw the difference with Freddie Michalak. He will be a great player of tomorrow.' Fabien Galthié tried all he knew to right the listing ship, but to little avail. 'It is not Freddie's fault,' said the captain. 'He is human, not a machine. We all dreamt of a different end. It was not to be.'

Jason Leonard passed his historic mark as the world's most capped player when coming on as a blood replacement for Phil Vickery in the fourth minute. He was on the field barely sixty seconds before reappearing later in the match. It was a game in which every little counted. This was a night for a mighty team effort. England did not disappoint on that count.

17 NOVEMBER
WE WANT TO GIVE FANS SOMETHING LIKE 1966 TO ENJOY AND REMEMBER
Matt Dawson

What an awesome night and what a night to be an England rugby player and supporter. A World Cup semi-final is something you always dream about and finally we delivered. It was tough and rough, exactly as we knew it would be, but our forwards were magnificent from the first minute and with that platform we were always going to win. We are not getting carried away – there is one massive match, the biggest game of our careers, to go – but just for now I am going to enjoy what we achieved at the Telstra Stadium and I hope you are all enjoying it at home as well.

Over the years I've made it a policy to deal with whatever hangover remains from a game on the Monday. If we have lost badly and things have gone wrong I mourn. If things have gone well I celebrate and savour the moment. Then the next day it's back to work as if nothing ever happened. It's the only way you can deal with what sport throws at you.

How did we get it right here? There were two main factors: first, we took a long look at ourselves on the video in a team meeting after our quarter-final win over Wales. We copped a lot of criticism for that performance, which is fair enough, but we didn't lose our confidence. We talked everything through – an honesty session, if you like – and plotted the way forward. Second, the management trusted us enough to believe us when the players said that we only needed a few short, sharp sessions in midweek training. We have done tons of work and got loads of fitness and conditioning in the bank. What we needed was to ease off and top up the batteries.

It paid dividends brilliantly. The pack tore into France from the start. And, from my ringside seat, I would say it's the most impressive pack display I have seen during my time with England. France have a terrific set of forwards and were looking to take us on, but we closed them out, stifled the life out of them. And, after weathering a bit of a storm midway through the first half, we came through with flying colours. It was never going to be pretty. When England meet France head to head it can often develop into a scrap. Add the tension of a World Cup semi-final, the weather and probably the slipperiest ball I have played with, and it was never going to be a thing of beauty.

Our fans were magnificent. I couldn't believe the sight when we ran on – how many were there, 25,000–30,000? The noise they made was extraordinary, the equal of anything I have heard at Twickenham. I am just so glad we have delivered for them. What a time they will enjoy in Sydney, and I understand there are more reinforcements on the way.

As a squad we are incredibly proud of what we have achieved in reaching the final, but are determined to take things one more step and bring home the trophy. We want to give the sports fans, not just the rugby fans, of England something to enjoy and remember. Nothing will ever equal the 1966 soccer World Cup victory, but we desperately want to offer up something of that magnitude. It's going to be a great day.

CHAPTER SIX:
2003 – THE FINAL

HELD IN SYDNEY

22 NOVEMBER
FIRST RELAX THEN COMES
THE TIME TO DELIVER
Matt Dawson

World Cup final week, as we always knew it would, just flew by. After the high of beating France, we needed a couple of days to come down so we could build again, and it was Wednesday before we had our first meeting about Australia. Only then did the reality of an imminent World Cup final dawn on us. I don't mind that, you don't want to be stewing away all week. We are fit enough – we couldn't be fitter, in fact – and we are determined. The focus is good and the opposition familiar. We know what has to be done and all we have to do now is execute it. We know Australia well through our annual games and, of course, they have a fair idea about our game. Yes, we have won the last four matches, but apart from our first-half performance in Melbourne in summer 2003, when we were exceptional, there hasn't been a fag paper between us.

Unlike most of the rugby world, and indeed the Australian press, we have always reckoned that if we reached the final the Wallabies would be lining up against us. You just look at the basics. World champions, at home, with everything to prove after a slightly iffy early season. They have risen to the challenge as we always knew they would, and we will be facing a much more formidable side than the team we beat in June. Their early wins over Namibia and Romania were no form guide at all, but what struck me about their performances in the matches that mattered – Argentina, Ireland, Scotland – was that they were only one poor pass or turnover away from really producing the goods. Their essential game plan was in good order and they really showed that against the All Blacks in the semi-final. They decided to attack the All Blacks' fly-half channel, and Stephen Larkham showed what a world-class player he is when in the groove. Australia went straight for the jugular, refused to kick possession away to the dangerous New Zealand backs, and were well rewarded for their efforts. My old sparring partner George Gregan was in fine form. In fact, he has looked in pretty good nick throughout, and I'm mystified by the criticism he has been copping. Anyway, that's not our problem.

It's time to draw in and focus purely on our game. The mood has been nice and relaxed, as it was before the French game, and the work has been kept down to a minimum, but the mental process began in earnest when we clocked back on after our day off. From that point onwards only the match mattered. Everybody handles the nerves their own way. Sleep – getting enough – is always my biggest concern before such a huge game. I get more sleepy as I get more nervous and could kip around the clock given the choice. I will happily doze all morning and all afternoon right up to the coach leaving for the ground. In fact, I normally sleep on the coach as well. I know the stomach will be churning, but that is totally normal. What I am hoping for is to feel nice and calm. There is nothing more to be said or done. It's time to go out there and help bring home a World Cup for England.

22 NOVEMBER
WOODWARD THE MASTER BUILDER HAS FAITH IN HIS FOUNDATIONS
Paul Hayward

When England lost their World Cup quarter-final against South Africa in 1999, they were dumped on the pile reserved for teams who cannot cope with pressure, forget to come up with a Plan B and have no idea how to slither and crawl their way through tournaments. The old story, supposedly. Alternating between gloom and hysteria, plenty of rugby folk thought Clive Woodward should pay for the calamity in Paris with his head.

Here England arrive at the Telstra Stadium in Sydney as favourites to win the 2003 World Cup, despite the presence of the defending champions at the other end of the paddock. There is not a single front-rank England player missing from the starting XV – and nor, said Woodward, are the pre-match favourites pining for anyone on the bench. Their record at the kick-off is twenty-two wins from twenty-three Tests. 'The preparation's been as good as it gets, and the support from England fans has been beyond words,' Woodward said. 'I keep pinching myself because we've arrived in the World Cup final at full strength. We're very pleased and proud of our preparations.'

When you hear the word 'preparations', you think of chefs cooking the right grub, buses arriving on time, grass being mown on the training ground and the media being fed with interviews at the appropriate times. But it runs much deeper than that. Preparation means walking into battle with a pack of forwards who have made 375 international appearances. Yes, 375 between eight men. It means yoking together thirty players and walking them through bonfires in London, Dublin, Melbourne and Wellington to see if they can cope. It means losing your place in the side if you have two bad games and not moaning to your agent or forming a gang inside the dressing room to 'get' the coach.

It means having six former captains on the pitch to transmit messages and maintain morale. You could also say it means sending the team down to Lympstone in Devon to train with the Royal Marines. Why? To show them real life-or-death courage and broaden their awareness of how their decisions affect those around them. Woodward's core idea was to turn a fifteen-man melee into a mutually dependent organism. In this meritocracy, it was easy for him to portray indiscipline as a crime against the team.

This may sound too English to tolerate, but according to these criteria Woodward has already established himself as one of the country's great organisers and team-builders. It would take a defeat by thirty points, a collective nervous breakdown among the coaching staff and an outbreak of systematic thuggery by the England players for that claim to be undermined. This is not to say that losing is OK ('Jeez – when will you Poms ever learn!'). The point is this: whatever the result, England will leave town with a template, a philosophy, a plan, a set of principles that will survive the result of the final. These are empty abstractions, you may cry. If so, abstractions have beaten the Wallabies four times in a row and knocked over the rest of the Southern Hemisphere.

The further he has marched at this tournament, the more Woodward has exuded certainty and control. Only the scare against Wales seemed to shake his conviction that the imperious form of the preceding eighteen months would carry England over the Rubicon. The best time to judge his mood was in the hours running up to this potentially epic game. With an Australian paper urging readers to honk horns and raise hell outside England's hotel, what did Woodward do? He made jokes. Good ones, too, about what the locals might have been trying to imply when they shouted 'boring, boring' underneath his window when he was in bed with Jayne, his wife. Under the camera lights, and with the questions bouncing in, Woodward managed to talk for fifteen minutes without making a single verbal error. He was funny, confident and sharp. If you listen carefully, you can assemble fresh evidence to support the claim that he has one incurable quirk. He has a talent for self-contradiction and following his own instincts, wherever they lead. But in the internal struggle between whimsy and circumspection, his wilder impulses are on the retreat. Keeping it simple has become his mantra.

'It's a brutal world we live in, but Test-match rugby is about winning,' he said. This late on, aesthetic principles have been packed away. It was with good reason that he told us: 'We're not Torvill and Dean.' England have played enough expansive rugby these past eighteen months to escape being parodied as the Flintstones, grinding their way into position for Jonny

Wilkinson to launch his kicks. But beauty is not an issue. Not now. Not with so much hard work on the line. The plan was always to beat Australia by any means necessary. Nor is this about St George on his high horse or rhetorical flourishes. 'I hear a lot about Churchillian speeches before the game and a lot of it is nonsense. You don't hear about these speeches when the team lose. In the moments before the game we'll be thinking about the kick-off, the restart and the first ten minutes of the game.' And always the references to the senior players: 'Martin Johnson and Lawrence Dallaglio will know how to handle this. They'll keep everyone's feet on the ground. I'll be in the box with Andy Robinson and Phil Larder [his fellow coaches], and we'll just be telling each other to think clearly. You've got to think straight in the pressure situations. If we get carried away we're not doing our jobs properly.'

With so much at stake, Woodward would have been forgiven for indulging himself, telling us how far he's come, how hard it's been, how much it means to him. But a voice inside was telling him: don't add to the pressure that is already there. 'No, it's not the most important day of my life,' he said emphatically. 'The World Cup will come and go. It's an important game of rugby, that's all.'

Gavin Hastings, once of Scotland, has talked about England's 'destiny'. Nice word, but not much use. Not to the England head coach, anyway. 'I don't think it's our destiny at all,' he said. 'We've been coming game by game. We've had a great four years since the last World Cup. We've only lost one or two games since then. So I don't think it's our destiny. I just think it's about eight o'clock tomorrow night.' Having smacked that one over the fence, Woodward then turned his attention to 1966, which was so long ago it might as well be 1066. The other day he talked about watching the England versus West Germany football game with his dad on an air-force base. That was then, this is now. Time to swat away distractions. 'It hasn't even crossed my mind. We're treating it as much as we can as another game. The ramifications of winning or losing will take care of themselves.'

Courtesy of some sadistic rule-maker, Woodward will watch the most important rugby match of his life from the inside of a box. Tournament regulations have kept him and his assistants caged behind glass. Imagine the hell of not being able to see your life's work unfold in real light, and having to listen to the muffled roars of the crowd through a window that manufactures distance between you and the legacy you did so much to create. One more win would make him the great reformer, a legend of English sport.

23 NOVEMBER
WILKINSON GRABS WORLD CUP GLORY
Paul Ackford

A wonderful, wonderful night. This occasion would have been compulsive if it had been played out on a scrap heap by two teams of nobodies, but to set it in a sensational stadium, with the world's finest rugby players at full stretch, and with so much at stake, was to elevate it to the ethereal. If there has been a more dramatic game of rugby of this importance, then I have yet to see it. And at the end of the longest game of the longest World Cup ever, the spoils go to England and Jonny Wilkinson. His drop goal twenty-five seconds from the last knockings of the second period of extra time confirmed England as champions of the world, by 20–17, and guaranteed his teammates long-lasting fame. As for the man himself, immortality beckons.

It would be ruinously crass to ignore the efforts of a magnificent Australian performance. They went into the contest decided underdogs, but refused to accept the tag. Apart from the first twenty minutes, during which Lote Tuqiri scored their only try, they were rushed, scragged and generally on the back foot. But, clinging hard and true to their sporting culture, Australia fought back. Twice, once at the end of ordinary time and once at the end of extra time, Elton Flatley kicked the Wallabies back on equal terms with nerveless penalties only for Jonny, the Boy Wonder, to step up and finish them off.

And just to show that this England team are worthy of a nation's respect and that rugby has more to offer than cash and status and self-glorification, there was a marvellous moment way after the initial elation of victory had ebbed away as the stadium was being readied for the presentation ceremony. Quietly, England's front-row trio of Jason Leonard, Steve Thompson and Phil Vickery went over to shake the hand of Australian prop Ben Darwin, whose serious neck injury, suffered in the semi-final against New Zealand, kept him out of the final. Sport at this level is rarely so inclusive.

The final was flooded with wonderful memories: the bravery of Stephen Larkham as he went off repeatedly to get a gaping mouth wound stitched; Jason Robinson's twinkling feet and the emotion he showed after scoring England's solitary try; the way Martin Johnson thundered into the Wallabies in the first quarter of the second half; the way Australia, in terrible trouble in the scrummage, rallied to force the game into extra time; the cool, calm Flatley.

And then there was Wilkinson. Is there no end to the story? Labelled a basket case earlier in the tournament, probed by a thousand putative media psychiatrists at dozens of press conferences, Wilkinson came through to win the World Cup for his country. It was his twenty-four-point haul that destroyed France and his drop goal that brought the Webb Ellis Cup to England for the first time. A smile flickered across his lips as the winner's medal was hung round his neck. He was probably thinking of the couple of kicks that flew wide of the posts.

And yet when England eventually regroup to reflect on the final, they will acknowledge that they should have been home and hosed long before Flatley breathed life into the Wallabies. Apart from the one lapse when Tuqiri exploited a seven-inch height advantage to out-jump Robinson and collect Larkham's cross-field kick to score, England's defence was rock solid. Stirling Mortlock, the scourge of the All Black midfield a week earlier, got no change out of Mike Tindall and Will Greenwood, and Larkham, so good at reading and slipping through gaps, was shut out, too. Australia's only way back into the match that they were losing 14–5 at half-time came courtesy of referee Andre Watson and a heavily penalised England scrum.

Watson pinged Trevor Woodman for refusing to go down for what would have been the final scrum of ordinary time to allow Flatley his kick. And if that decision had the air of fairness about it, there were plenty that were plain barmy. England were pulverising Australia in the tight yet they conceded five penalties in that area as Watson apparently refused to let the contest develop. It nearly cost England a World Cup, not to mention eviscerating one of rugby's great traditions.

England's other difficulty centred on the line-out. As they have done throughout the tournament, they continued to throw long and continued to miss the targets at the tail. Steve Thompson must take some of the flak as the missile launcher, but so must Ben Kay, the line-out captain, whose job it is to call the plays. It was Kay's fumble that led to the scrum and the penalty from which Flatley levelled the scores at 14–14 to force extra time. Flatley hit the kick with ten seconds remaining.

But enough of the brickbats. In a commendably cohesive and tight team performance, there were many who stood out for England. Matt Dawson and Lawrence Dallaglio had their best games of the World Cup, finally finding the link that is so important for continuity. Dawson also exposed a Wallaby weakness as he darted through the middle, and close to the sides, of rucks and mauls. Robinson was an electric livewire throughout, a constant thorn when running ball back at Australia. Josh Lewsey threatened early on when Australia were at their best, Ben Cohen got the better of Wendell Sailor in the battle of the big wings and Mike Tindall defended as well as he kicked, both of which he did brilliantly.

And Australia? They were shattered at the death. No shame in that for they punched well above their weight. It was sheer Wallaby cussedness that allowed them to hang on in as long as they did. Decimated in the tight, they had none of the go-forward they found in the semi-final. George Smith and Phil Waugh ploughed on but eventually they were submerged by a rampant England front five and the boot of Wilkinson.

The final sequence will go down in rugby folklore. Lewis Moody won a line-out, Mike Catt, Dawson and Martin Johnson drove or darted and Wilkinson swung his right boot as he has done so many times on training pitches around Australia. England were home. The cup was home. For four glorious years.

23 NOVEMBER
THE LIONHEARTS WHO LED THE WAY
Brough Scott

Jubilation, justification, rejuvenation: Martin Johnson held the World Cup in his hands and the enforcer's face lit into the sweetest smile as the years peeled off him. All those years, all those games, all those hits had led to this. As for Jonny Wilkinson, his brow, furrowed for so long during this tournament, was suddenly boyish in its triumphant happiness. He did the simplest, most obvious thing and it still went sailing between the uprights. He really was 'over the moon'.

Johnson and Wilkinson have hearts of oak, the pair of them: and they merit such an old-fashioned phrase precisely because they challenge old preconceptions. Sure, in their separate ways they are both the ultimate in strong, loyal, Englishmen formerly moated with unplumbable depths of English reserve. Yet now they are both acknowledged as giants of the modern professional era. Who dares stack such old virtues on some Cool Britannia bonfire? For here is fame without the short cuts of 'celebrity'. Here is worth measured more in value than 'earnings'. Here is courage seen but never stated. Here are boots and arms and bodies that do the talking. Here is immortality sought on the pitch rather than off it.

In the past few years, months, weeks and most of all in those one hundred impossible minutes of this final we have come to realise just how much we depend on Martin and Jonny. Clive Woodward has built up as fine a team unit as has pulled on an England jersey, if that's the right term for the torso-hugging white body glove of today. But shut your eyes and let the images crowd in, and seared forever into the retina is that last-minute

Wilkinson moment, the jink right for the drop-kick and the white ball spinning into history. It crowned the ultimate in *Boy's Own* heroics, but the memory also palpitates with the Johnson catalogue: the great catches in the line-out, the rumbling hits in contact, even that last power push that gained the extra second for the drop.

Johnson and Wilkinson have long been in our consciousness; best of all they are always high in that of the opposition. Having tried to rile Johnson as a primitive beast (to which he just gives one of his Neanderthal pouts), and to destabilise Wilkinson as some shot-through mental wreck after he scored only fifteen points against Samoa and missed a couple of kicks against Wales, the Sydney press reverted to puerile taunts of 'boring, boring'. They were, and let's use the words with careful relish, reduced to 'Whingeing Aussies'.

Part of the media frustration is the lack of skirt under which to peer. The biggest danger for anyone hitting the modern-day spotlight is to start trading fame for intrusion. Lawrence Dallaglio's 'honey trap' disaster was all the lesson Woodward's two superstars needed. We get to film and interview them, we read their ghost-written columns, but we do not get to know them. This should not be strange. In ordinary life it is good manners to be open and polite to strangers, but only a fool confides in every person with a tape recorder who sucks up to them in a hotel lobby. Profiles of Johnson and Wilkinson tend to be correct, not controversial.

Some of this is media savvy from two figures who are not natural song-and-dance men. But the other part is the better side of professionalism. The pressures may be immense but so too are the rewards and the resources to support them. Time was when training was fitted in after work, 'rehydration' was strictly pints of lager, and when both press and committee men earned more than the players who were patronised at having the luck to be on such a big stage. Now they are rightly treated as highly paid professional athletes with all the responsibilities and kudos that this can command. They are even allowed to advertise. Only a few years ago, to have seen the England captain and fly-half advertising razors and running kit would have been the end of life as Twickenham knew it. Yet who can argue that the respective commercial campaigns have not bolstered the Johnson and Wilkinson reputations as much as their bank balances? Before the Lions tour Martin Johnson's face had fangs inserted, now it just stares out hard and pitiless at every opponent's heart. Jonny Wilkinson and David Beckham's Nike rugby/football duet had more than a code-crossing charm: it reminded everyone watching just how infernally gifted a pair of feet belong to the England No. 10.

The commercials purport to take you closer to the real man; they actually return you to where they belong, to the pitch. That is where in this tournament both men have once again been immeasurably immense. During it Wilkinson was elected players' player of the year for the second winter running, but still set himself standards almost frightening in their intensity. If he missed a kick or took a wrong decision he was more upset than anyone. But he missed few, he tackled about four times his weight, he was the No. 10 every other country would have doubled the national debt for.

As for Johnson, he remains, quite simply, the greatest presence in the game. Of all the people in the tournament, of all the Englishmen in the world, he was the least likely to be pushed around. He may be England captain, an MBE, and a fine, generous and surprisingly genial citizen off the pitch, but on it he is hard, as hard as all the nails and oak timbers that ever made a Nelson battleship. Speed, athleticism and flair will always be the most visible part of the rugby armoury, but the basic ingredients start with contact and Johnson is quite happy to spell it out. 'There is a line,' he says in his quiet, almost soulful way, 'and I have been over it, most people have. Yet people do like the contact part of the game. You have to stand toe to toe with these guys and they respect you for it.'

Respect is the word. Respect for the game, for the preparation, for the rules, for the officials, even for the opposition. As the final drew ever closer we yearned back to that other World Cup in 1966 and to two other figures whose very presence lit up our lives, Bobby Moore and Bobby Charlton. Moore, as captain, had that walk, more bandy legged and less fearsomely brooding than Johnson, but a walk on to the pitch and towards the opponents that both reassured and inspired you. Charlton, like Wilkinson, was the weapon. But both pairs of players evoke another, even heavier word. It is courage. Think of what Moore and Charlton must have felt before they went out at Wembley. Imagine, more immediately, what it must have been like for Johnson and Wilkinson, knowing always that fifteen slavering brutes opposite were intent on making it hurt. Even with all the television close-ups, even when Wilkinson was flattened in the first half, have you for one moment felt that Martin or Jonny were quailing in front of the foe?

True courage has an honesty that illuminates both those around and watching it. Of course it happens everywhere, in the hospital ward, among the downtrodden in distant dictatorships, in many other places where it really is a case of life and death. But it also happens on the sports field, and rugby is the best of all in its brutal examination of the steel within the soul. Yes, courage remains the greatest of all the virtues. Here it took them both to the very end of the rainbow. In an ever more facile world, Johnson and Wilkinson have nailed the old-fashioned lie.

23 NOVEMBER

I MAY BE A MUPPET BUT I'VE WON THE WORLD CUP

Steve Thompson

I was at the bottom of a ruck when Jonny slotted that drop goal. I remember looking up and – boom – he had knocked it over. I saw the ball go through the middle of the posts and the referee's arm go up. Then I found myself hugging a couple of players. I don't even know who they were. In fact, I was so tired I wasn't so much hugging them as hanging on to them to stand up. The next thing I did was to look at the clock. There were about ten seconds left so I knew all we had to do was to win the kick-off and get it into touch.

I was just so exhausted at the end. The emotion of the win hasn't sunk in and I don't suppose it will for a few days. It was such a topsy-turvy game. I couldn't believe it when we were penalised at the last scrum of the game and Elton Flatley kicked the penalty to take us into extra time. It was a weird experience. There was no panic. We just thought that we had to carry on and we could win. Johnno told us that we had plenty of rugby left in us and that's how we approached it. The plan was to keep running at the Australians and keep hold of the ball, which we hadn't done all that well in the match. Johnno also said that we shouldn't just rely on the drop goals and the penalties from Jonny, that we had to make our own luck. The Aussies were very tired at that stage. Mike Catt showed that when he came on as a late replacement. He was breaking tackles the moment he took to the pitch.

I'm not quite sure what winning the World Cup will mean to me. I don't think it will hit home until we get home. Mentally and physically it will be good to have a rest and then I'm sure we'll get straight back into the club scene. I know something, though. The next couple of days are about drinking and having some fun.

It was a strange game. Even when Lote Tuqiri scored their try after six minutes I felt we were battering them in the scrum. Referee Andre Watson was quite clear about what he thought was wrong. He said we weren't binding properly and he'd put his life on the decision he made. I accept that but I thought we had the upper hand and were pushing them backwards.

It was massive to receive the winner's medal. I managed to spot my girlfriend, Fiona, in the crowd and that made it very special. The lap of honour, the support – it was all awesome. I know everyone says this sort of thing but that was the best day of my life. To be honest, it's been mad all week. I didn't sleep well after the semi-final against France. I reckon I got about six hours' kip on Sunday and Monday so I took sleeping pills for a couple of nights to make sure I was properly rested for the game. The other problem was my neck. That took until Thursday to loosen up after bearing the brunt of the French scrummage. But as the week wore on the physical issues disappeared and the mental ones took over. Relaxation has been the thing for me. I got it wrong against South Africa in the group matches because I built up for that game way too early. When I got to the stadium I found that I was exhausted from all the nervous tension and my performance suffered.

That's why I've tried to chill out. It's not been easy, mind. Popping out for a coffee with Lewis Moody, Joe Worsley and Julian White, a favourite pastime of mine, was almost impossible. What used to take half an hour took more than an hour because of all the back-slapping and autograph-hunting. I'm not complaining one bit, though. The support over here has been awesome and part of me quite liked the attention. Some of the squad used the back door out of the hotel to avoid the crowds but that did not last long. The press photographers soon discovered that exit route so we were forced to spend time in the team room playing computer games and watching videos. Tiger Woods's golf game was the favourite with Mike Tindall and Iain Balshaw, the hot shots, because they'd played it before. Even so, it was very competitive. Obsessive, too. I came down to the team room at 7 a.m. some days to find a couple of the lads, unable to sleep, staring at the screen. The alternative entertainment was *The Office*. That played non-stop on the video, keeping us amused.

I also tried to take my mind off the game by phoning home. My mates have been great. They seemed to sense that I didn't want to talk about rugby, so after the initial couple of questions we chatted about what they were up to. They've helped to keep my feet on the ground. My old friends know me as Wally (I changed from Walters to Thompson, my family name, some time ago) and they can't believe I'm on the telly and part of this England squad. To be honest they think I'm a bit of a Muppet. A Muppet who's won the World Cup, though. I think I'll remind them of that when I get home.

THRILLER PROVED A TRIBUTE TO PLAYERS' SKILLS
Tom Horan

Congratulations, England. I know exactly how you are feeling. If it was anything like when Australia won the World Cup for the second time in '99, Telstra Stadium officials would have faced a monumental task removing Martin Johnson and his teammates from the dressing room. It's a feeling you just can't describe or want to end, and we stayed in the bowels of Cardiff's Millennium Stadium drinking out of the Webb Ellis Cup for a solid three to four hours to savour the occasion. We knew as soon as we left that room the team members would disperse among family and fans, and the moment would be lost, so we weren't going to budge easily.

Apart from the birth of my children, it's the moment that I wish I could freeze in time. I knew how the victorious England players were feeling when they did a lap of honour and their expressions brought all the memories flooding back on why this is now such a magic tournament. Veterans Johnson and Jason Leonard seemed to have waited a lifetime to fulfil their dream. Kyran Bracken didn't come off the bench, but what a way to celebrate his thirty-second birthday. Beforehand I said to friends that I hoped every fan would leave the stadium talking about what a great spectacle they had seen rather than how boring it was. Every diehard fan will remember – for varying reasons – where they were when the amazing Jonny Wilkinson landed the drop goal that clinched England's first Rugby World Cup. It was one of the best matches I've seen – and I've seen a few over the years. That the players, in the constant drizzle, could turn on such a thriller was a testament to their skills.

For Australia's press to have labelled England boring in the lead-up was unfair. They have been the best team in the world for more than two years and you don't get there by being able to turn it on only on the odd occasion. They are certainly the hardest to beat. They have achieved such momentum through the management excellence Clive Woodward has put in place that these days losing is now a lot harder than it once was, even if at times here you suspected they were trying hard to do just that. I'd doubt very much whether there is a true rugby fan in Australia who would now pick fault in Wilkinson. He's simply the best player I've seen, full stop. He's got everything and he is humble with it. While he has his share of natural flair, he has got to where he is through a mind-boggling schedule of hard work that leaves you knackered just watching him.

I spoke to George Gregan briefly after the game and he was gutted. But, like me, he conceded England fully deserved their victory. I was in the Australia team who were pipped by Rob Andrew's drop goal at the death in the 1995 World Cup, but that was in the quarter-final, not the final. Still, it hurt. In these quarters you tend to talk about the rivalry between Australia and New Zealand, but the one with England is gathering momentum at a frightening pace. Coach Woodward had orchestrated four straight wins over the Wallabies going into the final, and I think contests between the two countries are going to have an even greater intensity in future.

Besides Wilkinson, I thought Mike Catt had another good game when he came on and Mike Tindall was sensational in taking the pressure off his match-winning fly-half. In the end the clock just ran out on Australia, but they can hold their heads high. They never fully recovered from their last twenty minutes of the opening half, but Lote Tuqiri was outstanding, Stephen Larkham had three trips to the blood bin but kept coming back for more, and Phil Waugh and George Smith never shied away from their workload. Waugh was probably Australia's player of the tournament.

Now the teams can look ahead to the 2007 Cup and, despite a few old hands retiring, you can bet England will not be short on talent when it comes around. Australia must now ensure that their search for new faces is relentless because to stay at the top level will require more than just marketing nous. For the moment, though, England can afford a well-earned celebration.

24 NOVEMBER
ANDREW'S SHOUT REFLECTED FINAL'S TUMULTUOUS CLIMAX
Jim White

The reaction in the Radio 5 Live commentary box at the decisive moment of the Rugby World Cup final mirrored precisely what was going on in front of televisions across the country. As the commentator Iain Robertson was saying 'and Wilkinson drops for World Cup glory' (not quite 'they think it's all over', but not bad) behind him you could hear a screamer, later identified as the former England player Rob Andrew, belting out a long, impassioned 'yes-yes-yes-yeeeeeessss'. As it was a male voice, we could rule out Meg Ryan reprising her orgasmic yelps from *When Harry Met Sally*.

Andrew's shout was replayed throughout the afternoon

across the BBC radio network, and we all knew exactly how he felt. I for one have never sat through such a tense, tortuous and ultimately tumultuous two hours of televised sport. Even if, in return for negotiating such a climax to their tournament, the organisers will now be obliged to spend the rest of eternity in the bowels of hell being probed by hot pokers, they got themselves a bargain. Interviewed before kick-off, Clive Woodward refused to accept the ITV reporter's hyperbolic suggestion that this was a game that could change lives. 'It's very, very important. But no more than that,' Woodward claimed. Even the soon-to-be Sir Clive, though, could not argue with the notion that this was a match that changed rugby.

Throughout the autumn the game has enjoyed a domination of the airwaves previously undreamt of in the reign of football. Throughout the hours of coverage, there have been moments of pure pleasure such as Rupeni Caucaunibuca's tries for Fiji, the sight of Ieaun Evans almost expiring in delight at Wales' unexpectedly convincing performances and Brian O'Driscoll's mid-air juggling as he scored for Ireland against Australia. There have been moments too of low farce – the England and France players peeling those pec-hugging shirts off each others' backs to swap at the end of the semi-final, the Scotland players' ill-judged twitching during their national anthem before the game against France and anything Austin Healey said.

But for much of it, you didn't have to be a devotee of rugby league to think that, as a television spectacle, the fifteen-man game would be much improved if viewers had a vague inkling where the ball was for much of the time. Until the final, that is. Then, in delivering a sporting contest of unbridled drama, rugby seized its moment. It really will not have mattered that a huge television audience had not one clue between them as to why the referee Andre Watson awarded the Australians a penalty in the last second of normal time. As it happens, even those more familiar with the rule book than the facial features of their own spouse will find it hard to appreciate that decision. Rugby may be a sport which has ninety-two different laws governing how the ball should be returned into play once it has crossed the touchline, but this was one of those rare days when such joy-cramping bureaucracy was soundly defeated by the theatricality of the event.

There were many reasons for it, not least the admirable Australian characteristic of refusing to accept defeat. The conviction with which George Gregan and his team played was matched only by their graciousness. Seeing the warmth of the Australian players as they congratulated their English opponents at the end of the game brought those of us anxious to wallow in Antipodean defeat up short. If they know how to win Down Under, they also know how to lose.

But the fact is, the tournament officials could not have planned the ending better. The final in all its draining emotional intensity is the image we will remember the World Cup by – not the hours of one-sided bullying in the group stage. Did anyone really enjoy Australia scoring nearly 150 points against Namibia? In the end this World Cup has been crystallised into the cathartic thrill of one moment of sublime skill by its most visible practitioner. You cannot buy an image like that. That is a lesson the advertisers, who pockmarked the tournament with exhortations to buy their goods, could do with learning.

IT HURTS TO ADMIT, BUT CHAMPIONS ARE WORTHY OF ACCLAIM
Peter FitzSimons

Dear Poms – And that'd be right, England, wouldn't it? You had to go and do it, didn't you? It wasn't enough for you just to win the World Cup at our expense, no, that would be too simple. You had to do it in a fashion to drive us Australians mad. Instead of a quick, clean, clinical kill, leaving us, say, twenty points shy – with no possibility of being haunted for the rest of our lives about how close we got – you had to tease, didn't you? You had to leave it until the last twenty-eight seconds of a hundred-minute game before finally administering the *coup de grâce*.

Do we do that to you in the Ashes, huh? Do we tease you until the final session of a five-day Test? No – we decidedly do not. For the last fifteen years or so, we have made it a point of honour to put you beneath the sod after about three days, and it's only ever four days at the absolute most. See, we Australians don't like teasing, we think it's unsportsmanlike. OK, maybe on the subject of Tim Henman we have been a little guilty on occasion of fooling around, by letting him into the Wimbledon semi-finals, but we never, ever let him get all the way to the final – because that would be downright rude, doing it in your country 'n' all. Ditto, the World Cup of cricket. We usually don't let you within a bull's roar of the final, but when we do, we usually make appropriately short work of you.

And then there was the fashion in which your blokes played. Out-bloody-rageous. See, if it had been sixteen-man rugby, as coach Clive Woodward unveiled at the beginning of the tournament, we could have complained until the cows came home. And if it had been a one-man effort, as we in the expert rugby media had all been fearlessly predicting – giving the ball to Jonny Wilkinson and asking him to kick it until his nose bled – then you really would have given us something to whinge about. But, nothing of the sort. In the unkindest cut of all, the English team played fifteen-man rugby, ran the ball every bit as much as we did, spread it as wide as we did, and showed every bit as much courage as the Wallabies. Martin Johnson's men played – and I really can't put it any higher than this – like Australians. Had you played it any other way, we could have said things like 'well, maybe they won, but would you really want to win a World Cup by playing that sort of dull rugby? We Australians would rather lose than to have a hollow triumph like that'. But, you didn't.

Speaking of Johnson, he is yet another one who got my goat. After the match, instead of being a surly brute whose opening remarks could be boiled down to 'nyah-nyah, nyah-nyah', he was magnanimous in victory and gracious to a fault. Even Woodward, get this, gave our Eddie Jones a hug. And don't even get me started on your tens of thousands of supporters. Afterwards in the bars and on the boulevards they partied till dawn, but didn't make any trouble at all. Overnight, not one Englishman got himself in any trouble with the police. Instead, they were good-hearted, free-wheeling folk who were just about impossible not to warm to. There is, in short, seemingly no way out that I can see, or any other Australians can see.

Cannon to the left of us,
Cannon to the right of us,
Cannon in front of us
Volley'd and thunder'd,
Into the valley of Death,
Rode the six hundred.

In sum, you English have left us with absolutely nothing we can possibly say, or whine about, other than – Gawd, this hurts – 'Well done, that is a very fine rugby team you have there, and they are worthy heavyweight champions of all the world.' And having said that, I am now going to report you all for submitting an Australian, all Australians, to cruel and unnatural punishment, making us say things that we will regret all our lives.

Yours sincerely,

Disgusted

Sydney

25 NOVEMBER
LETTERS TO THE SPORTS EDITOR
IN PRAISE OF POMS

SIR – Irony is a funny thing. In the final of the 2003 Rugby World Cup, Australia struggled to keep the English score in sight with a weapon that we, the Aussie public, had derided as an English invention: the kicking boot. Elton Flatley, the Wallabies' kicker, kept the Aussies in touch by kicking penalties. Isn't this just what Australian rugby fans accused Jonny Wilkinson of doing? Boring rugby? My side lost but I found it anything but boring.

At the start of the tournament, rumour had it that Jonny was the best rugby player in the world. He didn't pass the ball a lot and he certainly didn't run with the ball at all. He just kicked the ball an awful lot. Carlos Spencer, on the other hand, did look the best player in the world. But in the final Wilkinson stepped up to the mark and, under what must have been enormous pressure, just ripped that title away from everyone. He did it all. He ran the ball strongly and effectively. He passed the ball. He tackled like a mongrel and even took a hit that would have floored many bigger players for the count. Of course, Big Jon also kicked the winning drop goal with seconds to spare in extra time. Incredible.

When the final whistle blew, I cannot say I was disappointed. I had just watched a fabulous game of rugby – deserving of a World Cup final. As much as it hurts me to say it, the best team won on the night. The Poms are deservedly world rugby champions.

Kim Hewitt
Gorokan
New South Wales
Australia

SACK JONNY

SIR – As I watched Martin Johnson accepting the Webb Ellis Cup, I could not help noticing a slight rumble in the ground. Closer investigation revealed it was William Webb Ellis turning in his grave. Why? Because, when in the process of inventing the game, he is said to have picked up the ball and run with it. He didn't pick up the ball and kick it.

Running seems largely to have gone out of the game since it turned professional. England are not alone in this, of course; they're just the worst. Scoring tries seems now to be an afterthought. Kickers like Jonny Wilkinson must be forced out of the game. The emphasis needs to be placed firmly back on running rugby. To that end, the rugby league system always has been preferable, with only two points for a penalty and one for a drop goal. Moreover, penalties should be given only for foul play. I am sick of paying good money to watch the Wilkinsons of this world waste vast amounts of playing time on taking kicks at goal.

Noel Sinclair
Bexhill
East Sussex

26 NOVEMBER
LETTERS TO THE SPORTS EDITOR
DEFENDERS OF THE FAITH

SIR – Oh, there had to be one, didn't there! I don't know what match Noel Sinclair had been watching, but it clearly wasn't the World Cup final in which England ran the ball more than the Aussies, tackled harder and broke through the gain-line more often and if not for the referee would have won comfortably. As a final point, even if a dropped goal had been worth one point, England would still have won 18–17, so let's not be curmudgeonly. Celebrate for once.

Gary Stark
Kettering

SIR – In his letter lamenting the kicking aspect of the union game, Noel Sinclair provides the solution to his own problem: namely that he should take to following the league code.

I also wonder whether advocating getting rid of Jonny Wilkinson is a treasonable offence yet?

Arabella Smith
Guildford
Surrey

2003 RESULTS – Quarter-finals: New Zealand 29, South Africa 9; Australia 33, Scotland 16; France 43, Ireland 21; England 28, Wales 17. Semi-finals: Australia 22, New Zealand 10; England 24, France 7. Third-place: New Zealand 40, France 13. Final: England 20, Australia 17.

CHAPTER SEVEN: 2007

HOSTED BY FRANCE, SCOTLAND & WALES

26 AUGUST
PLAYING AT THE WORLD CUP FULFILS A LIFELONG AMBITION
Matt Stevens

I may be one of the youngest in the England World Cup squad but I am five years older than the Rugby World Cup. Given the importance of the event, it often surprises me that this competition is of such recent birth. On the brink of my twenty-fifth birthday, the RWC is celebrating its twentieth birthday. I feel we have sort of grown up together, and I, for the first time, have been invited to the party. It is a nearly lifelong dream come true.

I can't honestly claim to remember the first World Cup when New Zealand won in 1987. Yet I suppose rugby was part of the air I breathed in South Africa. My father was an avid supporter of our provincial team, now the Sharks. The stadium where the Sharks played is famous for its family atmosphere, and rugby matches were day-long events which started with picnics in the surrounding fields and car parks and stretched into evening 'braais', spontaneous mini-matches among parents and children, and the inevitable impassioned analysis of supporter experts over beers and boerewors.

During the summer holidays I often stayed with my grandparents in the Cape. Our neighbours were the ex-Springbok captain, Morne du Plessis, and his wife and children. I was unaware then of Morne's god-like status in the rugby pantheon, but he was a hero to all the neighbouring children because he gathered us together for beach trips and games in the park.

Even if Morne had not later been revealed to me as one of the great players and leaders in rugby, his gentleness and enthusiasm provided an extraordinary role model for a young child. In later years I have valued his advice concerning my career and his insight and leadership when he has intervened in the thorny and complex politics of rugby transformation in South Africa.

By the time of the second World Cup, I was on the brink of playing junior provincial rugby, glued to the television broadcasts of the RWC, and increasingly aware, because of South Africa's exclusion, of the entanglement of sport and politics. I watched my first live World Cup game in Durban, at the stadium where I played in the car park as a young boy – Kings Park, as it was known in 1995. It was the semi-final, possibly more famous for the fact that it was nearly called off because the pitch was flooded than for the highly contested game between France and South Africa.

I gather you didn't have to be a South African to appreciate the symbolic enormity of South Africa's winning of the 1995 World Cup and signifying, through Mandela's goodwill, both a potential for national unity and reconciliation and a triumphant re-entry into international sport. But, as they say, you had to be there. Not necessarily at the stadium itself, but in

South Africa, where it seemed as though the whole country spilled on to the streets in dizzy hope and celebration. It is hard to question the cathartic joy of that 1995 South African moment, or the other that I have witnessed at close quarters, England's triumph in 2003, which brought hundreds of thousands, unprecedented in an English rugby celebration, on to the streets of London. I think there are gradations of sports supporters from the *aficionados* who support everything from school and junior club teams to regional clubs and international sport, to those who will only watch seasonal finals and international Tests, to those who will only watch rugby if it is the World Cup.

Whether one approves or not, size does count and so does patriotism. The World Cup certainly gives rugby exposure to new or flagging audiences and it has proved its ability to bring magic and unity, however briefly they may last, to countries. I found many of the heroes of my youth watching previous World Cups. Now I will have the honour of playing with and against some of them. I have already been quite outspoken about how highly I rate the chances of England's squad, and I presume some people will dismiss my opinions as youthful and subjective even more readily than they did the upbeat predictions of Will Carling. Yet I take comfort from the fact that none of those people have been training with me or the England squad for the past two months. I think they forget that we are one of only two teams fielding players who have won a World Cup already. I think they forget the intangibles that come into play simply because it is the World Cup and we are defending the title.

When I think of the World Cup, I feel the same excitement I did when I was ten years old. That ten-year-old believes with all his heart he'll be putting on that World Cup final jersey and scoring that all-important winning try. Of course, I'm a professional and know that each game is an important stepping stone out of the pool stages and later into the quarters and semis. But what must underscore any player's clinical approach is raw, unbridled passion. I have seen that in the England squad and so, apart perhaps from actually scoring the winning try, I must agree with the ten-year-old in me.

2 SEPTEMBER
ALL BLACKS LOOK A SURE THING, SO WHAT CAN GO WRONG THIS TIME?
David Kirk

Believe it or not, sometimes it is tiresome to live in Australia. In particular when discussion of the Rugby World Cup comes around and some wag with preternatural insight notes that New Zealand have only won one Rugby World Cup and then proceeds to gag, gurgle and dribble with his hand around his throat, eventually wrestling himself free to general hilarity, I grow weary of the land of the bouncing kangaroo. Or at least Wallaby supporters.

The All Blacks are once again red-hot favourites to win the World Cup in 2007. It seems that the only thing that gives other nations and bookies comfort is history. New Zealand have indeed only won one Rugby World Cup. And that was the only tournament in which the All Blacks did not start as firm favourites. So, the logic goes, just because they are the best team doesn't mean they will win. Look what happened in London, Johannesburg, Cardiff and Sydney. Bummed out, choked, didn't perform when it really mattered. The same will happen this time.

If history is to be our guide we should start by absorbing the benefits of hindsight. The All Blacks may have gone into the World Cups of 1991, 1995, 1999 and 2003 as favourites but they shouldn't have. In 1991 the team was clearly ageing and struggling for form. The Wallabies had rebuilt after the Jones era and the 1987 disappointments. A young, hungry team on the way up should have been identified as the team to beat. The 1995 All Black team was a genuinely great team that should have won. They ran into an extraordinary set of circumstances with a gastric illness the night before the final and a Springbok team surfing a wave of national rebirth that carried them through. The 1999 team was talented but lacked crucial leadership and composure. The Wallabies were better going into the tournament and certainly once it unfolded. In 2003 England were top of the world rankings, had beaten the All Blacks in New Zealand that very year and should have been favourites.

In 2007 results support All Black favouritism. The Tri-Nations trophy and the Bledisloe Cup are both safe and sound in Wellington, and regular victories over France, every United Kingdom nation separately and the British and Irish Lions all confirm the number one world ranking. The 2007 All Black team has depth, leadership, strong set-pieces, the best fly-half in the world and great try-scoring power out wide. There is little doubt they should win and we all know it. But what could stop them?

Let's run through a few options. How about the weather? It used to be that some teams played much better on dry grounds than wet ones and vice versa. Big, slow forward packs and strong-kicking fly-halves ground out victories in the pouring rain that they could never have achieved in sunshine. The weather will not determine the winner of the 2007 Rugby World Cup. Changes in the laws and the professionalisation of the game have homogenised player shape, size and playing styles. Everyone plays more or less the same way these days. The team who does it better wins, not the team who does it differently.

How about injuries? Any team who suffers a run of injuries to their top players will be materially affected, but the All Blacks are surely less exposed to this than any other team. Australia are particularly vulnerable. If any one or more of Gregan, Larkham, Mortlock, Vickerman or a prop gets injured, Australia will be doomed. South Africa have only a few world-class players and limited depth, likewise the UK nations. France have rotated and developed their players so much that we more or less have no idea who is in their top team, so who knows if injuries will hurt them? The All Blacks have three of the best five props in the world, three of the best six second-rowers and adequate replacements everywhere else. Perhaps they are most exposed at fly-half, in the loose-forwards and at centre, but it would take an extraordinary run of injuries to seriously affect the overall performance.

What about playing away from home? Many countries have poor records in that respect. Unfortunately for the rest of the world, New Zealand are not one of them. Their performance away is second to none in world rugby. The home advantage will, however, play an important role. France traditionally do not travel particularly well. At home, however, the Tricolours inhale the passion of a full stadium and transmute it into a raw, physical intensity that is truly frightening and very often effective. To win the World Cup, the All Blacks will have to beat the French nation as well as the French rugby team.

Two possible causes of an All Black failure remain: referees and self-doubt. Referees will play an unhealthily prominent role in the World Cup. The two problem areas will be the tackle, degenerating as it does into rucks, mauls, pile-ups, scrags, wrestles and every other indescribable tangle of legs, arms and penalty opportunities. My view is that at most breakdowns, both teams could be penalised for any one of about four different infringements. It's a lottery and different referees draw different names out of the hat at different times. The other key area is the scrum. Referees nowadays seem loath to referee the scrum in favour of the stronger team, believing, it seems, that the scrum should serve as an efficient way to restart the game, rather than as an advantage to be exploited by the better team. Referees often effectively de-power the scrum by penalising the stronger scrum when the weaker one collapses or disrupts to avoid a pummelling. All teams will need to adapt to referee interpretations as matches unfold. A failure to read a referee and adjust will mean penalties, field position and – in a tight match – could be the difference between winning and losing. The All Blacks will be refereed more tightly than any other team, just because they are the All Blacks.

Finally, self-doubt. How could a team with such talent and confidence engendered by years of dominance have self-doubt, you may ask? It is not as simple as that. Confidence, mental toughness and self-belief are intellectual and emotional constructs. On the one hand, individuals and teams need to have a strong belief in their superiority. A knowledge that they are, on paper, faster, stronger, better. The task then becomes to do what you are capable of doing on the field. If things are not going right, keep believing in the facts of faster, stronger, better and keep doing it. Time is on your side. The opposition, who may be playing above themselves, will eventually falter, the laws of physics will kick in. Don't panic. It will happen. But self-belief is also emotional. In the face of overwhelming odds – two minutes to go, two points down, at the wrong end of the field – teams with the self-belief necessary to win a World Cup genuinely believe they will. All they need is the ball and a plan. I don't know if the 2007 All Blacks have what it takes in rational and irrational self-belief. I sure hope they do because if they don't, the next Wallaby supporter that fakes choking to me is going to find my hands around his neck helping him to get the job done properly.

8 SEPTEMBER
FRANCE ARE SHAKEN TO THE CORE
Brendan Gallagher

Argentina – gloriously, deservedly and courageously – sent France's Rugby World Cup into turmoil with a sensational 17–12 win over the hosts in the opening game at the Stade de France. The team that nobody in world rugby will embrace did their talking on the pitch with the best and most complete performance in their history, producing one of the biggest upsets of the World Cup. They dominated the contact area, defended with discipline, attacked with flair whenever possible and but for a couple of scruffy dropped-goal attempts and two missed penalties by Felipe Contepomi, would have won by more.

Juan Martín Hernández, as had been suspected, brought opportunism and an unpredictability to the Pumas' game, sending France scurrying in all directions in a pulsating first half. The gifted Argentine often does not know what he is going to do next, so new is he to the fly-half position, but he is a world-class footballer with a dazzling future. With the more direct and experienced Contepomi on his shoulder and the ageless scrum-half Agustin Pichot at his impish best, Argentina were firing from the start. They were, too, defending like a team with decades of resentment at being excluded from competitions involving the senior nations to work out of their system.

Contepomi and David Skrela swapped early penalties before Argentina – mixing Garryowens and cross-field kicks with fluid handling – pressed on with another two from the Leinster man. The French crowd remained loyal, but their patience was tested in the twenty-seventh minute when Ignacio Corleto raced forty yards for an invaluable interception try after alert work by specialist poacher Contepomi. France hit back through Skrela but failed to dominate up front, and as half-time approached, after as good an opening forty minutes as the World Cup has seen, Contepomi and Skrela swapped penalties to leave France still eight points adrift.

Bernard Laporte's side began strongly after the break but again Argentina held firm – defending heroically in one prolonged passage as France looked to barge their way over. Discipline, all the time discipline. This was an Argentina we have not seen before. Skrela did peg back one final penalty as the tension grew – there has never been such a crucial game so early in a World Cup – and France showed their attacking intent by producing their two jokers in the pack, Freddie Michalak and Sebastien Chabal, mercurial but considerable talents both. Hernández kept testing Cédric Haymans but his kicks began to lose accuracy and France's experimental full-back regained his composure. It was from such an ill-directed high ball that France counter-attacked and Corleto was penalised for not releasing. But Michalak fluffed his kick horribly.

Both sides were at a standstill now, a legacy of that extraordinarily draining first half, and you could see the mental process slowing almost to a halt as they headed for the final whistle. Contepomi could have sewn the game up with a final penalty but, frankly, who cared? Victory was theirs. 'It was a marvellous match; it was tough. The French came at us head-on. We are overcome with happiness, but we shouldn't get above ourselves because it is only the first match,' Argentine coach Marcelo Loffreda said with splendid restraint. Loffreda was right, of course, but this win was truly significant. It was the night Argentina finally joined rugby's top table, even if they had to gatecrash the party.

10 SEPTEMBER
ENGLAND ROAR LIKE KITTENS
Martin Johnson

It's a long old tournament – six weeks of thumping commitment – and the huge demands on stamina and fitness would make it remarkable if the players got through it without at times feeling weary, jaded, and physically and emotionally drained. But not before it has even started, surely? We'd been hearing for a week, from various pundits and the England camp itself, that the players had had quite enough of all the talking, and couldn't wait to actually get out there and play. Well, they're still waiting, and so is everyone else. Release the English lion from its cage and listen for the roar? You must be joking. What we actually got was the kind of pitiful mewing you'd expect to hear from a kitten stuck up a tree.

The United States are a powerful sporting nation, but not

in rugby union. The sport there has a mostly amateur player base of 80,000, of which nearly forty per cent is female. They've heard of the World Series all right, but not the World Cup, and if you asked most Americans what they thought of a maul, they'd say it was a great place to do their shopping on a Saturday afternoon. But you'd have been hard pressed here to identify which team was the highly drilled, sophisticated, professional outfit, and which one was on expenses of fifty quid a day. The United States had nothing to offer but hard work and a blood-and-guts defence. Yet, their expected second-half capitulation was actually a 7–7 draw, and two of England's three tries in the 28–10 win came when an expulsion to the sin-bin had left the opposition with only fourteen men.

ITV clearly feel it is nothing less than their patriotic duty to open every World Cup programme with a clip of Jonny Wilkinson's World Cup-winning dropped goal, but much more of this and it would be more appropriate to replace it with the swinging right boot of the England coach being delivered, with some feeling, to some well-deserving backsides. Saint Jonny is, of course, confined to a spectators' role at the moment, so injury prone he could rupture a tendon taking the top off a boiled egg. But anyone still harbouring the belief that his return alone will transform England into another team of world-beaters clearly resides with the pixies.

Wilkinson, whose prowess as a kicker of penalty goals has somehow persuaded some people that he's actually a mixture of Barry John and Phil Bennett, could perhaps make a small difference, but only in the way that a stick of chewing gum would have helped plug the hole in the Titanic. In fact, if England really want to be less creative than they were here, the best thing they could do is to get Wilkinson fit enough to replace Olly Barkley at No. 10. The one area in which England tug the forelock to no one in this World Cup is in the art of looking backwards to the last one. 'If only we had Wilko' has been a constant lament, and now they have decided that Lawrence Dallaglio is the same dynamic player he was in 2003. Dallaglio was, as ever, oozing with passion. His eyes bulged, and he constantly thumped himself in the chest, but it's during the game that England need all this – not while he's singing the National Anthem.

Dallaglio finished the match in the sin-bin, which is where his captain might have been earlier had the referee not missed a scything hack by Phil Vickery that brought to mind World Cup glory only in the sense that it was right out of the Nobby Stiles manual. Before the game, England's captain said: 'We're desperate to show people what we can do in a game.' Well, they did, and he was spot on. Desperate is precisely what it was. All the talk has been whether England can beat South Africa in their second pool match, and thus progress to a quarter-final against one of the lesser teams, rather than Australia. Ye gods, on this form they'll be lucky to beat Samoa, and you wouldn't be entirely confident of them seeing off Tonga either.

However, amid all the gloom, it is perhaps as well to focus now on what professional sportsmen are fond of calling 'taking the positives out of the game'. In which case, given that the bookmakers rated England's chances of retaining their World Cup at 33–1 before the tournament, you certainly can't accuse them of failing to live up to expectations.

LAMENTABLE ENGLAND'S TITLE DEFENCE LIES IN TATTERS
Mick Cleary

England's world champions crown lay rusted and battered in the Stade de France gutter after a performance that mocked their status as defenders of the title. At 36–0, this was their worst World Cup defeat and the first time they had failed to score a point since 1998. No pace, no threat and no hope. It was a humiliating experience for those on the field and a deadening one for the thousands of England fans who had made the trip. The chariot is destined for the knacker's yard. It is the low road now for England towards the knockout stages, a route fraught with danger and obstacle, while South Africa stride out on the high road with glory in their sights.

After winning the toss and the anthems, England promptly lost their way. They infringed at two of the first three line-outs and made a complete pig's ear of defending the narrow side in the fifth minute. South Africa won the line-out, nudged it forward, but in a thrice had switched play to J.P. Pietersen. A quick shimmy and he was away. Fourie du Preez gave great support, stumbled when tap-tackled by Robinson but had enough savvy to bide his time and throw the try-scoring pass on one knee to flanker Juan Smith.

It was a devastating blow for England. They needed stability and reassurance; instead, it was the same old nightmare – chasing shadows, making mistakes, looking edgy. Mike Catt missed a drop goal, put a ball out on the full and then missed touch from a penalty. Profligate. In between, Francois Steyn had banged over a penalty from forty metres. That was 10–0 within ten minutes. The Boks were in the groove, while England were in a muddle.

Midway through the first half they managed to shred the Springbok scrummage – no mean feat – winning a ball against the head. What did they do with it? Scrum-half Shaun Perry drilled the ball straight out. There was little spark or initiative or quality in England's play, excepting the occasional trademark zig-zagging run from the rear by Robinson. He alone looked likely to cause problems. He alone in those early stages threatened to take the game to South Africa. Good sides make the opposition think; England failed to. South Africa were alert to everything. Du Preez was quick to see the possibilities when the Boks were awarded a penalty in the twenty-first minute. He walloped the ball downfield, England were caught napping, Jaque Fourie swooped on to the ball and was only lassoed by Josh Lewsey at the death, losing control as he reached to touch down. A close call.

England knew that they had to come off the ropes if they were not to suffer an early knockout. Any opponent can sense weakness – a Springbok can sniff it from a hundred paces. South Africa hit hard and early. They ought to have had more faith in their own ability and less concern about England. Instead they fluffed three dropped goal attempts. They had the pace and wit to trouble England, that much was evident. And that much was brought to bear just before half-time. England were turned over in contact, the ball bobbled loose, Andy Farrell took a swipe with his boot. Too late. Du Preez had latched on to it, swivelled away, made huge yardage in a flash and put in a perfect try-scoring pass to Pietersen.

South Africa were 20–0 ahead at half-time. It was a fair reflection of the disparity between the sides. There was already a forlorn end-of-empire feel about England, from the sight of Lawrence Dallaglio, surplus to requirements, putting in extra training prior to kick-off to the tumultuous cheers which greeted big-screen footage of Wilkinson potting that goal. That was then and this was now. South Africa were a different class. The second half was all too predictable, Montgomery landing three penalties and Pietersen skipping over after yet another devastating break from Du Preez. Easy pickings.

17 SEPTEMBER

BRILLIANT GEORGIA PUSH IRELAND TO BRINK
Brendan Gallagher

This was an extraordinary, gut-wrenching and logic-defying game that left two rugby nations on the very brink. As a gladiatorial spectacle it probably won't be bettered in France this World Cup, and the Bordeaux crowd were beside themselves with nerves and excitement. It was a game that took Ireland to the precipice of World Cup elimination before their campaign proper had even started and before some fans had even left the Emerald Isle. It was the occasion and contest in which Georgia announced themselves emphatically to the rugby world.

An apparently routine game in Bordeaux developed into one of the great World Cup epics and, for long periods of the second half, one of the greatest upsets in sport, let alone rugby, was on the cards. As the estimated 15,000 Ireland fans present will testify, the best team on the night lost, narrowly, by 14–10. *C'est la vie*, but let's not allow history to be rewritten in the years to come. Ireland were second best and scraped home by the skin of their teeth, by virtue only of their calm and well-organised defence, the one part of their game in full working order.

The Georgians had done marvellously well in Lyon in midweek to fully extend the predatory, in-form Pumas, but this was infinitely better and eye-opening – a Herculean effort but also a very clever and well-planned performance from their second XV against a team ranked sixth in the world. Georgia deserved to win for their courage and physicality alone, and spent most of the final quarter hammering away at the Ireland line, almost a metaphor for the way in which they have struggled manfully to get the rugby world at large to cave in and recognise their love for the game, and need for assistance.

To put it in perspective, with nearly eight hundred caps Ireland were the most experienced side to take the field in a Test, and ran on after the mother of all wake-up calls against Namibia. Ireland were pumped up and determined to justify their coach's faith in them. Instead they spent most of the night firmly planted on the back foot as Georgia's magnificent warriors up front tore into them. The classy Merab Kvirikashvili at fly-half manoeuvred his troops around the pitch, though he did eventually overdo the dropped goal attempts. He struck four, none of them bad misses, but with seventy per cent possession in the second half Georgia should have stayed patient. Easier said than done in this car crash of a game.

Ultimately Ireland scraped home with tries by hooker Rory Best and full-back Girvan Dempsey – the latter a well-worked effort of rare quality possession – while Georgia had to be content with an interception try from Giorgi Shkinin and a penalty and conversion from Kvirikashvili. 'It's not mission impossible to qualify but it's looking a hard job,' admitted Ireland's coach Eddie O'Sullivan. While Ireland ponder,

Georgia's captain Ilia Zedginidze must be granted the final word: 'It was inspiring. Obviously this score could allow Georgia much more opportunity and propel us forward. As a national team we are not that confident. When we talked about Argentina we had much more confidence. In future matches we can show more ambition. We were tense against Ireland, but the day will come when we are more relaxed. I'm looking forward to this day.'

30 SEPTEMBER
NOBODY STOOD UP
WHEN IT MATTERED
Ieuan Evans

One of the darkest days in Welsh rugby history. It was that bad and that depressing. Having been on the receiving end myself as Wales captain when we lost to another Pacific Island, Western Samoa in the 1991 World Cup, I know exactly how they will be feeling after losing 38–34 to Fiji, and how much captain Gareth Thomas, on a day that should have been a celebration of his one hundredth cap, will be hurting. I am crestfallen. You look at the quality of players we have and the huge amount of experience, especially in the back line, and you wonder how on earth we can be so devoid of leadership, composure and clarity of thought and deed.

It has been a really bad World Cup for Wales, who have only performed in patches. There was a purple patch at the start of the second half here, when they fought back admirably. They had the momentum, but still they could not exert control, despite having massive dominance at the set-piece and particularly the scrum. It was almost as if they were over-excited by their try-scoring in the second half. Having hauled themselves back and ahead, that was the time for someone to say, 'Right, let's not go looking for trouble. Do not give them chances because Fiji know how to hurt you.' What happened? Wales gave Fiji more chances and they took them, gratefully. Why did Wales not take the game by the scruff of the neck with calm authority and composed decision-making? The car was running down the hill, but nobody was at the wheel. Do not stop playing if on a roll, but play at the right time and take the appropriate decisions. Know when to offload, when to pass, when to kick.

Well done, Fiji. Seru Rabeni and Vilimoni Delasau were magnificent. But Fiji are not that great a side, so sadly it is not about praising Fiji, but burying Wales, for they were that poor.

The damage was done in that lamentable first half, where Wales were amateur in everything they did. They lost composure, shape and the plot. In the opening minutes they blew several chances, with both Tom Shanklin and Stephen Jones ignoring overlaps. Back in Suva they would have prayed for this sort of game, for it played right into Fiji's hands. The one thing you do not do against South Sea Islanders is play it loose and fail to dominate, with no pattern in attack and passivity in defence. Wales were standing off Fiji and that allowed hugely powerful and quick runners like Rabeni and Delasau to wreak havoc crossing the gain-line, and they duly did.

Wales quite simply panicked. You have to work as a team, as a collective, and take the steam out of a side like Fiji. Far too often Wales were isolated, going it alone, peeling off rucks and running straight across the field, and were predictably hit very hard by some of the most physical tacklers in the game. Meat and drink to the Islanders. Individuals were trying to do too much, rather than working together to sap the energy of Fiji and see them off. Wales were knocked back in the tackle and turned over. The number of turnovers was shocking. It was carnage out there at times despite Welsh dominance at the scrum. The decision-making was awful, hanging on to the ball too long, or not picking the right pass. Once again our kicking game was woeful, with sliced kicks and no yardage. Fiji like nothing better than open spaces and putting big, fast men into the holes. Haven't Wales seen Fiji playing Sevens, for goodness sake?

Let Shane Williams show his individualism and do his own thing because that is what he is there for, but elsewhere you need method. When Wales won the Grand Slam last, back in 2005, they played a free-flowing game, but they had runners and support in numbers. Wales should have played the territory and run the game in Fiji's twenty-two. With control and patience will come points. Conceding twenty-five points in nine minutes, Wales were chasing and fretting. Where was the leadership? Who was in charge? Passes have to take the opposition out, especially if they tackle like Fiji. You know the Islanders will commit and indeed over-commit to the tackle and come flying in. You have to attack the inside shoulder and take the man out with the pass.

At the start of the second half Wales certainly took advantage of the extra man with flanker Akapusi Qera in the sin-bin. I think lock Kele Leawere should have joined him for a late tackle on Alix Popham. Wales started to make Fiji turn, putting ball behind them and forcing them back with kicks. Wales were finally exerting a bit of control. Shane Williams's brilliant try was the spark that was needed, but Wales were being far more accurate and clinical in everything they did, with passes well directed and options well taken, picking off the defenders and holding their depth. But then no sooner had they regained the lead and the initiative than they lost it and the plot again. Coach Gareth Jenkins will be judged on the World Cup and is big enough to take the criticism, but it is the attitude of the players that concerns me most. Wales had the very ingredient that should have won the game, experience, and nobody stood up. That defeat to Western Samoa was one of the worst experiences of my life. Another dark day in Welsh rugby and once again the blow was delivered from the South Pacific.

7 OCTOBER
THE NIGHT OUR GODS BECAME MERE MORTALS
David Kirk

The All Blacks didn't play badly, but they didn't play well enough. For long periods of this quarter-final they played better rugby than any other team in the competition is remotely possible of playing. Their ball retention, their pace and audacity was often a joy. That they couldn't turn this into points and a comfortable victory was a testament to the sustained intensity of the French defence and their own inability to stop trying to create the perfect form of rugby and just win the match.

It is unbelievably frustrating to sit here and review this defeat, 20–18. If you look at the All Black scrum it was clearly superior to the French scrum. The line-out functioned well and the continuity play was excellent. Byron Kelleher played as well as I have seen him play. Dan Carter in the first half was all class, making the right decisions, kicking well, firing out his flat passes, putting Luke McAlister into the gap for his try. Jerry Collins, Richie McCaw and Rodney So'oialo clearly outplayed their opposite numbers, and while they had few real opportunities the outside backs did all that was asked of them. No one played badly. If no one plays badly in a great All Black team they should win. But they didn't. The glory of sport. The despair of not knowing what more you could have done.

It is not fair to quibble about selections after a match like this. Who knows what other players would have done in the same circumstances? It is to my mind true to say, however, that the rotation policy has not worked the way the coaches and selectors would have liked. For all the endless hours of training and honing of different combinations so they work on the field, some combinations simply work better than others. Some players simply gel in a way that means the pass sticks or the gap is found or the right decision is made. With the margin of error so fine at World Cups it is the team management's responsibility to find those combinations and stick with them. I am old-fashioned, I know, and really a long way from the intensity and nuances of professional rugby, but I think playing the best team regularly is important. It is possible to have too much talent.

France certainly played well. They brought a simple game plan to Cardiff and a lot of heart. They picked a full-back who could kick the ball back and a forward pack who would compete everywhere. They were particularly effective on their feet driving line-outs and mauls and in stifling the All Black midfield. Perhaps most impressive of all was their lack of mistakes. They were under the hammer time and time again in the second half and they held their nerve. No penalties, no cheap points.

It is a shame that the match turned on refereeing decisions. Wayne Barnes's decision to show McAlister a yellow card and his missing of the clear forward pass which led to France's final try determined the outcome of the match. The players deserve better than to have refereeing decisions determine the outcome of matches. But the All Blacks always knew they would be refereed more closely than other teams at the World Cup. It comes from setting the pace. If you are doing things faster and better than other teams, referees will always be looking to see if there is some judgement they can make on this seemingly superior ability.

Did the All Blacks adapt effectively? Could they have done more? The answer is yes, but there is no one area of the game, no easy, obvious lack of quality or technique to put our finger on. The failure is in a collective lack of capacity to kill a match stone dead when ahead. We may well ask is this a failure? Is it a failure to want to embrace a style that is nerveless and an aspiration that is beyond what has gone before? The answer is no for gods and yes for men. Unfortunately in Cardiff our gods became men.

8 OCTOBER
ENGLAND'S TURNAROUND A TRIUMPH FOR CLEAR MINDS
Mick Cleary

As the klaxons and horns blared across an exultant Marseille night, Jonny Wilkinson managed to walk through the throng unnoticed and unmolested. It won't last. The whole of France will be paying attention to him from here on. To him, and to those heavy-duty England forwards who mushed Australia 12–10. The French need no telling of the threat posed by Wilkinson and his pack. They know it, and they have dealt with it.

Even so, England's dominance in the quarter-final at the Stade Velodrome was such that France will be forced to spend many hours laying flesh bare on the scrummaging machine if they are to counter the blasting power of Andrew Sheridan and his white-shirted chums. In 2005 at Twickenham Sheridan did a one-man demolition job on Australia. Here he had seven mates in concert with him. If anything, this was even more commendable. Simon Shaw had his best game in an England shirt while Lewis Moody injected the necessary cur-like venom at the breakdown. Australia were turned over nine times, a startling ledger of loss. Australia had improved on their scrummaging yet still England took them apart. The Wallaby problems began at the tight scrum and ended in various parts of the field. The fault-lines exposed up front were exploited all over the pitch.

Australia were 'flustered', in the words of departing coach John Connolly. In all phases, England rattled Australia: with their ferocity at the breakdown, with the sturdiness and accuracy of their set-pieces and with the breadth and imagination of their attacking game. They challenged themselves to deliver and, by so doing, tested Australia at every turn. There were errors and mishaps, but the transformation was astounding. England's real point of failure was in their finishing. At least three try-scoring chances were wasted. Wilkinson, too, will not be wholly satisfied with four successes from seven attempts. He still struggles with the World Cup ball. That apart, England were classy and assured.

Where did it come from, this voraciousness, this cohesion, this all-round excellence? Rebuked from without, England had also been severe on themselves. 'There was a big buzz in the dressing room,' said Martin Corry. 'We were just not ready to go home. It wasn't just that we owed fans and others a performance, we also owed ourselves a performance. We'd put so much into the preparation that we couldn't face leaving with a splutter. All that adversity, too, all that knocking, brings you together.'

Even so, the about-turn is remarkable. England insist that they did no more than tinker with their blueprint in the wake of the 36–0 defeat against South Africa. There is no doubt that there is more clarity to their play, and here there was more balance. They duffed up Australia and also took it wide. It was a potent combination. Wilkinson and Catt dovetailed well, spraying passes or dinking kicks. Their minds appear less cluttered, their spirits less worn down. Perhaps that drubbing did them some good. 'I'm sure it did have a part to play,' said Rob Andrew, the Rugby Football Union's elite rugby director. 'It was an appalling performance and an appalling result. It demanded a reaction.'

If there was one single moment that encapsulated the rage within England, and the listless complacency within Wallaby ranks, it was in the twenty-fifth minute when Chris Latham fielded a routine clearance kick from Peter Richards, briefly on the field as a blood replacement. Latham took the ball and was instantly swamped by Mike Catt and Paul Sackey. Within seconds a phalanx of white shirts was steaming into the ruck. Turnover to England, shame and anxiety for Australia. 'We were determined to put bodies on the line and really give it a go,' said Catt. 'No one expected us to get here. This group of guys is really close and we all turned up today.'

For all their dominance, England could not shake off Australia on the scoreboard. Half-chances went begging, a bombed pass to Catt here, an infuriatingly elusive kick through for Sackey there. They also had to contend with unsympathetic refereeing in the early stage. Two penalties went against England at the scrum, even though they had the measure of their opposite numbers. Technically Alain Rolland might have been right: morally, he was wrong. Wilkinson fluffed a couple of kicks towards the end of the first half, having passed Gavin Hastings's all-time record of 227 points with his second penalty. Stirling Mortlock, though, was also misfiring, notably with his final effort from long-range.

That was a heart-stopping moment for the entire England camp, from coaches through to the thousands of followers up in the stands. But England's resolve and shrewdness rightly carried the day. They had given their all, they had not panicked when Lote Tuqiri bagged his first (and last) try of the tournament in the thirty-third minute, and they had come back at Australia with some trickery of their own. Has there ever been a like occasion when an English national team in any sport have hauled themselves off the canvas to such stunning effect? Truly, a knockout.

12 OCTOBER
LETTERS TO THE SPORTS EDITOR
WHERE AUSSIES RULE

SIR – There seems to be some impression Up Above that all, or, at least, most of us Down Under are crying ourselves rivers enough to end the drought over the loss of an international rugby match somewhere in France. Truth is that most of us couldn't give a pile of macropod droppings about our fat toffs playing your fat toffs or anyone else's fat toffs. Rugby is a minority sport played in wealthy private schools and their alumni in some professions in two state capitals, with the other sort of rugby-for-dummies being much more prevalent in those areas.

The majority of us prefer Australian (Rules) Football, the game of our own, a three-dimensional, free-flowing, multi-skilled sport with a much more varied scope for spectacular athleticism, and about to celebrate its sesqui-centenary in 2008. Australian Football League crowd figures bear this out, with the AFL average nearing 40,000 per game, about twice the figure for other sports here, and behind only those for the American NFL and Bundesliga soccer. So, no, we're not at all broken-hearted.

Leonard Colquhoun
Tasmania

8 OCTOBER
SCOTS DENIED AS ARGENTINA MARCH ON
Brendan Gallagher

Argentina, suffering from a bad bout of stage fright as the tantalising sight of a World Cup semi-final appeared on the horizon, hung on grimly to claim what was justly theirs against a Scotland side who finally roused themselves in the final quarter and hinted at what might have been. So the Pumas' extraordinary World Cup odyssey continues, despite this 19–13 win being comfortably their sloppiest performance of the campaign to date. Territorially in command for most of the evening, they grew more nervous as the game progressed and over-elaborated almost to the point of paralysis. In the end they needed a couple of magical interventions and huge touch-finders from Juan Martín Hernández – a long way short of his best but still influential – and the cool head of Gonzalo Longo at No. 8 to see them home and get the party started.

The full inquest, however, can wait. For now they can wake up and relish their achievement of reaching the semi-finals of the World Cup for the first time. 'We were very tired and Scotland played really well, so we just stuck with it,' Agustin Pichot, Argentina's captain, said. 'We are very pleased to be in the semi-finals but it hasn't sunk in yet.' For Scotland, this was about the limit for a hard-working and formidably fit team who alas lacked the X-factor to make them serious contenders for a final-four spot.

As well as the inevitable nerves on only their second World Cup quarter-final appearance, Argentina had to deal with the knowledge that back home a football-mad country had ground to a halt just to watch the rugby. The football authorities had even switched the biggest domestic game of the season – the Buenos Aires derby between River Plate and Boca Juniors – to an early start to clear the airwaves. It was the biggest day in Argentine rugby history by some distance.

No pressure then as Longo, making his fiftieth Test appearance for the Pumas, led the team out. Unsurprisingly there was a nervous start from both sides, though Hernández nearly started where he left off against Ireland, firing a forty-yard dropped goal attempt narrowly wide. Though restricted by a thigh injury, Hernández put up a few trademark bombs which encouraged the French crowd to side with Scotland, and the game got going. Felipe Contepomi pulled an early penalty attempt wide and moments later Dan Parks made the Pumas suffer by finding the target from fully fifty yards. First blood to Scotland.

Argentina, though, finally started to get in the groove and work through the phases, taking 'ownership' of the ball as they cranked up the pressure. Scotland, though tackling well, began to leak a few penalties and this time Contepomi was on target. First he thumped the ball home from forty-six yards, and then was on target from an acute angle when Scotland were penalised for not releasing. The Pumas were building up a head of steam but they also needed a stroke of luck for their next score after Longo charged down a clearance kick from Parks. There was still plenty to do for the Pumas' No. 8 with two Scotland defenders in close attendance, but Longo still managed to win the race to touch down.

Though Contepomi added another simple penalty after the break, the Pumas became curiously error-prone, spilling simple balls and conceding silly turnovers from what appeared to be solid possession. The nerves were jangling – so close to a World Cup semi-final yet still so much to do. It was predictably Hernández who got them back on track again with a terrific long touch-finder and then, as the pressure built, a sharply taken dropped goal. As the hour approached Scotland went for a final throw of the dice, bringing on Craig Smith, Scott MacLeod, Kelly Brown and Chris Cusiter. Scotland needed to score next, which they did courtesy of Chris Paterson's sixteenth consecutive successful penalty kick in this tournament, after Rodrigo Roncero had needlessly strayed offside at a ruck. Then, in the sixty-third minute, they finally hit the turbo and in a frenzied and sustained attack forced Cusiter over in the corner. Naturally Paterson converted to set up a thrilling, if chaotic, finish. Argentina held on, however, and next they will hope to show all those football fans back home what the oval-ball game is really about.

13 OCTOBER

STILL A WORK IN PROGRESS BUT PUMAS' RISE IS NO SURPRISE
Hugo Porta

The success of the Argentina team during the Rugby World Cup is not something that has come about by chance. Argentina have a group of players who are at the very top level in the sport. In fact, this band of brothers have shown that they have the ability to play as an extra participant in either the Six Nations or the Tri-Nations. I also have no doubt that this is what the International Rugby Board would want. But perhaps that is not what Argentine rugby wants – rugby is still a work in progress at home.

But this squad are armed with the physical and technical skills to take on the best nations and beat them. The players still start as amateurs, and are coached by amateurs, but if they are good enough, they can move to the two best professional leagues in the world – in England and France. Ally that with a coach, Marcelo Loffreda, who has been in place for eight years, choosing his players as they mature – with two months' preparation in Pensacola in the United States prior to the tournament – and we can see why we have what it takes to cause disarray against the so-called 'bigger' nations. Perhaps Loffreda going to Leicester is another sign that we are on the up. The fact that we don't lose out physically any more, man for man, in any tackle or set-piece situation, means we have a chance against any team in the world.

Winning the opening game of the Rugby World Cup against France opened the horizons of possibility for the entire squad. We now have better odds of winning than England do, which is just incredible. What has happened in Argentina during the tournament is outstanding. These players have captured the imagination of the nation because they come from an amateur sport. We have only 360 rugby clubs in Argentina, but they are often heavily involved with work in deprived communities, and the spirit and valour which the game espouses is getting wide exposure.

Now, when the Pumas go on to the pitch, it is more than just fifteen players, because the weight of the nation pushes behind the team. Argentina will grind to a halt when the Pumas take to the pitch against South Africa. We also have special players in the likes of Juan Martín Hernández, at No. 10, who could have been a footballer. The Argentine players must trust their mental strength; we are capable of beating anyone, and the fact that we have already travelled further in this tournament than any side in Argentine history is dangerous for the opposition. If we can match South Africa physically, and continue our defensive play, which has been as good as any other nation, we will have a chance of reaching the final, provided we ally that with our natural flair and intelligence on the field.

14 OCTOBER
WILKINSON KICKS ENGLAND INTO FINAL ON NIGHT OF THE TITANS
Paul Ackford

It was a game to tell your grandchildren about. A game so close and tense and taut that it almost went beyond enjoyment. One man turned it England's way. No prizes for guessing the name. Jonny Wilkinson kicked England into another World Cup final. Four years after he saw off France with his boot, here in a sensational match he kicked England into a second successive climax, 14–9. England were heroes to a man because for long periods of this match they had to defend and dig themselves out of their own territory. But this is a team with bags of character and when it mattered, when it really, really mattered, they forged towards the French line for Wilkinson to deliver two decisive knockout blows. This England story has now gone beyond fairytale and turned into the stuff of legend. Four weeks past they were nowhere, dishevelled, disorganised and helpless, yet now they can do what no country has done and hang on to the Webb Ellis trophy. Magnificent.

England got off to the most sensational of starts when a delightful chip by Andy Gomarsall forced Damien Traille into a howler. It was a classic case of a man caught out because he was unaccustomed to the position in which he was selected. Traille was slow to read the flight of the ball, slow to get to the bounce of it and slow to react when that bounce worked beautifully for England and popped up into the arms of Josh Lewsey. And there was another great opportunity for England when Mark Regan, of all people, charged down a lazy clearance kick from David Marty to force a five-metre scrum. England's front five started where they left off in the quarter-final and drove and drove and gradually began to roll France backwards, only for Nick Easter to lose control at the base of the scrum and for France to escape downfield.

The issue for England, after the first ten minutes, was those opening exchanges were by far their finest. Wilkinson went close with a long-range penalty and a speculative drop goal, but the rest of the first half was a sustained period of French territorial domination. It was a pretty mixed effort, to be honest, from France. There were passages of wonderful handling, with Yannick Jauzion the rock around which the attacks were built, and there were fine examples of tactical kicking from Lionel Beauxis. But in between, especially during the last ten minutes of the half, were passages when France looked lethargic and wasteful.

It didn't help that they lost Fabien Pelous midway through the half. Sebastien Chabal added his customary aggression, but Chabal is primarily a back-row forward and France missed Pelous's intensity and hard work. With Pelous on board and with the first-up tackling of Serge Betsen, France forced English errors at the line-out and elsewhere. A Martin Corry knock-on eventually set up a successful penalty chance from Beauxis, and another well-struck shot enabled France to go in 6–5 ahead at the interval.

That lead was extended when Beauxis added his third penalty after a very dubious refereeing decision by Jonathan Kaplan. Beauxis had made a fine break and was halted by Wilkinson when Easter was judged to have entered the ruck from the side. It did not appear that a ruck had formed and Easter was well within his rights to attack the ball as he did. England responded well. Mathew Tait, who had made a couple of half-breaks earlier in the match, was freed up wide on the right. Jauzion got back to tackle Tait but gave away the penalty in the process, and Wilkinson banged over the kick to bring England back to within a point of France.

The match then entered its decisive period. Freddie Michalak, the architect of victories over Ireland and New Zealand earlier in the tournament, replaced Beauxis. A clever kick from

Jean-Baptiste Élissalde set up an attacking scrum, and when that was defended well Élissalde hurled out a huge reverse pass which Cédric Heymans gathered to set up the position from which Michalak fired a horrible, floppy drop kick. It was that kind of match, a Test full of unforced errors and players unable or fearful of grasping the opportunity to turn the game. There were periods towards the end of the game when both sides kicked poorly, each intent on banging the ball as far away from their own twenty-two as possible.

Yet there was no escaping the tension which built in the most excruciating manner. Wilkinson tried a snap drop goal which banged against the left-hand post and back into play, and then Jason Robinson ran through four French would-be defenders before Jauzion nailed him with a last-ditch tackle. As the game lost its shape while players cascaded off the bench to replace spent or injured bodies, the spectacle became even more gladiatorial. Both sides knew that the next mistake could be the one to cost their country a place in the World Cup final. Even the spectators were cowed into silence for large chunks of the match as if an intervention of the wrong sort might break the concentration on the field. France commanded the territory but England tended to force the turnover when that pressure threatened to smash their World Cup dream to bits.

France went close again when Corry got heroically to Chabal after Julien Bonnaire palmed a hanging Jauzion kick to Vincent Clerc. Lawrence Dallaglio entered the game, yet always, always there was the single, solitary point separating the teams. Until seventy-three minutes and fifty-two seconds. That was the amount of time which had elapsed when Dimitri Szarzewski tackled Robinson high and Wilkinson coolly knocked over the penalty. And it was Wilkinson again who sent his country into the final when he smacked over a drop goal with his left foot. Four years earlier Wilkinson's right foot created history. Here it was his left which clinched the match. Remarkable man, remarkable game, remarkable tournament.

19 OCTOBER
LETTERS TO THE SPORTS EDITOR
FRIEND IN THE NORTH

SIR – I met a charming Frenchman called Patrick in Harry's Bar in Rue Danou and, with my friends, spent a long time discussing the merits of Northern and Southern Hemisphere rugby. Patrick was determined that what really mattered was not who won, but that whichever team won, they had to go on and lift the cup for the North. So I decided on a bet. 'England win and you can give me your French jersey [size doesn't matter in rugby, everyone wears extra large] and I will wear it at the final. France win and I will give you mine.' Back in Harry's at 11 p.m., Patrick and I duly celebrated. He gave me his shirt. Thank God we won – I had no other clothes. Will I be wearing a French shirt for the final? Yes, but under my English one. *Vive le Nord,* and *Allez les Blancs.*

Geoff Collyer
Farningham
Kent

15 OCTOBER
HABANA LEADS WAY FOR SOUTH AFRICA
Mick Cleary

It was not pretty, nor was it convincing, but South Africa are back in a World Cup final for the first time since they lifted the trophy on home soil in 1995. They had more thrust, a touch more opportunist class when and where it mattered, and will fear little about meeting England, whom they thumped in the pool stages. Self-belief will not be an issue for the Springboks, even though their game has become fractured and inconsistent. Their four tries in a 37–13 victory, three of them scored in the first half, came from turnovers. South Africa will need to raise their performance levels. Argentina's great adventure is over. They gave their all but lacked their customary devil and cohesion. They left behind stirring memories. More was the pity that they could not make more of an impression in their first semi-final.

Four weeks earlier, South Africa looked remorseless against England. Their pack was unremitting in all phases, while scrum-half Fourie du Preez ran the show behind with dazzling ease. And then it began to slide. The Springboks still won their games but with less and less assurance. They knew only too well that they were fortunate to get past Fiji in the quarter-finals. They needed an early break to settle nerves, and they got it when Du Preez intercepted Felipe Contepomi's pass and raced home from sixty-five metres in the eighth minute. It was a blow to Argentine hopes, for they had gone against the grain just before then, counter-attacking from the rear through strong-running full-back Ignacio Corleto who combined with his left wing, Horacio Agulla. They chanced their arm, and saw what happened. No wonder that they were reluctant to be yanked out of their cautious comfort zone. Pressure rugby brings dividends. Adventurous rugby brings risks and pitfalls. The Pumas, though, persisted.

It was to cost them dear. Their concentration levels were poor, their control visibly lacking. It was far from a classic performance by the Pumas, who seemed afflicted by stage fright. Millions of new converts were tuning in to watch back at home and they were fluffing their lines. It was all rather disappointing. Three turnovers, three tries to South Africa. It was a damning return. The game seemed as good as won by the time the teams went down the tunnel at half-time with the Springboks leading 24–6.

Argentina had actually pegged back South Africa to 7–6 around the half-hour mark with two penalty goals from Contepomi. It had been a scrappy, fitful opening. Then Bryan Habana's class came shining through. Schalk Burger, flirting with trouble every time he came clattering into the breakdown, managed to turn over Argentina. A long, two-man cut-out pass and the ball was on its way to Habana. A chip over Lucas Borges, a chase, a gather, and Habana was on his way, touching down for his seventh try of the tournament to draw level with Australia's Drew Mitchell as the World Cup's leading try-scorer. On the stroke of half-time it was the men who had led the charge for Argentina in France, half-backs Agustin Pichot and Juan Martín Hernández, who proved fallible. A dive pass from the base was fumbled at fly-half and South Africa devoured the loose ball, Francois Steyn feeding his partner, Jaque Fourie. Burger lent support to send back-row colleague Danie Rossouw over the try-line.

Much has been made of Argentina's capacity for playing with their heart, for their sense of brotherhood and generosity to one another. All those elements are part of their game. But they have also been playing with the head. They are a clever side as well as a passionate one. Normally they are shrewd and opportunistic, as well as tough and durable. They were unable to bring those elements into play. And they paid the price. South Africa had to be no more than engaged and alert to get their scores.

Argentina needed instant succour in the second half if they were to get anything from the match. They had come too far to fold so easily. They had to give an account of themselves. They did, but they needed a sympathetic nod from television match official Tony Spreadbury, who ruled that Manuel Contepomi had not lost control as he touched down. The play was slipshod and splintered. Montgomery knocked over two penalty goals while the poacher, Habana, scooted in from seventy-five metres with a trademark interception three minutes from time.

21 OCTOBER
BRAVE ENGLAND KICKED INTO TOUCH AT THE LAST
Paul Ackford

No second successive World Cup for England. It was a hugely worthy effort. They worked and bashed and probed all game, but they were up against a South African side who matched them defensively and matched them in obduracy. England never gave up, even when they lost influential figures like Mike Catt, Jason Robinson and Phil Vickery on the hour, but they never found the key to unlock the Springbok defence.

There was no doubt that England were unlucky. Mark Cueto had what appeared to be a legitimate try disallowed by the television match official, and there were other instances when a different interpretation might have produced a different decision but, on the balance of play, there can be few complaints from England.

South Africa did what we knew they would. They competed for everything and they held on to their discipline when England came at them in waves. It was a triumph for captain John Smit and coach Jake White, who had orchestrated this campaign from four years out, and it was a fitting reward for a host of fine players. Victor Matfield, Juan Smith, Bakkies Botha, Percy Montgomery and Smit all had fine matches. We never saw the electricity of Bryan Habana, but this was a World Cup final and they are always tight.

And at the end the best side in this World Cup prevailed, 15–6. South Africa have been the class outfit. They have faced down all challenges and challengers and they have done so with dignity and no little class. England made them work very hard to earn their triumph, but they are worthy winners and the trophy is in good hands for the next four years.

The first half was unbelievably ferocious. It wasn't pretty rugby, and at times as the game descended into an extended kicking match it wasn't particularly edifying to watch. But there was always the strong sense of a gladiatorial battle. And for the first thirty minutes the contest went to script. England lost the first two line-outs on their throw and struggled for the rest of the half to secure comfortable possession while Andy Sheridan applied enormous pressure to the Bok scrummage. England's tactics were laid out for inspection in the first ten minutes, as first Andy Gomarsall then Jonny Wilkinson put up a series of hanging kicks dropping just outside the twenty-two into territory defended by South Africa's back three. Percy Montgomery wobbled occasionally but he, J.P. Pietersen and Habana defended stoutly.

South Africa weren't that much more adventurous. There were moments of invention, notably when Butch James nearly got away after he held on well to a chip kick and Francois Steyn evaded the tackles of Jonny Wilkinson and Phil Vickery on a damaging run at the end of the half. But for much of the early moments it was mistakes that tipped the encounter. England made the first when Wilkinson unaccountably went wide inside his own twenty-two and Mathew Tait was penalised for holding on. Montgomery knocked that one over and he finished the half with another successful strike after Steyn had set up a punishing series of drives from Botha, John Smit and Danie Rossouw. In between Wilkinson got one back when he landed a marvellous shot from wide out on the touchline after Paul Sackey had been nailed by Pietersen.

The real drama was left to the first minutes of the second half. Tait ripped through the defence with mesmeric footwork. England rucked the ball quickly and then Wilkinson went left with a tip pass to give Cueto a chance to squeeze in at the corner. It looked for all the world that Cueto had managed it, but the referee went to the television match official, Australian Stuart Dickinson, who ruled that Cueto's left foot had drifted into touch. Wilkinson banged over the penalty because Schalk Burger had deliberately careered into the ruck from an offside position, but it was a grievously unkind blow to England.

England's fortunes dipped again later when Jason Robinson hobbled off to be replaced by Dan Hipkiss. They had already lost captain Vickery, injured in the frantic effort to scrag South Africa at the end of the half. And when Catt was also forced off ten minutes after the interval there was a clear sense of England's wonderful World Cup effort crumbling into dust. Yet England refused to buckle. Mistakes crept into their game, but Wilkinson marshalled them well, Nick Easter and Corry drove hard, and Hipkiss skipped and darted across the defensive line. And England hung on to what had sustained them for so long in this competition: a refusal to buckle coupled with a strong sense of self-belief.

They were also up against easily the most physical side they had faced in the knockout stages. South Africa weren't the fluent team who had destroyed England in the pool round, but they were highly disciplined and they defended with organisation and real power. Burger banged away at the breakdown all evening and Botha, Juan Smith and Rossouw were equally industrious. They also had the rub of the green. On the hour Steyn banged over a penalty when England were punished for crossing. It was a kick which put the Boks almost out of reach, nine points ahead. But moments earlier Alain Rolland had ignored a similar manoeuvre when two South Africans appeared to impede English defenders. If that had gone England's way Wilkinson would have had a kick to get within three points of the Boks. Decisions and moments like that turn big finals. It certainly turned this one.

The other factor was that England could not make the big plays. With ten minutes to go they forced a line-out five metres out from the Bok goal-line, and George Chuter overthrew, handing the advantage back to South Africa. It was almost England's last chance. They emptied the bench. They cranked up the effort. Wilkinson tried and failed with a dropped goal. They had one last valiant but futile rumble from a line-out, and their World Cup was over.

22 OCTOBER
SWEET CHARIOT HAD TO TURN SOUR IN THE END
Martin Johnson

Ah well, at least we'll now be spared the argument as to where it stands in the list of the world's greatest unsolved mysteries. Number one: the *Mary Celeste*. Number two: the Loch Ness Monster. Number three: How on earth did England win the 2007 Rugby World Cup? The combination of a stadium situated in the middle of nowhere and another French rail strike didn't make life any rosier for English supporters as they trudged forlornly away into the night, and any form of primitive transport back into Paris would have been welcome. But finally, as we all thought it had to sooner or later, the sweet chariot itself had also ground to a halt.

Up until the final, England had become the great survivors. Cast away on a desert island with a box of distress flares, but no other apparent means of sustaining life, they'd somehow managed to knock up a bijou beachfront apartment, and were dining out on coconut cocktails and grilled swordfish. It was, though, too much to expect that they could actually win the tournament playing what you might call loincloth rugby, a compelling argument for the Darwinian theory of man's descent from the apes. Never has a team received so many bad luck messages before a big game, on the basis that the rest of the world didn't fancy having chimps for champs.

Mind you, South Africa more than played their part in turning the final match of an otherwise captivating tournament into a desperate advertisement for modern international rugby. A kick-off close to bedtime, for the usual television-driven commercial reasons, made the urge to have someone turn off the floodlights so we could all get some sleep almost overpowering. There is a modern trend in all sports which presupposes that spectators are not capable of enjoying themselves without the provision of artificial entertainment, which is why you can't get through a one-day cricket match without having more parachutists descend from the sky than were deployed at Arnhem. Here it was a French band, who burst into action every time there was a stoppage in play. The choice of music was a cross between old-time dancing and the kind of Pathé newsreel ra-ra-ra that used to accompany those old British black-and-white wartime films, when the heroic tank commander (usually Sir John Mills) drove his Jeep triumphantly into town after liberating Benghazi.

'The Great Escape' only featured in the chanting from England's supporters, except that this time there wasn't to be one. Gordon Brown made the trip over, presumably to remind us that England had reached the final on a manifesto of austerity, thrift and, above all, a heavy taxation on the loyalties of all those who like a bit of joy in their rugby. For all their admirable resilience and team bonding since their horrific pool defeat by South Africa, England have had more in common with a 1940s Churchill than Brown, in as much as they have nothing to offer their people other than toil and sweat. In four matches against the top-tier nations in this World Cup they've scored one try. They nearly scored another early in the second half, following the only piece of genuinely exhilarating running rugby in the entire game, from Mathew Tait. It was, though, ruled out on video evidence, and though there was the consolation prize of a Jonny Wilkinson penalty to bring England within three points of the opposition, they never threatened to do anything quite as exciting again.

South Africa offered precious little in this department either. All through this tournament Wilkinson has queried the pressure in the official World Cup balls, which is perhaps not surprising. It must be hard to keep the things properly inflated when the wind is being knocked out of them by ferocious application of the boot, and the only evidence of dazzling rugby came from players trying to spot the ball as it descended from the floodlights. It's the modern way, it seems. Hoof the ball upfield to gain territory, and wait for the opposition to make a mistake running it back. Except that the opposition doesn't run it back, it does precisely the same thing.

England might conceivably have won the game had they had sixteen players, as they briefly did in the second half when a spectator – whose choice of shirt suggested that not all New Zealand supporters have yet made it home – ran on and joined an English ruck. He will probably end up in court, with his French lawyer trying to get him off on the grounds that his urge to inject a bit of *joie de vivre* into the game constituted a crime of passion.

21 OCTOBER
NOW WE'RE GROWING UP
AS A NATION
Nick Mallett

This victory was not as spectacular as South Africa's win in 1995. There was no sign of the wings of a jumbo jet skimming the roof of the stadium or of Nelson Mandela in the No. 6 jersey bringing the rainbow nation to its knees in admiration. But it may just have a longer-lasting effect. It may be a more meaningful symbol of what is possible if we believe in trust and fairness and finding the right people to do the job.

You feel that perhaps now in South Africa we are finally growing up as a nation. We have won this World Cup by looking outwards, by talking to the world and talking to each other. It is an incredible achievement given our history of circling the wagons, and Jake White, the coach, and John Smit, the captain, should be given the utmost credit. It wasn't so long ago that the politicians and administrators came after White. But he stuck it out and has handled the huge pressure of the job with remarkable dignity. There is no harder job in rugby than coach of South Africa, because not only are you supposed to win, you are supposed to bind together so many different cultures and satisfy so many different agendas.

Perhaps White's greatest strength is his open-mindedness. By nature, he is an inclusive man and he has brought a togetherness to this squad that was lacking in 2003. I can imagine a time when there would have been howls of anguish at the thought of bringing an Australian on to the coaching team, but White's appointment of Eddie Jones was a masterstroke. Jones has brought to South Africa not just technical ability, but confidence, gregariousness and a knowledge of playing in a World Cup final. We didn't see too much of the Jones fluidity in the final, but it was never going to be that sort of game. South Africa have won previous games at this World Cup through the brilliance of their strike runners, but this game was about rigidity and direct rugby. It was about being able to revert to traditional strengths and toughing it out.

In these sorts of matches the margins are tiny, and there were two moments that decided the game. The first came in the first half when Jonny Wilkinson missed a drop goal from just to the right of the posts. For a player like him it was a very good chance and he will be inconsolable at the miss. The second moment was 'that decision'. A moment of brilliance by Matthew Tait opened South Africa up, England moved play to the blindside intelligently and at first glance it looked as if Mark Cueto had squeezed in. It was a hell of a decision; the margins were millimetres and milliseconds. But Stuart Dickinson decided it was too close to call. In previous matches those sorts of fractional verdicts have tended to go to the attacking team. Perhaps it is that inconsistency that will needle England, rather than the rightness of the television official's call. But in those two moments England lost eight, perhaps ten points.

It is hard to be critical of England. They played the game that they had to and those two reversals cost them their chance. But few would argue that South Africa were the better side. Juan Smith and Schalk Burger were enormous in defence with some huge hits. The back three, after a couple of early wobbles, just got better and better, and J.P. Pietersen and Bryan Habana helped out Percy Montgomery superbly. The performances of the wings in defence are a telling symbol of the unity of this team. As some of us suspected, the line-out was another telling factor. South Africa won all thirteen of their throws, but were able to steal ball off the England line-out on seven occasions. That is an awful lot of possession in a tight game and Victor Matfield deserved his man of the match award.

But perhaps most telling of all was the captaincy of Smit. His throwing in was immaculate, he helped shore up the scrum and he put in more than his share of tackles. However, he is much more than a rugby player. He is the leader of this South African team and they all respect him immensely. Back in 2005 Burger and Butch James might have exploded on so big an occasion, but here they played with a control that is a testimony to Smit's captaincy. The hooker may not be as tall as the last three men to hoist the Webb Ellis Cup, but Smit is just as big a man as Martin Johnson, John Eales and Francois Pienaar. He never runs a teammate down and always backs his coach. He has the one hundred per cent support of his squad, an unbelievable statistic in a South African team. The country has seen how close this squad is and has responded by giving it total support. In rugby South Africa has come together – one game, one nation. It may not be as emotional as 1995, but somehow it promises to be more lasting.

21 OCTOBER

NO SUCH THING AS A BLUEPRINT FOR SUCCESS IN EXCITING NEW WORLD
Paul Ackford

World Cups are invariably watersheds. They tend to signpost the nature of the rugby which will dominate the next four-year cycle. Not this one. How can it? This tournament has been fascinating for the very reason that no clear themes have emerged, no blueprints to determine how the sport will develop leading into Rugby World Cup 2011.

Consider this explanation for New Zealand's early exit from Eddie Jones, the Springboks' technical adviser: 'They had an unnatural obsession with the World Cup and I think that might have cost them,' Jones said. 'You learn as you go along and if you've too much focus on the future it can detract from what you're doing at a particular moment. They didn't build a team. They built a squad. Under pressure it's like if you're wicket-keeping to Shane Warne and you've kept to him a number of times. You know then what he's going to bowl. If you haven't, you're not quite sure. Maybe you didn't pick the look he gave you when he ran in, and you miss the ball. That's why regular combinations are so important.'

Jones has a point here, one that neatly encapsulates the way Argentina, South Africa and Australia have approached the tournament, with settled sides and momentum built on an intimate knowledge of each other. But France and England do not fit that pattern. England's selection was all over the place before, and during, the first few games of this World Cup, as was France's, where Yannick Jauzion was in then out then in again, and where Damien Traille switched position on a whim. No lessons there for 2011 in terms of evolving a team.

No lessons either in identifying a style of play which is successful in World Cups. Fabien Galthié, the former captain of France, has stressed that possession can be counter-productive, that it is easier to win games by defending ferociously and forcing turnovers. In the so-called bronze final between France and Argentina, France won sixty-five per cent of the ball yet lost the match by five tries to one. Some observers have viewed the re-emergence of a dominant scrum as an essential cornerstone of a successful side. And while that has certainly been a factor in England's progress, South Africa were under the cosh against Argentina in the semi-final yet cruised past them, and New Zealand were on top against France in the quarter-final and lost. Fiji couldn't beg a stable scrum platform against Wales but still prevailed.

Even the attacking philosophies have differed. According to Jones, England have revisited a style of rugby more appropriate to the early 1990s, one built on grinding the opposition down, establishing field position and kicking goals. Argentina, it could be argued, did much of the same in the middle part of the competition, yet it was only when they took greater risks, which they did in both their matches against France, that they became a truly dangerous side. Fiji, on the other hand, got as far as they did because there was no distinctive pattern to their play other than to give it a go from anywhere.

But if there have been few distinctive trends to follow on the pitch, at least there is consensus as to what must happen off it. Eddie Jones again: 'The Island sides [Fiji, Tonga and Samoa] have done well off the back of International Rugby Board investment. The IRB should get credit for that, but I think they need to take it a stage further. I believe they need to target around five or six nations, including the Islands, because we need more countries with the ability to knock off a top side. Japan obviously has the potential to be one of them because of their socio-economic status, but they've got to be serious about rugby and they're not at the moment. I don't think they commit to an international programme and they'll only do that if they get to host a World Cup. The United States is another one. The potential there is enormous, and in terms of Europe you've got to look at one from Georgia, Romania or Portugal – probably one from the first two – coming through. Do an inventory of those countries, work out which has the most potential to go forward and target them with resources and finance. Then you've got six nations who can push the countries ranked six to ten in the world.'

And perhaps that is the lesson of this World Cup, the watershed moment if you like. Celebrate the fact that it hasn't thrown up a methodology for success on the pitch. International rugby would be a dull old game if that were the case. But celebrate also the progress the likes of Tonga, the United States, Georgia and Fiji have made. And move mountains to ensure that they are even more robust and competitive in New Zealand in 2011.

2007 RESULTS – Quarter-finals: England 12, Australia 10; France 20, New Zealand 18; South Africa 37, Fiji 20; Argentina 19, Scotland 13. Semi-finals: England 14, France 9; South Africa 37, Argentina 13. Third-place: Argentina 34, France 10. Final: South Africa 15, England 6.

CHAPTER EIGHT: 2011

HOSTED BY NEW ZEALAND

6 SEPTEMBER

DESPERATE KIWIS ARE CENTRAL TO THE SUCCESS OF THIS WORLD CUP
Mick Cleary

In the Land of the Long Black Shroud, the mourning for failed World Cups past continues. You might argue that New Zealand's obsession with trying to snare the Webb Ellis Cup is bordering on the demented. Talk of what the All Blacks have to do if they are to throw off the yoke of twenty-three years of underachievement dominates airwaves and colonises acres of newsprint in New Zealand. From the woman polishing the chrome fascia in the hotel lift to the barista in the corner café in Dunedin, they all want to know what it will take to lift the curse.

New Zealanders are right to be so preoccupied. They should care; it does matter: the World Cup is that significant on rugby's landscape. It is still the benchmark against which all other achievements are measured. The lustre of the Springboks may have dimmed in the Tri–Nations, but they are lauded, for a few weeks longer at any rate, as world champions. And the All Blacks are still also-rans when it comes to the World Cup. Their solitary success came in the first tournament in 1987, when they had home advantage and the rest of the world barely flickered an eyebrow of interest as to what was going on in New Zealand and Australia. It is a miserable ledger, a stain against their name.

Back then a World Cup was a novelty concept, frowned upon by diehard amateur administrators in the Northern Hemisphere. They agreed to it as a sop to their brazen cousins from south of the equator. Indeed, Eden Park was barely half full for the opening game between New Zealand and Italy. By the time All Black wing John Kirwan weaved his way past six Italian tacklers on an eighty-metre run to the try-line, the world no longer needed persuading that this was a good thing. It still is. The World Cup has brought status and global credibility to rugby union. It has created interest beyond its normal narrow confines, drawn in a new audience, and given a taste of exalted competition to many lesser nations.

Of course, there will be those who question the right of countries such as Namibia or Russia to be here. And they would be wrong to do so. The very richness of a World Cup comes from its cosmopolitan make-up. The Pacific Islanders, Canada and the United States have all brought colour and zest to World Cups. Western Samoa revealed themselves to be a nation of note on the world stage when beating Wales at the 1991 World Cup. Argentina's rise to the point of being allowed to sit at the top table with the Tri-Nations sides in 2012 owes much to their stirring passion plays at each World Cup, culminating in their third-place finish in 2007.

And this time? Well, it would be futile to argue that the time difference between New Zealand and the mass markets of Europe will not impact on the tournament's profile. It will. There are also legitimate concerns about pricing and the knock-on effect on visitors. The onus then is on the event itself to force its way into the sporting consciousness, through the drama of the contest, the elan of the play and the unveiling of new heroes. There has to be a narrative that matters and there has to be a true sense of something worthwhile happening. That is where the four million Kiwis who are fretting about the All Blacks enter the equation. If their connection with the event begins and ends with the fortunes of their own team, the tournament will be a dud. If there are swathes of empty seats, or rows of Kiwis wrapped up in their own self-absorbed world and not giving a damn about Japan or Italy, then the World Cup is in trouble. The litmus test will be how the locals in Dunedin respond to the men in black. England, that is. They are playing in their back-up dark kit against Argentina. If the Kiwis take England to their hearts in some measure, that will be as big an achievement as the real men in black finally winning another World Cup.

8 SEPTEMBER
JOHNSON PAYS HIS RESPECTS
TO A BROKEN CITY
Mick Cleary

Martin Johnson stood in the middle of the pitch at Lancaster Park, Christchurch. The clock high up in the Hadlee Stand read 12.51. It has been like that for seven months, ever since the very earth on which Johnson stood heaved and bucked, spewing out 500,000 tons of liquefied silt into the city, the destruction claiming the lives of 181 people on that dreadful day, 22 February 2011.

Johnson's tour of Lancaster Park ought to have been in preparation for England's opening World Cup Pool B match against Argentina, which was due to be staged there. Instead the England manager was there to pay his respects to the city's dead and offer support to those trying to rebuild shattered lives. Christchurch, the most famous of all rugby cities in New Zealand, was due to host seven matches. Instead, the World Cup has gone elsewhere. For a brief moment, Johnson, along with injured captain Lewis Moody, four other players and scrum coach Graham Rowntree, reminded Cantabrians of what might have been. The ground moved, and continues to move with more than eight thousand aftershocks still rumbling, to terrible effect since that summer's day. Amid the gaping holes and mounds of displaced turf, Johnson offered his sympathies.

It may have been but a gesture but Christchurch took note. It was a touching, yet grim scene, horror-movie stuff in a way, as if an arm might reach out from beneath at any moment and drag Johnson under. 'It was a no-brainer for us to come here and show our support,' said Johnson, who had never played at Lancaster Park, though he sat in the stands shortly after being called out as a replacement for Wade Dooley on the 1993 Lions tour. Rowntree had been on the bench for the first Lions Test in 2005, the night that Brian O'Driscoll was tip-tackled out of the tour. That seemed a tragedy at the time. What little we knew of perspective back then.

'When you see such a sad scene as this, at such an iconic stadium, well, it's not about rugby then, is it?' Johnson said. 'Rugby is very much secondary. For us, we don't get affected. We can move on and play somewhere else. Let's hope that we'll be back playing here one day.' Chances are he will not. The AMI Stadium, as it is now known, is on the verge of being condemned. The two towering stands, rebuilt over the last decade at a cost of £52 million, have both shifted on their axis. Already plans are in place for the star-studded Crusaders, with All Blacks Richie McCaw and Dan Carter in the ranks, to be temporarily relocated to the 20,000-capacity rugby league ground at Addington.

As for this World Cup, it is but a distant thrum. A fan zone set up in Hagley Park has a rather forlorn air about it. That is why England's visit had such resonance. 'It was important to bring a little bit of Rugby World Cup here,' said Moody, who had expressed similar sentiments when visiting a city hospital earlier. Australia, coached by a famous son of Christchurch, Robbie Deans (one of the stands is named after his family), as well as the All Blacks, will also visit. England have led the way.

'This is both a proud yet also a sad moment to see you here,' said Christchurch mayor Bob Parker as he greeted the England delegation at the stadium. 'Our hearts rose last 4 September when the first quake struck but the stadium was untouched. We could still host England and the Rugby World Cup. Then hearts went through the floor when a quake came roaring in from the opposite direction, taking lives and changing the landscape forever. It will take ten to fifteen years to completely rebuild our city. But we want to turn this into something positive. We're going to make a good fist of it, create a low-rise sustainable city. Out of adversity can come good things.'

More than a thousand buildings will eventually be demolished. Right throughout the city are visible signs of ruin. The Red Zone in the city centre is like a film set, with no unauthorised access and thousands of buildings either damaged or awaiting inspection. We took a haunting forty-five-minute tour, with rubble piled high and such illustrious landmarks as the cathedral in a state of collapse. It will take £15.6 billion to rebuild the city, four per cent of the entire country's GDP.

Across the city, Mike Esposito was typical of many locals, struggling to come to terms with what had happened and then to make ends meet. Esposito is managing director of Welcome Abroad, a company that runs five tourism businesses. The company usually caters for half a million visitors a year. That is down to fifteen thousand. He used to employ eighty-five people; now only twelve are on his books. He talks of how hard it was to lay people off at a time of such crisis for everyone, of how kids in the city are now beginning to suffer hair-loss as delayed trauma sets in. And yet there was a note of defiance in him, too, a sense that one day Christchurch will be back in business and trading as it once used to. 'We're doing the hard yards and knuckling down,' said Esposito, who runs the city's tramways, punts on the Avon and tours in and around the area. 'All our stars seemed to be aligned and then the world changed. Our development project for the tramway stopped a hundred metres short. It's still not open. Your head spins at times. There's bewilderment, but wry smiles, too. You can lose your bearings in a city that once you knew so well. But we'll get through it.'

The International Rugby Board has launched an appeal fund to help with the restoration of rugby facilities. 'We really appreciate such help,' McCaw said. The appeal will also help make the Christchurch community feel that they are not alone in all this. For a while, Johnson and McCaw were on the same side, part of a rugby family just trying to help.

10 SEPTEMBER

IT HAS TO GET BETTER AFTER OPENER FAILS TO STIR SOUL
Paul Ackford

The six-year-old Canadian girl asleep in her mum's arms had it about right. 'Did she enjoy it?' I asked, as we made our way towards the exit. 'The opening ceremony more than the game,' Mum said. She knows her rugby, that little one, because the seventh global gathering started with barely a whimper as the All Blacks tonked Tonga 41–10. No great surprise in that. There was little chance of an upset when the side ranked first in the world played the team in twelfth place.

Rugby doesn't really do upsets very often. But the match lacked bite, edge. It failed to stir the soul and that was disturbing. At its best that's what rugby does. The intricacies of the game are so complex, so convoluted, that, frankly, no one understands what's going on. The officials pretend that they do and, by and large, the players give them the benefit of the doubt because otherwise anarchy reigns. But rugby has never been about rules and regulations and technicalities. There has to be an emotional connection for the sport to work convincingly.

The Tongans had theirs before a ball was kicked when the hooker, Taufa'ao Filise, led their war dance, the Sipi Tau. The passion was palpable then. Tonga even broke a few pernickety World Cup rules by advancing on the All Blacks with murderous intent. The All Blacks stared back implacably before performing their haka. There was a whiff of cordite in the air. This one appeared to mean something. You could see it on their faces, in the theatrically aggressive gestures which accompany the war dances.

There was emotion and promise in the build-up to the opener, too. Six thousand Tongans greeted their team at the airport. On the morning of the match the waterfront area of Auckland filled with buxom, scantily clad Tongan women caterwauling their support for their rugby players. Starting early and loud, they cranked it up and up and up. Wandering between them and gangs of nomadic Argentines, French and South Africans, it was impossible not to feel stirred by the obvious excitement and interest which the Rugby World Cup was engendering.

But that was the trouble here. That connection was not maintained. As the game commenced, when rugby itself and equality of competition became the issues rather than colour, the interest dissipated. It survived the opening ceremony. The little girl was right. When the monstrous Jonah Lomu held the hand of the small boy and walked towards a huge, glistening, golden replica of the Webb Ellis Cup, all those dreams and all those expectations were still possible. They were all in the future. But after twenty-four minutes when the All Blacks were fifteen points to the good, after twenty-eight minutes when the first of the Mexican waves lapped itself round the stadium, after thirty-one minutes when the All Blacks had grabbed their fourth try and a bonus point, the reality had hit home. This was a very good team not having to play at all well to beat a very poor team thoroughly convincingly. That's not an authentic sporting contest. It's more a coronation, an affirmation of what is expected, and that's not very exciting at all.

And so the interest turned not to who was going to win, but to how good these All Blacks are as they seek to land their second World Cup after an indecent gap of twenty-four years. Dan Carter and Richie McCaw seemed in decent nick but we knew that. The All Blacks have plenty of competition in their back three after full-back Israel Dagg and wing Richard Kahui each scored a brace of tries. But we knew that, too. Graham Henry, New Zealand's coach, awarded his men five out of ten after the game. That seemed about right but, if truth be told, we couldn't really judge because there hadn't been a proper contest.

Relief was the word which best summed up the start of this World Cup. Relief that all the tickets were eventually sold for the match, even if touts were offering them at face value on the roads to Auckland harbour. Relief that Carter and McCaw had survived unscathed. Relief that a tournament had ridden, and risen above, the setback of the devastating earthquake that destroyed much of Christchurch. By far the most heartfelt emotion on a very flat night came from New Zealand Prime Minister John Key. Lomu and the small boy had just walked towards the Webb Ellis Cup, which appeared to hover over the Eden Park pitch. 'Enjoy the rugby,' Key said to his congregation, as the cameras and phones flashed their acknowledgement. 'And go the mighty All Blacks.' And go those All Blacks did. But it wasn't a great advertisement for the game of rugby itself. This Rugby World Cup will get better. It has to.

11 SEPTEMBER
SLOPPY ENGLAND GIVEN WAKE-UP CALL
Paul Ackford

Can England win a World Cup playing like that? Not a snowball's chance in hell. This was a huge wake-up call for Martin Johnson's squad because for large tracts of the match they were outplayed and out-thought by an Argentine effort which once again bordered on the heroic. Were it not for a lamentably poor kicking effort by Martín Rodríguez and Felipe Contepomi, who between them missed six shots, England could, and possibly should, have started their campaign with a defeat instead of a 13–9 victory.

Not that they were much better in the kicking department. Jonny Wilkinson, brought back into the fold precisely for his ability to accumulate points, had a nightmarish evening, butchering five himself. That's worth saying again. Wilkinson had his worst outing ever, missing five shots at goal, two of them falling into the get-them-in-his-sleep category, to take England to the brink of the biggest shock of the tournament so far.

But let's not turn this contest into an inquest as to which team had the more fallible kickers. Argentina were quite magnificent. To push England as hard as they did, to neuter them up front, to get in behind their defence, which they did at the start of the second half and again in the final seconds of the match, was just marvellous. Better, they did this having lost their tactical leader, Contepomi, after twenty-six minutes, and with their spiritual guru, the thirty-eight-year-old Mario Ledesma, recovering from a clattering from Courtney Lawes which left the hooker senseless. Most teams in those circumstances would have folded, but most teams aren't Argentina.

Yet England survived, thanks mainly to the bustling intervention of Ben Youngs, who scored the game's only try and injected pace and provided belated direction to an attack which was largely shapeless. A fine Ben Foden run off a clever Wilkinson pass apart, it was difficult to think of too many England raids which were constructed with intelligence or clarity. Some of the old bad habits surfaced, such as big forwards cluttering up the midfield. Delon Armitage and Foden were England's most aggressive and incisive backs and Manu Tuilagi smashed as only a young, strong man can, but, frankly, some of the stuff offered up by Japan in their game against France was more coherent than England's efforts.

There could well be repercussions, too, following the encounter. The referee's microphone picked up James Haskell making allegations of eye-gouging as the final whistle sounded, and Lawes will no doubt attract the attention of the citing officer following a crunching, possibly late, tackle on Gonzalo Tiesi which ended that centre's involvement, and a knee which accounted for the stars in Ledesma's eyes. Haskell was keen to downplay the incident afterwards, blaming his reaction on 'over-exuberance' in the heat of battle. But with the Rugby World Cup authorities keen to be seen stamping down hard on acts of foul play, Lawes could be facing an anxious wait.

Johnson has also got other issues to ponder. Why, for example, did his team concede so many different penalties in so many different aspects of the game? Dan Cole was the guy sent to the sin-bin towards the end of the first half, but his indiscretion was simply the last of a long line. Johnson's anger as player after player handed the advantage back to Argentina at crucial stages in the match was as intense as it was justified. That, Wilkinson's inexplicable series of misses, and a defensive display which allowed Rodríguez and Marcelo Bosch to rip England to bits at the start of the second half, just when they needed to start hard, need to be fixed promptly.

There was some good stuff up front. Haskell did as much as anyone to rein in Argentine physicality, Tom Croft had a fine match in the line-out and the England scrum improved significantly when replacements Matt Stevens and Dylan

Hartley took advantage of the fatigued Rodrigo Roncero and Ledesma's absence. Ledesma, by the way, at his fourth and final World Cup, shook the referee's hand as he left the pitch. The guy really is a class act.

It must also be said that this was a true and brutal Test match. Each attacking or defensive effort appeared to leave a trail of bodies in its wake and the medics will be earning their money as both teams attempt to rehabilitate battered bodies. That was what made this spectacle so compulsive. Unlike the opening flop of a game, the contest was intense and vital. Argentina have to take credit for that. Against Wales in their warm-up match, the Pumas were flabby and disinterested. In a tight, compact, atmospheric stadium in the middle of Dunedin at the start of a World Cup they came alive. The surprise was that, alongside the sensational efforts of both locks and a back row in which Juan Martín Fernández was staggeringly good, Argentina played some rugby. Bosch livened up their midfield when he came on and both wings troubled England deeply. Another surprise, less palatable this time, was that their scrum came under pressure in the final quarter.

England's performance was nothing like good enough but, as Johnson was keen to stress afterwards, teams who find ways to win matches in World Cups when not playing well, especially late on, often are there at the end. What Johnson was at a loss to explain was how, in a stadium closed to the elements, with nary a breath of air to add complexity to the art of goal-kicking, one of the best exponents in the history of the sport had such a wretched evening. Wilkinson had no answer to that imponderable either.

CHAPTER EIGHT: 2011 259

16 SEPTEMBER
AMERICANS CRACK THE CODE TO SECURE 'SUPERPOWER' VICTORY
Brendan Gallagher

The Russian and American combatants may have disappeared into a squally night to enjoy a beer together, which is possibly a first in international sporting relations between the two nations, but it is a compliment to both teams that ultimately this was just another World Cup match. All the pre-match talk was of the 'Superpower shoot-out' and renewed Cold War rivalries, but once the US Marine marching band had done its stuff and the anthems had been sung, this quickly became a rugged and enjoyable Pool C encounter, played in miserable conditions but with a passion that warmed the cockles.

The Eagles won, by 13–6, because they were the better and more experienced side and produced the only try of the game – a first-half cracker by scrum-half Mike Petri – but they had to work like dogs to break down Russia's heroic defence. It was all getting a little tense in the final ten minutes when Russia somehow found the energy to start pressing hard themselves. The Americans also clearly cracked the code for the Russian line-out, not through espionage and a 'dirty tricks' department, but by old-fashioned detective work, breaking down almost frame by frame the videos of their last two meetings with Russia in the Churchill Cup and putting two and two together. The result was that they stole the ball at six Russian line-outs, priceless possession in a game that was always going to be decided by a score, two at the most.

'We are taking part at the Rugby World Cup for the first time in our history and it was our debut match so there were a lot of emotions and we took these with us on to the field,' said Russia coach Nikolay Nerush. 'To beat the United States in this match would have been really difficult for us, but we showed that it is at least possible. I am very proud of our effort – we lost the match but we didn't lose ourselves.' Nerush is right to be proud, and a high-powered delegation in the stands, headed by Russia's Deputy Prime Minister Alexander Zhukov, who also heads the country's Olympic Committee, will have seen enough to know that Russia have a future in the game if the government funding that has been promised materialises.

10 OCTOBER
DISMAL CAMPAIGN PETERS OUT IN PANIC, CONFUSION AND SURRENDER
Mick Cleary

The disturbing realisation that the level of England's play, far from progressing, had actually regressed did not take long to take root. Where was the sharp-eyed sense of opportunism that had seen Ben Youngs announce himself so thrillingly on the international stage barely twelve months before, twice showing Australia a clean pair of heels? Against France in this quarter-final we saw only panic. The same was true of several other players, from the manic gesticulating of Chris Ashton when things are not going his way, to the edgy, fretful play of Toby Flood at inside centre, the man who had seemingly broken England's reliance on Jonny Wilkinson by starting ahead of him for twelve Tests in a row. During that time, England eviscerated World Cup semi-finalists Australia, beat current darlings-of-the-hour Wales, in Cardiff, and won their first Six Nations title in eight years. And what did England do? They reverted to the norm, dropping Flood, promoting Wilkinson only then to fling the pair together just seventy-two hours before their biggest game in four years. What happened to that slavish devotion to Shontayne Hape or the use of Mike Tindall as a makeshift No. 12? England appeared to make it all up at the last minute, and it showed in a first half of comic proportions. The upshot was a 19–12 defeat.

There was a clownish feel to many of the errors made by England, with balls thudding into the shoulders of supposed attacking runners, or hitting the turf instead of hands. The opening half an hour was a pantomime, far from the intended rendition of consummate skill. England were fretful, clunky, stressed and inconsequential, all of which was manna from heaven for a France side seeking salvation. How can England have gone from smooth, accomplished performers to such an indecisive lot, bereft of fluency and self-belief? England have lost their bounce and edge. Their rugby has been all rather tortured. There is little doubt that the likes of Ashton and Ben Foden are frustrated about how their own involvement has diminished.

England backed Wilkinson's sense of pragmatic game management to bring home the World Cup booty and it did not work. His presence cramped the team's attacking game. By the time they discovered it, it was too late. Tries by Vincent Clerc and Maxime Médard were easily conceded, another sign of English unease given that defence had been their strength in the pool stages.

There were many irritants on the night, some minor, but with significant consequences. Why, for instance, does Wilkinson not wallop the ball huge distances from penalties from hand? He made only about twenty-five yards from one such clearance from inside England's twenty-two midway through the first half. France stole the line-out, doubled back on the attack from where Clerc got past three tacklers to score. If Wilkinson's punt had been another twenty-five yards upfield, the danger would have been minimised.

It was the lack of cohesive drive that really dragged England down. Manu Tuilagi was the lone stand-out performer, several times busting through. But even later, when Flood made inroads, the final pass was forced and lost. England had no one to match the shrewdness or imperiousness of the Biarritz duo of Imanol Harinordoquy and Dimitri Yachvili, whose box-kicking game tormented England as it has so often done in the past. This was not an irresistible French performance, gilded as it had been by genius in 1999, or summoned from deep within as it had four years before in Cardiff. France played with verve initially but that was it. England ought to have been able to deal with what was against them, but they gave France too much leeway. Second-half tries from Foden and Mark Cueto gave the scoreboard a flourish, but the truth is that England were comfortably beaten on the night. They had made it all too easy for France, a fact that will haunt them forever and a day.

10 OCTOBER
RAMIFICIATIONS FOR SOUTH AFRICA AS WALLABIES STEAL IN
Brendan Gallagher

Few games at this World Cup have produced a more intense bout of head-scratching than this quarter-final. Australia had just twenty-four per cent of territory, they spent almost the entire eighty minutes on the back foot and they were forced to absorb wave after wave of South African pressure. And yet, by the end, somehow it was they who progressed, 11–9, to the semi-final.

There were significant consequences for South Africa, with the captain John Smit, second row Victor Matfield and coach Peter de Villiers all announcing their retirements immediately after the game. The departures of Smit and Matfield – the latter described by Smit as the 'greatest Springbok ever' – were expected, but not so De Villiers. Cynics might argue that given South Africa's failure to advance further, and the volatile rugby politics in the country, he was merely jumping before he was pushed. At least he had the satisfaction of leaving at a time and place of his choosing and to coincide with two extraordinary players who served him so loyally, not least when times were difficult and the flak was flying.

'It's a sad occasion, stepping down, and you are never prepared for when it ends. You want it to be a fairytale, you want it to be in a final,' said Smit, who captained his team for a remarkable eighty-third time here. 'I have been blessed to play and captain the Springboks and although I am devastated now, I have always been proud to be a Springbok. It was a sad way to end but when you look at the players that are left and coming through we are in a good place. I spoke to all the guys afterwards and told them to remember this game and how it feels to lose by millimetres.' De Villiers was gracious while reserving a parting shot for his critics. 'It was a brilliant journey and something that none of you [media] guys could take away from me,' he said. 'I wanted to be the best I could be and that is the way I want to be remembered. There is a time to come and a time to go and the journey for me is over. I enjoyed it. I am privileged to have been in a position to help my country.'

Any team who defend as heroically, and for as long, as Australia did here have earned the right still to be in contention in the closing stages of the match. They enjoyed some luck, especially in referee Bryce Lawrence's laissez-faire control of the breakdown, which saw Australia's openside, David Pocock, appear to get away with offending at will. But equally their sheer bloody-mindedness frustrated the Springboks into making some poor decisions and turning the ball over with untypical regularity. The absence of South Africa's long-range kicker, Frans Steyn, who was injured, was also telling.

Australia led 8–0 early on thanks to captain James Horwill's try, which came after Schalk Burger had spilled the ball near his own line, and a James O'Connor penalty, but after that South Africa quickly seized control of the play. The Springboks – who had fielded the most experienced starting line-up in Test history with 836 appearances between them – dominated territory and possession, and the boot of Morne Steyn edged them ahead 9–8. That advantage should have been extended but errors, notably Jean de Villiers's forward pass to set up a disallowed try for Pat Lambie in the second half, prevented them forging further ahead. It proved costly. In the seventy-fourth minute, South Africa conceded a dubious penalty for pulling down at the line-out and the cool O'Connor made no mistake with his kick.

16 OCTOBER
WALES' FIGHTBACK WILL BE THE STUFF OF LEGEND
Mick Cleary

How rotten. How unfair. Who could possibly raise a glass to salute France for reaching their third Rugby World Cup final? Even the players' mothers must have thought twice about it. There was neither merit nor glory in their 9–8 victory, but there was finality. They are through, and the game should weep. Poor Wales. How the soul bled for them, for their heroic grandeur not just in surviving for sixty-two minutes with fourteen men, but for playing all the rugby. It was a ludicrously knee-jerk decision by Alain Rolland to dismiss Sam Warburton for a tip-tackle, one that completely ruined the game. Why did he not wait and consider? He was too quick on the draw. Yellow, yes: red, no. Any match, let alone a World Cup semi-final, is for the players and the fans, not for the hidebound detail of disciplinary protocol. The contest, as well as the spectacle, was grievously scarred by Rolland's pedantry.

As for French flair? Forget it. This was *l'anti-jeu*, the negation of all that rugby should be about. There was no grace, no soul and no ambition. They reduced the game to its bare bones, taking no risks, refusing to chance their arm and simply kicking, and not very well at that. They were fretful, crabby and utterly without charm. They are welcome to their final.

That France made more than twice the number of tackles that Wales made shows the paucity of the French approach. Given that the Welsh line-out was fragile, that the scrum was under the cosh after tight-head Adam Jones was forced off after just ten minutes, Wales did well to generate any sort of momentum.

But they did, nobly and defiantly, rallying themselves after the shock of the dismissal, spurred by their sense of each other as well as by the realisation that they were facing a bunch of scaredy-cats. But the sporting gods were to deny them. Justice was nowhere to be seen at a subdued Eden Park.

Wales might well have sneaked home no matter the forces ranged against them. They missed eleven points from three penalty shots and a conversion attempt. They were denied only by the narrowest of margins after Stephen Jones's conversion of Mike Phillips's fifty-ninth-minute try hit the nearside post. Leigh Halfpenny had a pot from a metre inside his own half with four minutes to go. It dipped just under the crossbar. Where was a favourable gust when you needed it? In the frantic closing stages, Wales went through twenty-seven phases but could not engineer a final shot at the posts. The Fates are a miserly bunch. You might argue that missing kicks shows a lack of skill. And you would be right. Wales did have their chances but could not take them. If it were just a matter of these blemishes settling the outcome, then so be it. But matters were shaped by another's hand.

How much blame can be attached to Wales' young captain? A fair bit, for he overcommitted to the type of tackle that has been outlawed for some while. Warburton knows that there is zero tolerance and he would have deserved rebuke for getting sent to the sin-bin. Wales, already under duress after the loss of their Lions prop to a calf strain, might well have imploded at the sight of their talismanic leader trudging to the sidelines. But they did not. They kept their nerve and they held the line, not that France came remotely close to threatening it.

There were some magnificent rearguard performances to savour: from twenty-year-old No. 8 Toby Faletau to the battling

Phillips at scrum-half, who strove and urged, giving his side hope from unlikely circumstances when he arced past the outstretched arms of lock Pascal Papé to score midway through the second half. Phillips managed to touch down almost halfway to the posts. It was not a difficult conversion but Stephen Jones must have had its significance on his mind for he pulled it slightly, thudding into the woodwork. It felt like the miss might have been important at the time and so it proved. The Scarlets' fly-half had replaced James Hook early in the second half as Wales realised that they needed territory. It was Jones's adroit kick that teed up the position from where Phillips scored.

It was all to come to naught. Wales had the plaudits, France had the booty. They are the first team to get this far with two defeats in the pool stage. They have been riven by discord and lambasted for the divisive comments of their coach, Marc Lièvremont. Small wonder that he waved away criticism of his team's style. He had found vindication through the result and will now seek to bring the Webb Ellis Cup to France for the first time. France lost to New Zealand in the inaugural World Cup final in 1987, and to Australia twelve years later. Revenge would be sweet indeed, but on this form you can only see the winner coming from the Southern Hemisphere.

As ever, there was plenty to admire in the all-consuming play of Thierry Dusautoir and the cleverness of scrum-half Dimitri Yachvili. He ceded kicking duties to Morgan Parra, who slotted three penalties from three attempts. Both he and Jones fluffed dropped goal chances. Parra contributed the only decent French break when he brushed past an impeded Jamie Roberts early in the second half. There was precious little else to savour. This is not a gilded generation of French players but they have a chance to claim a historic accolade. They will have to show more if they are to trouble their final opponents, and much more if they are to take hearts and minds with them. Wales had it within their grasp. It was snatched away on a technicality. Rolland was right by the letter of the law. Well, damn the letter of the law. We have all been deprived as a result.

22 OCTOBER

GATLAND TAKES HEART DESPITE WALES ERRORS
Mick Cleary

There was to be no consolation for Wales, only desolation. In six days they saw their World Cup dreams reduced to dust, with not even the compensation of ending as the third-best team in the tournament, beaten 21–18 by Australia. Yet if their bodies tired, giving rise to a rash of handling errors, no one can question their soul. This was a team rich in character, a virtue shown tellingly in the last sequence of the game, Wales scoring a try that they had no right to be able to do. The clock was almost three minutes into overtime when Leigh Halfpenny touched down after thirty phases, a lung-scorching effort, a statement of defiance, for victory was beyond Wales. This was the first time they had lost three matches in a World Cup but the mood can only be upbeat. They have given of themselves, played with joy and toughness, and left a lasting impression.

As they stood in a scattered circle awaiting the medal ceremony, they looked weary and crestfallen, and that was before they learnt that they have slipped further down the International Rugby Board rankings to eighth, below Ireland and Argentina, who were knocked out in the quarter-finals, the Irish being roundly beaten by Warren Gatland's side. The madness of statistics. Three defeats by a total of five points, a deficit that a reliable goal-kicker would have made up on his own. That fallibility has cost Wales dear. It will take time for compensatory thoughts to take root, but they will.

Gatland, the Wales coach, said: 'We were not as quite emotionally up for it as we have been for other games, and that showed. Our performance was a little bit down from what we are capable of. But Australia are one of the top sides in the world and they are one of the best defensive teams in the competition. We are disappointed, but we have to take a lot of positives from the way we have progressed as a team.'

Even though there was a terrific finale to the match, you do wonder at the wisdom of it, as it is a burden on wholehearted players. Australia had injuries to contend with, fly-half Quade Cooper collapsing in agony midway through the first half with no one near him, his anterior cruciate ligament giving way. He was on crutches at the presentation ceremony with teammate Kurtley Beale hobbling around after departing earlier with a recurrence of a hamstring problem. There were bodies everywhere getting treatment during the game.

Wales' fatigue was the more evident and had a bearing on the outcome. Australia had a day less to prepare but they opted to make eight changes to Wales' three. It showed. Wales lacked the snap of their early games, an assurance on the ball and in contact, several times spilling possession. They seemed unable to match the tempo of the opposition. Wales paid dearly for their flawed goal-kicking, with James Hook and Halfpenny again the culprits. Hook missed a sitter just after half-time, the sort of blunder that characterised his play. He looked a shadow of the player he was.

If there were fears that Wales would be hopelessly adrift without the suspended Sam Warburton, they proved largely unfounded. Former captain Ryan Jones put in a colossal shift, forcing turnover after turnover and proving to be a real presence. Toby Faletau was shifted across to openside from No. 8, and though he was resolute, he did not manage to help deliver as much quick ball as a more natural openside such as Warburton might. Wales managed only intermittently to get their attack on the move.

Australia began at such a rattle, working Berrick Barnes over the try-line within twelve minutes, that you feared Wales might take a pounding. The Wallabies ran everything, looking to stretch and test Wales at every turn. This was no add-on match for them, a going through of the motions. Beale had already limped off by the time Barnes, who was sharp and menacing, was put over by a delightful pass from Cooper. But when the maligned Wallabies fly-half hit the turf in the twenty-second minute, Australia reined things in a bit. So, too, did the crowd, giving Cooper a round of applause.

Wales had to survive on scraps, that and an outrageous bit of good fortune. Somehow referee Wayne Barnes and his two assistants did not rule on a monumental forward pass, more an American football throw, from Hook to Shane Williams, the wing having to stretch his boot to toe it downfield and gather to dive over in the forty-ninth minute. That put Wales in front, 8–7, but Australia's ascendancy showed in the two penalties and a Barnes dropped goal that put them clear. Stephen Jones got three points back before the Wallabies effectively put the game beyond Wales with a well-worked try from Ben McCalman in the seventy-fifth minute. Only moments earlier George North had saved a certain try when stripping Adam Ashley-Cooper on the try-line. Wales refused to fold, as their final try showed. And that attitude will take them far.

22 OCTOBER
MY FINAL MEMORY? THE TEAM, TOGETHER, ALONE
Will Greenwood

Stare into the eyes of an All Black during the haka and you see a deep, cold darkness. Some will say it is nothing more than adrenalin-dilated pupils. Others will tell you it is a trick of the light. The foolish will claim it is a hint of nerves. They are all wrong. What you glimpse is a man's soul – and it draws you in. As you face the challenge of the haka you find yourself tumbling into a stare, like Alice down the rabbit hole. The noise of the crowd disappears and your mind fills with the deafening voice of a nation asking you one question: 'These boys will do whatever it takes to win. How far are you willing to go?'

And at that moment, on that field, no matter how you got there, you have to decide. What are your limits, where do you draw the line, how much pain can you endure? During the haka before the semi-final against Australia, you could feel the pulse that has been driving this country's team. The crowd stamped their feet and joined in, the two temporary stands in the stadium moved to their beat, swaying with intent, threat and danger. The players fed the crowd with their display of togetherness and the crowd fed the team with a power surge of support. I doubt I will witness anything like it again. This was twenty-four years of pain and hurt bubbling and simmering.

This was the understanding that since 1987 it has been a pretty thankless task being an All Blacks supporter.

The desperation to reach the final was palpable on the streets of Auckland beforehand, with no excitement about the game, just a desire to fast-forward time. They knew they were on the cusp of a moment that could change their collective history. The irony is that should they go all the way – and New Zealand supporters already seem to be doing a mental lap of honour – then for all its life-changing impact there is a very good chance the players will not remember too much about the final. You remember the lead-up, you remember the hours spent turning yourself into a machine, working on skills, your fitness. Every bead of sweat, each repetition, all those quiet nights reminding you that a World Cup is not about the will to win, it is about being willing to prepare to win.

This New Zealand team have earned this moment; they have been on their emotional and mental journey. I played against Ma'a Nonu when he won his first cap in 2003 and his transformation as a player tracks the development of the team beautifully. He started as a flat-track bully who could see only one way to win and that was by going straight through or over the opposition. Now he can do it all: change his lines, pop up in unexpected places, offload deftly and, if he has to, go at it like a bull in a china shop. The team around him have also developed balance and they have options to win in different ways. This has allowed them to carry many styles of player but all with the same aims – being error-free, building pressure, taking chances, keeping the grip on their opponents' collective throat. Aaron Cruden banging over a dropped-goal was a final acknowledgement of the value of an attitude that embodied everything they had hated about rugby – sometimes taking three points will suffice.

If France are going to have any chance they need to find their own sense of unity, which seems to have eluded them in this tournament. I wrote them off well before the final and I have learnt my lesson. They can be dangerous, but only if they find calm in the midst of the battle. When they lose their heads, they lose. They beat Wales not with emotion but with a death squeeze that was almost English in its lack of imagination and dumb reliance on kicking. Here they will have to play out of their skins and conquer their fear. Every changing room knows fear. Courage is not a lack of fear. It is having the strength to feel it and still go out and do what is needed.

World Cups are won by teams who can look around their changing room and have that one quiet moment, that one second when they know beyond any shadow of doubt that they are among friends who will stand by them no matter what. The time will come when the coaches have left and the subs are waiting in the tunnel, when the door shuts and the fifteen stand together, cocooned from the hysteria outside. The captain will walk into the middle, the huddle forming around him for that team moment, the tactile bond which is by its very nature reassuring, the feeling of togetherness, of safety in numbers, the primeval urge to stay together believing everything will be all right. There will be a rattle of studs on the floor as this mass of bodies sways one way and then the other, the huddle moving like a wave as the hugs come and are released. The smell of sweat and muscle cream, no great speeches, only the promise from the captain to leave the field a winner. Then the silence again, the hugs and the look, that look, from every player. It has to come from one to fifteen and if they get it right it will never be forgotten.

When I am asked what I remember about my World Cup final, this is the moment I mention. The match itself I have never watched. My mental pictures are only flashes: the missed tackle on Stirling Mortlock I can't deny; the knock-on in the Australian twenty-two that will not disappear. Yet I cannot remember much else except for that moment in the changing room, that still second of invincibility, of knowing that right there, right then I would not trade any one of our players, no matter who was offered. It was a beautiful feeling.

The final itself will be very different, a fury of emotion, noise, speed and lightning-quick incidents. If players lose focus, if they forget their promise to their team and to themselves, they will fail. The only way they can win is to make sure that when their moment comes they stare straight back – and do not blink.

24 OCTOBER
A NATION BREATHES AGAIN AS ALL BLACKS CLING ON
Mick Cleary

A nation would have gone into collective meltdown if this one had slipped by and, boy, it so nearly did. How close, how gripping and how utterly absorbing this match was, the best World Cup final there has been, full of character, sinew and dramatic uncertainty. And at the end, there was the Promised Land for New Zealand to claim, territory that this entire country has craved since the inaugural tournament was won at this venue twenty-four years earlier.

If the 1987 final was the routine coronation of the finest side of that (and perhaps any) era, then this was a true contest. Any concerns that this game would be a one-sided dud were dismissed even before a ball had been kicked. From the moment that France advanced on the haka in an arrow-shaped formation, hands linked, with Thierry Dusautoir as the spearhead, the underdogs played with deep-rooted passion as well as cleverness. They so nearly pulled it off. To the losers, the critical acclaim; to the victors the spoils. There is no doubt who got the better deal. There was little glory in the manner of the All Blacks' 8–7 victory, but at the end they had the pot, and that was all that mattered. No wonder the New Zealand coach, Graham Henry, leant across to touch the cherished trophy when asked for his views on the match. He did not need to say anything. He touched the gleaming cup once again. That was what it was all about.

It had taken graft rather than genius, fortitude rather than flair, proof that this was a team of many parts. In times past, the All Blacks had choked when the going got tough. Twice in previous World Cups, France had proved the bogeymen. Here, New Zealand trembled but they did not collapse in a heap. They were obliged to hang on grimly, and if Craig Joubert, the referee, had not been so generous to the host nation, then perhaps France might have completed the transformation from pool-stage chumps to champs. If François Trinh-Duc's forty-eight-metre penalty in the sixty-fifth minute had not drifted just right. If Morgan Parra had not taken a knee to the head from Richie McCaw and been forced off. 'If only', as ever, is the inscription on the medals of the losers.

France's back row of Imanol Harinordoquy, Julien Bonnaire and the *nonpareil* Dusautoir trumped their celebrated counterparts, their set-piece became more and more dominant, and centre Aurélien Rougerie hammered every black shirt that came his way. But it was not enough, and given that Wales had fallen by the same margin to France in the semi-final in similar circumstances, perhaps there was a perverse justice in it all.

While France were the unlikely heroes of the match, those being acclaimed were the All Blacks, but this was not their finest performance. They lacked composure and were exposed at the line-out. They were fortunate to get an early try from the unheralded source of prop Tony Woodcock, who steamed through a gaping hole in the France line-out to touch down in the fifteenth minute. It was not so much that the All Blacks were on edge, paralysed by the expectation heaped on them, but that they were rocked by a France side who we had not seen for eighteen months, never mind the previous seven weeks. There was also a substandard showing from scrum-half Piri Weepu, who missed eight points through missed kicks. Their injury jinx at fly-half also continued as they had to use fourth-choice Stephen Donald after Aaron Cruden suffered a knee injury after thirty-four minutes. Donald kicked the winning goal from in front of the posts in the forty-fifth minute.

So often we have lauded the brilliance and sparkle of these All Blacks. Here it was time to salute their fibre and bloody-mindedness, their refusal to fold when under pressure. All that was shown when France came at them with sustained ferocity early in the second half. New Zealand were on the ropes after Dusautoir touched down in the forty-sixth minute, the try stemming from an opportunist attack triggered by an interception from Trinh-Duc. The replacement fly-half converted, and the comeback was in motion. The All Blacks still had a one-point advantage but they appeared flaky up front and vulnerable behind.

France grew in stature, with Harinordoquy all-consuming, and the scrum beginning to take a toll. Yet New Zealand survived. Perhaps the experience of 2007 helped get them through, the fear of feeling that desolation again. Perhaps it was destiny. More likely, it was a combination of good fortune and steadfast defence. France had minor openings but could not capitalise. New Zealand gained territory then ran down the clock with close-quarter drives. It was pragmatic, restrictive and negative, yet the crowd, the country, did not give a damn. The time ticked past the allotted mark, a penalty was awarded, Andy Ellis booted the ball high into the stands and bedlam broke out across the land.

23 OCTOBER

THE GOOD, THE BAD AND THE RUGBY
Paul Ackford

It wasn't the best World Cup. That title remains with South Africa in 1995 when Nelson Mandela, a suicidally low-flying jumbo jet and the confirmation of Jonah Lomu as a superstar combined to catapult rugby union to a global status it had never previously enjoyed. But this one in New Zealand was pretty damn good, its success encapsulated in the hold it had over a nation, the warmth of the welcome, the cultural fit, and an overwhelming sense that watching rugby in New Zealand just feels right. If there was one gripe, it was that Eden Park, with one stand still sitting on a tower of scaffolding, couldn't quite deliver the majesty of experience offered by the great rugby cathedrals of the world. But the smaller venues were top-drawer.

The rugby generally was top-drawer, too. This was a tournament which, by and large, rewarded teams who played. True, France got to a final with barely a creative note in their repertoire, and England, apart from romps against Georgia and Romania, plodded blankly on, but other countries had more about them. Wales, pricked by a group of youngsters whose lack of inhibition was their most refreshing feature, were attacking two minutes and forty-two seconds into overtime in their final match for Leigh Halfpenny's try. Relentless, brave, but unsuccessful for the third match in the tournament, it sort of summed up Wales' World Cup. Australia, when they had some possession – which they manifestly weren't able to gather against New Zealand, South Africa and Ireland – showed what a delight they are to follow. Japan had their moments, as did Tonga, Canada, Italy and Argentina.

Much of the credit for that turnaround from the turgid, kick/chase rugby which polluted the 2007 World Cup lies with the administrators who tweaked the laws and the officials who policed them. There were a few examples of human error, but in terms of management of the game, in terms of consistency of approach, the players knew what to expect from referees. Only one match, South Africa's quarter-final against Australia, provoked orchestrated howls of protest over a referee, Bryce Lawrence, who went off-script to concoct a breakdown which degenerated into chaos. The other major talking points were punctuation marks in games in which the officiating was generally well received.

The tournament has, though, refined the pecking order of positional importance. Forget outside-halves, who either fell foul of injury (Dan Carter and Rhys Priestland), or failed to flourish (Quade Cooper and Jonny Wilkinson). Flankers are rugby's new black, and openside ones at that. Most of the debate going into matches centred on the relative merits of the teams' No. 7s. It seemed that every country had a belter. From Namibia's Jacques Burger, through Georgia's Mamuka Gorgodze and Samoa's Maurie Fa'asavalu, and on via Heinrich

Brüssow, David Pocock, Sam Warburton, Sean O'Brien and Richie McCaw, flankers were the main men: frustrating, creating, dictating.

Even from this distance, England's campaign has lost none of its awfulness, though this has nothing to do with their record. Quirkily, France made the final with two defeats, Wales came fourth with three, yet England, derided and unloved, came up short just once before heading home. But it was the way England failed to acknowledge their deficiencies which was most worrying. Had they gone out firing in their quarter-final then most of the fuss over off-field issues would have subsided. But the sight of passes hitting retreating players' backs or being flung in front, behind, anywhere except at their intended target against France is difficult to excuse or forget.

England are not the only team in need of regeneration. South Africa are also at a watershed, needing to build an identity around youngsters Pat Lambie, Frans Steyn, Bismarck du Plessis and Francois Hougaard rather than soldiering on with the old sweats. Some reputations suffered. Bryan Habana, unlike Shane Williams, had little influence on matches, and the Beast, Tendai Mtawarira, never quite got out of his cage. Ireland, too, have come to the end of their particular road. Like England, Ireland persisted with an outside-half whose summer days are behind him. Ronan O'Gara had his moments, but the best outside-halves have to interest defences ball in hand, and Wilkinson and O'Gara lacked the instincts and the expertise to do so when it counted.

Only one team ticked that box, as it did most of the others. Forty-eight teams might have turned up to this tournament but it was only ever about one group. From the moment they trounced Tonga through to the final, New Zealand were the only story in town. Cory Jane and Israel Dagg's night on the pop aside, theirs was a dignified, well-ordered procession. Bumps along the way, major ones like Dan Carter's groin, minor ones like Kieran Read's ankle, were negotiated with calm assurance. Those issues, McCaw's and Mils Muliaina's one-hundredth caps, and the conclusion of Graham Henry's association with the All Blacks after 103 matches, all consumed a nation and a watching world. But it never intruded, never detracted from the experience because the nation was evidently infatuated with the notion of rugby again, showering support and hospitality on teams and venues across both islands. And because the All Blacks were always worth watching.

That was the lesson from this tournament, the realisation that Test rugby does not have to be a stodgy affair decided by experience. The stars of this World Cup were young men – Dagg, George North, Pocock, Warburton, Aaron Cruden perhaps, Lambie, James O'Connor, Jamie Roberts. They brought the excitement and the adventure, just as New Zealand have demonstrated that risk and reward are not incompatible bedfellows in important matches. The All Blacks notched forty tries from their seven games. Wales, their closest rival, were eleven scores adrift of that mark. Good on you, New Zealand. As a country and as a team, you've done world rugby proud.

2011 RESULTS – Quarter-finals: Wales 22, Ireland 10; France 19, England 12; Australia 11, South Africa 9; New Zealand 33, Argentina 10. Semi-finals: France 9, Wales 8; New Zealand 20, Australia 6. Third-place: Australia 21, Wales 18. Final: New Zealand 8, France 7.

ACKNOWLEDGEMENTS

There is a considerable scrum of people who have helped push this book towards the try line – or at least in range of a dropped goal. My thanks go to: Robin Harvie, who commissioned the book for Aurum Press in the first place; Melissa Smith and Lucy Warburton, my hard-working editors at Aurum; Cerys Hughes, publishing manager at Telegraph Media Group, for her guidance; Gavin Fuller, Lorraine Goodspeed and the rest of the *Telegraph* library, who have facilitated my research and continued to amuse me during my visits; the writers – and photographers – who travelled around the globe watching, and some playing in, the seven World Cups to date on the *Telegraph*'s behalf, and keeping readers informed and entertained; and the production staff, who handled the copy with the care and deliberation of Jonny Wilkinson lining up a kick at goal. You've all done very well.